A World Unto Itself

A World Unto Itself

The Political Memoirs of Don Jamieson

Volume II

Don Jamieson

Edited by Carmelita McGrath

Breakwater
100 Water Street
P.O. Box 2188
St. John's, NewfoundlandA1C 6E6

The Publisher is indebted to the Department of External Affairs, Ottawa, and in particular to Alan Lever, for their assistance with the research and development of this book. Special thanks to the Jamieson family and, in particular, to Barbara and Heather, for their assistance and support, and for the use of photographs in this book, taken from the private collection of Barbara Jamieson.

The Publisher acknowledges the support of the Canada Council, which has helped make this book possible.

The Publisher acknowledges the financial contribution of the Cultural Affairs Division of the Department of Municipal and Provincial Affairs, Government of Newfoundland and Labrador, which has helped make this publication possible.

Cover Design: Angela King-Harris

Cover photograph courtesy of Don Hollett

Canadian Cataloguing in Publication Data

Jamieson, Don, 1921-1986.

The political memoirs of Don Jamieson

Includes index.
Contents: v. 1. No place for fools - - v. 2. A world unto itself.
ISBN 0-920911-68-4 (v.1). - - 0-920911-79-X (v.2)

1. Jamieson, Don, 1921-1986. 2. Politicians - - Newfoundland - - Biography. 3. Politicians - - Canada - - Biography. 4. Newfoundland - - Politics and government - - 20th century. * 5. Canada - - Politics and government - - 20th century.
I. McGrath, Carmelita. II. Title. III. Title: No place for fools. IV. Title: A world unto itself.

FC626.J35A3 1989 971.064'4'0924 C89-098594-4
F1034.3.J35A3 1989

Donald C. Jamieson
1921-1986

One

In Newfoundland, September is the most pleasant month of the year. An always capricious summer mellows in its old age, makes every day count, and tarries as long as possible.

September, 1966, ran true to form and provided perfect conditions during my first campaign for election to the Canadian House of Commons. Because mine was a safe Liberal seat, I could succumb to a mood of guiltless indolence and adopt a cavalier attitude toward my bid for votes. The result was a most pleasant holiday for my wife Barbara and me.

I was contesting a by-election in the constituency of Burin-Burgeo, an area consisting of dozens of small settlements and a few larger centres, all located within sight of the sea along hundreds of miles of Newfoundland's south coast. From earliest times, it has been a major fishing district. In 1966, most places were still isolated; to reach them in the time available, I chartered a small seaplane operated by an experienced pilot.

Although Barbara and I knew the coast well, it was our first extensive tour by plane. The experience was memorable and breathtaking. From the air, the magnificent scenery appeared dramatically enhanced: countless dark islands mirrored in the calm ocean, dun-coloured barrens dappled by silver, shimmering ponds, bald coastal cliffs, their scarred, deeply etched faces pierced here and there by the sheltered harbours and high-walled channels around which the people made their homes.

Our visits to these secluded villages proved to be a delightful and unforgettable experience. The generous, hard-working people were the soul of kindness; everyone turned out to greet us. While there was serious talk, our biggest problem was a surfeit of hospitality. Since we could not visit every home, most of the people would crowd into whichever one we chose after agonizing over how not to offend anyone. The mood of the gatherings was invariably festive. There were community problems, of course, but discussion of these was disposed of quickly. Then came music, food and, sometimes, "a drop of the hard stuff."

The attitude towards liquor varies widely along the coast. Temperance zealots may frown privately on the habits of their more earthy neighbours, and may even occasionally attempt to wean them away from the demon rum. But tolerance is never in short supply, and even among those who eschew strong drink, there are many who can be persuaded to take "a little something against the cold." Such invitations can come at any hour. One morning at nine, we were greeted in a community by a group of men just back from the fishing grounds. They produced a five-gallon can of "white lightning"—whisky blanc—smuggled from the nearby island of St. Pierre. This tiny French possession has long influenced life on the coast. Best known as the shipment port for astonishing quantities of spirits during Prohibition, the island and its neighbour, Miquelon, have been slaking the thirst of the people of southern Newfoundland for centuries. Our hardy hosts that morning clearly subscribed to the well-entrenched principle that it was the inalienable right of the people of the coast to obtain their liquid refreshment from St. Pierre without paying anything as patently absurd as customs duties.

Amid a great deal of winking and oblique references to the frustrated Mounties who struggled in vain against the illicit trade, the fishermen mixed huge belts of the colourless pure alcohol with hot water and sugar. Barbara and I were clearly expected to follow suit, which we did with considerable trepidation. We even observed the ritual of downing the entire potion in a single lip-smacking gulp. My wife all but collapsed and I was rendered speechless for one of the few times in my career. The fishermen chortled delightedly and, to our dismay, promptly set up another round. The remainder of our visit is best left unreported except to record that the scene of this inhumane initiation was called, appropriately, Stone Valley.

To minimize such risks to life and limb, and also because we were in a holiday mood, we decided after Stone Valley to take our sustenance in private whenever possible. Each morning, Barbara stocked a picnic basket with an assortment of delicacies and a bottle of choice wine—duty paid. Each lunch hour, we searched out an attractive picnic site and, having moored the plane, enjoyed a splendid repast. Surely, no politician on the hustings has ever had it as good! Lounging in warm sunshine and blissful seclusion, we were content in the knowledge that our campaign odyssey was an assured success.

One day, however, trouble came from an unexpected quarter. Our picnic site was idyllic: a small, uninhabited island, its wide expanse of white sandy beach fringed by a green meadow. On landing, we had sighted a dark object which we had taken to be a boulder, but our meal was barely spread out on the cloth when the object moved. It was a large, black ram placed on the island for summer grazing. Incensed at our invasion of his domain, the creature pawed the ground, snorting loudly and ominously. Barbara screamed and bent over to pick up the picnic supplies. The target she offered proved irresistible. The ram raced across the beach, head lowered and huge horns thrust menacingly forward. He butted Barbara in the rear, sending her sprawling. Even worse, having been deprived of female companionship for months, he proceeded to bestow his affection on my startled wife in an all-too-obvious fashion.

Abject coward that I am, I immediately raced for the plane moored at the shoreline. The pilot followed suit, pausing only long enough to grab the picnic cloth by its four corners with everything left inside. Poor Barbara, abandoned most ungallantly, scrambled away from her molester, and all three of us piled into the plane with the ram in hot pursuit. There we remained until the beast's ardour cooled. At the first opportunity, we freed the plane for take-off and evacuated the beach with the alacrity of wartime commandos. Only after we were safely airborne could we see any humour in the incident, and even then Barbara did not share in our laughter; she was too busy denouncing our lack of chivalry.

An election campaign drags interminably for most candidates, but I ended our tour with genuine regret. We had made hosts of new friends, enjoyed many unique and exciting experiences, and victory was assured. On election night, the only speculation concerned the size of my majority, and this turned out to be one of the largest on record. Yet I had held only one formal meeting, used no advertising or organization, and made no promises. The vote of confidence I had received was unmistakable; it also contained a message. Despite the low-key campaign in September's balmy days, major problems were already looming in my new constituency, and the people of Burin-Burgeo were looking to me to deal with them.

Two

Adjusting to my new role as Member of Parliament was a painful experience. There were times when I came close to quitting. I had been involved in politics literally since childhood, and was considered a seasoned activist. My backroom experience was of no help, however, as I sought to learn the ropes in Ottawa.

Parliament is a world unto itself. It may be the most exclusive club in Canada; certainly there is a unique camaraderie among its members. But most House of Commons friendships are fragile, even among natural allies. The mood of amiability is shallow and intermittent, ebbing and flowing to the rhythm of partisan events and the clash of conflicting ambitions. Like many clubs, Parliament is tacitly committed to an immutable pecking order, with the privileges of membership employed frequently for self-preservation and aggrandizement.

Initiation does not produce instant comradeship. There is an apprenticeship to be served, a time of testing as the veterans eye the new recruit and ruthlessly assess his potential. A sink-or-swim attitude pervades the corridors of power, a feeling that the new arrival must make it largely on his own to be worthy of recognition. It is less a matter of animosity than of calculated indifference compounded by the preoccupation of members with their own problems. The initial result is a depressing sense of isolation, even loneliness, as the freshman MP struggles to find his way in a strange new environment.

For me, the problem was especially acute. My high-profile background in private broadcasting caused some to question my reasons for entering politics. Columnist Doug Fisher echoed a widespread view when he labelled me an elected lobbyist for the Canadian Association of

Broadcasters, an organization I had led for four years. The many Liberals in the Walter Gordon camp saw me as a right-winger, and openly anticipated my opposition to the directions in which they were attempting to steer the Liberal Party and government. Charles Lynch, a respected media pundit, was the first of many to forecast my early appointment to cabinet, and Ottawa insiders, with their insatiable appetite for gossip, had me feuding with Richard Cashin, a fellow Newfoundland MP, over the succession to Newfoundland's lone cabinet seat. This seat was held by Jack Pickersgill, whose retirement was being forecast widely throughout the capital.

I ought to have known better, but I was caught unawares by such talk. I had no grand design; there were no deals with the Prime Minister or anyone else, and while my interest in broadcasting policy was keen, I was not about to launch an assault on the Canadian Broadcasting Corporation or beat the drum for private interests. Yet within days, I was being warned that friends of Cashin were lining up to prevent my entry into cabinet; there were passing, unflattering references to my business connections. Judy LaMarsh, who as Secretary of State had responsibility for broadcasting policy, was her usual blunt self, warning me that there was no goddamn way I was going to influence her decisions on broadcasting matters. I began to wonder what I had let myself in for.

My feelings of doubt intensified as I set about the routine task of establishing an office and prepared to deal with the already mounting requests for assistance from my constituency. After polite applause and a few handshakes at my first caucus, there was a brief meeting with Mr. Pearson—I could no longer call him Mike as I had done for years. Then I was on my own. Jack Pickersgill was as considerate as I could expect of a busy minister, and the help of his staff, especially his private secretary, Audrey MacQuarrie, was invaluable. The government House Leader, George McIlraith, got me an office. With his renowned talent for understatement, George confided that it was not the best office on Parliament Hill, but it was in the Centre Block, and that, he assured me, was where the action was. He was more right than he knew!

The single room was directly beneath the chamber of the House of Commons. When members applauded by pounding their desks, the walls shook, windows trembled, and conversation became impossible. Before I became inured to the uproar, I assumed it heralded some event of great moment. I would race upstairs only to find routine business in progress and members applauding as much out of boredom as anything else. Since applauding was an ingrained habit, my secretary, Janet Blair, and I felt as if we were working amidst a continuous thunderstorm.

If George McIlraith put me in the centre of the action, he was a complete cop-out when it came to furnishings. Since I had come in through a by-election, he explained, there was not much furniture left from which to choose. Once again, he grossly understated the case; what came up from the storage room resembled nothing more than the leftovers from a garage sale. I promptly took Miss MacQuarrie's advice and, with her help, bought my own furnishings. All, that is, but the water cooler. Here, as with the other furniture, I drew a decrepit reject, an inverted glass container on top of a battered sickly green base. Periodically, as the ice cubes in the bottom melted, giant bubbles formed in the water and erupted with a rumble that sounded for all the world like the emissions from a very upset stomach. I felt obliged to explain the phenomenon to visitors, lest they suspect that my secretary or I had committed a dreadful breach of etiquette.

The lowly state of my office facilities should have convinced anyone with half an eye that I was receiving no special favours and that reports of my influence were grossly exaggerated. Nevertheless, the rumours persisted and the few who sought me out deep in the bowels of the Centre Block decried my low estate but assured me knowingly that I would not be there for long. I had reached the same conclusion, but for different reasons. I was about ready to throw in the towel and go home.

I was not alone among the newcomers. By then, Jean Marchand was in the cabinet and Gérard Pelletier was still on the back bench. A few seats away from me sat Pierre Trudeau, who had been appointed to the largely symbolic post of Parliamentary Secretary to the Prime Minister. As I became familiar with my new life, I saw little evidence that the "Three Wise Men" from Quebec, as they had been dubbed earlier by the media, were having any significant impact or, for that matter, were enjoying themselves more than I was. Marchand, an excellent speaker, made the occasional intervention in the Commons. Pelletier, who was still writing a regular newspaper column, often while seated in the Commons, had gained some publicity as co-chairman of the committee assigned the task of dealing with the controversy over the CBC program, "This Hour Has Seven Days." He said hardly anything in the House, however, or in càucus. As for Trudeau, I was in Parliament for weeks before I even saw him. He had been named one of the handful of MPs attached to that autumn's session of the United Nations General Assembly. Consequently, during my first weeks in Parliament, Trudeau was almost constantly in New York.

I found it amusing many years later, when I was Secretary of State for External Affairs, when a Liberal MP, assigned by me to the same post Trudeau had held, complained about a briefing he had had from Geoffrey Pearson, the former prime minister's son. Pearson, he felt, had belittled the Prime Minister by saying that as a delegate, Trudeau had done little in New York but have a good time. However, Pearson was not being critical of Trudeau; he was merely telling the MP to prepare for a dull assignment and a lot of free time at the United Nations. Conditions may have improved since then, but traditionally, the delegates chosen from the Commons and from non-governmental organizations were given few major responsibilities. Some would, from time to time, make a niche for themselves with one of the UN's innumerable committees. If, however, they decided to take a more relaxed approach, they were seldom missed and rarely criticized. Obviously, the fun-loving Trudeau had opted to make the most of being in New York and, as far as anyone can remember, his contribution to the work of the United Nations was far from memorable at that time.

Only after the 1966 General Assembly closed did I see much of Trudeau in or around the House of Commons. Neither he nor Marchand nor Pelletier made any obvious effort to assert "French power." Indeed, the entire Quebec caucus was fairly docile from late 1966 to early 1967. Many of its members had outside work in addition to their parliamentary duties. I was surprised to discover, for example, that several MPs, mainly those from Quebec, were still members of their city and town councils. Others were carrying on extensive legal and medical practices. Still others were quite elderly and not especially eager to plunge into contentious issues.

In addition, of course, the Quiet Revolution was already well launched in Quebec, and the euphoria of the coming centenary, much of it centred on Expo '67 in Montreal, was starting to build. It was not a period when members from Quebec were likely to become too agitated over federal issues affecting their province. Already, many veterans were talking openly about getting out when the next election was called. Obviously, in such a mood, there was little disposition to bend over backwards to accept a newcomer.

In the House of Commons, I was as ignorant of procedures as I had been of the mysteries of the Latin Mass when, as a Protestant child, I had attended my first Catholic service. Then, to avoid embarrassment, I had simply followed the lead of those around me—standing, sitting and bowing along with everyone else. I fell back on the same tactics in the House, shouting aye and nay in concert with my seatmates, albeit a little tardily. For all I understood of the proceedings, I could have been voting to start another war. Only when I caught the eye of the congenial and unflappable party whip, Bernie Pilon, and received his nod of approval did I experience a heady sense of participating in the nation's business, and of saving the government from ignominious defeat.

Pilon was one of the first to befriend me. It was not simply the newcomers who did not understand the procedures, he assured me. There were members of long-standing who visited the House so seldom that they scarcely knew the location of their seats. In a minority

Parliament, they were the bane of Pilon's existence, but if they showed up for key votes he was satisfied. He even respected some of the no-shows if they passed his acid test of being good constituency men. He called them the "wedding and funeral brigade" since, invariably, they excused their absences by reporting their attendance at one or the other of these events. A convinced grass-roots man despite his duties, Pilon maintained that, in terms of political kudos at home, a funeral was worth two weddings. Always arrive late at the church, he advised me, and go straight to the front pew; that way, there was no chance of being overlooked. While I enjoyed Pilon's gentle cynicism, it did nothing to enhance my regard for my new calling. My self-esteem took another beating during an important vote one evening when I offered to help the whip "round up the strays," as he put it.

Drinking is much less prevalent among MPs than is sometimes suggested, but every political party has a few in the ranks who imbibe to excess, especially during night sittings. A member who sat near me had this failing, and he rarely survived the dinner hour in one piece. Usually, he retreated quietly to his office and fell asleep. On the night of this particular vote, however, he was nowhere to be found. Pilon, having consulted his numerous lists, concluded that the government's margin would be too close for comfort. The errant member must be found, a task assigned to me with the stern reminder that the fate of the government depended on the success of my mission. While the division bells rang interminably, I roamed the parliamentary precincts in search of my elusive colleague. Having had no luck in the Centre Block, I raced through the connecting tunnel to the West Block where a discreet guard, suspecting that my quarry might be engaged in a little private contemplation, directed me to a small second floor room equipped as a non-sectarian haven for private prayer and meditation. There I found our stray member blissfully asleep and, in the subdued light, looking more dead than alive. Quickly I led, pushed and dragged him to the Commons and, with the help of others, planted him in his seat. Immediately, he passed out again, his snores a rude intrusion on the silence as the Speaker took his place to call the roll. There were several votes in sequence that night, and each time the Clerk, an old and wise parliamentary hand, reached the sleeping member's name on the list, he paused momentarily while a seatmate and I hoisted our inebriated colleague to his feet and tilted him slightly in the direction of the Chair. Such was my first assignment at the very heart of our cherished democracy: to help sustain the government with the votes of a member who did not even know he was there.

If some members were so little concerned with the nation's business, the same could not be said for others. The difference was largely due to the rebuilding job spearheaded by Walter Gordon, Keith

Davey and a few others who, by 1966, had assembled an impressive group of younger Liberals determined to make changes. Often referred to as "Gordonites," many were extremely active and geared toward reform. In the autumn of 1966, they had plenty to be active about. The Liberal convention of that autumn and the caucus meetings preceding it saw major, often acrimonious, debates on social policy issues. Particularly divisive was the question of the timing of the introduction of Medicare. Mitchell Sharp, then Finance Minister, supported the need for a slow approach. Walter Gordon—who had resigned from cabinet because he had given "bad advice" to Pearson on calling the election—was still influential and opposed Sharp's approach. The sides were very evenly drawn, both in the convention and in caucus, making this one of the first major post-war divisions between what can loosely be called the "right" and "left" wings of the Liberal Party. The argument, as always, was about the availability of funds, and although Sharp won, it was a temporary victory. Indeed, it was during this period that the federal government became more and more involved in costly social programs. Only later would federal-provincial issues relating to Medicare surface; in 1966, these issues were marginal.

For better or for worse, much of the thrust of social reform, including the contentious question of universality, pre-dated Trudeau's term as prime minister. The largest growth in major welfare and related programs, including those involving cost sharing with the provinces, took place during the Pearson years, with Walter Gordon and those who shared his views spearheading the drive and gaining a great deal of non-Liberal parliamentary and public support along the way. The achievements and failings of the Trudeau era are another matter, of course, on which I will have more detailed observations later. At this point, I merely want to record that the principal elements of Canada's social security structure were in existence before Trudeau's term in office.

When Pearson appointed him Justice Minister in 1967, Trudeau's rising public profile was not due to any emphasis he gave to the welfare state. Rather, he literally leaped to prominence with his controversial law reforms, particularly those relating to the freedom of the individual. His expression—borrowed, it is now said, from a newsman—"The state has no place in the bedrooms of the nation," is likely to remain the best remembered of all his utterances.

The enthusiasm and skill with which Trudeau chose to tackle the first of his projects as Justice Minister surprised Pearson, as it did many others. Although Pearson supported Trudeau and was as reform-minded as anyone, his principal concern remained the improvement of relations with Quebec in the context of the entire constitutional issue. Earlier, he had fought hard, and with eventual success, for a distinct national flag and, less successfully, for changes to the national anthem. He had established the Royal Commission on Bilingualism and Biculturalism and, in many other ways, had sought to close what he saw as a widening chasm between Anglophones and Francophones in Canada. The principal reason he chose Trudeau as Justice Minister—with Marchand's full support—was to prepare for the constitutional conference he was planning for the next winter, not merely as the climax of Centennial Year, but as his last major act as prime minister. When this effort came in 1968, Trudeau completely lived up to Pearson's expectations. In the intervening months, however, he chose to begin building his reputation in a totally different area of ministerial responsibility.

Whether by accident or design, Trudeau's approach and willingness to challenge old taboos matched precisely the heady Canadian mood of 1967. By and large, federal politics was surprisingly tranquil during much of the build-up to Centennial Year. The mood of the people—generally conciliatory, genial and optimistic—affected most parliamentarians. There was a general disposition to avoid confrontation whenever possible and to shelve contentious issues. This aim was not always attained, of course. One exception came shortly after I took up my seat.

This involved my first appointment to a parliamentary committee. I wanted to be named to the Committee on Broadcasting, and Jack Pickersgill assured me there would be no problem. Instead, however, I found myself a member of the group studying Pickersgill's massive, staggeringly complex and innovative bill to reconcile the confusing grab-bag of transportation legislation then on the books. Pickersgill undoubtedly saw the bill as the crowning achievement of his career. More than that, it would become evident later that Jack had craftily written into the legislation the source of his post-parliamentary employment—the chairmanship of his proposed Canadian Transport Commission. Thus, there was more than one reason for his anxiety to see the bill enacted quickly, and in one piece.

When I told Jack that, for what I understood of the bill, it might as well be written in Sanskrit, he replied candidly. It was good that I felt ill-informed, he told me, since I would not be tempted to voice my opinions and prolong the proceedings. As if that was not message enough, the committee chairman, Joe Macaluso, quickly reinforced it after I had been bold enough to risk an occasional intervention. Lay off the questions, he told me, because they only served to keep the opposition going: just sit there and vote on cue.

Although he was a tough chairman, Macaluso was a likeable colleague, and we soon became good friends. Sensing my frustration and chagrin over my role as a mute cipher, he confided that the reason

I had not been named to the Broadcasting Committee was Pickersgill's concern that, once involved in issues I knew something about, I would promptly lose interest in the transportation bill, and Jack needed all the supporters he could find to get his precious measure enacted. So I was exposed to another entrenched parliamentary tradition: the system of rewards and punishments, of mutual back-scratching and long-remembered slights and favours.

Pickersgill was, of course, a master practitioner of the art. With nothing better to do, I watched his skilful manoeuverings with growing, if grudging, admiration. He was present for every committee meeting, patient and conciliatory in his responses, yielding on inconsequential points but holding fast to the basics of the legislation. Jack Horner, then a Conservative and an informed opponent of many of the bill's proposals, asked me during one session: "How can you beat that guy? I say 'The Minister is totally ignorant of the facts,' and all Pickersgill replies is, 'I agree with the Honourable Member.' What's left to say after that?" As things turned out, Horner found a great deal more to say, despite his frustration. The hearings dragged on for several weary weeks. In the end, however, through skill, tenacity, incredibly hard work and brilliant tactics, Pickersgill prevailed.

His only setback occurred not in the committee, but after the bill was reported back to the Commons. Through a foul-up, Bernie Pilon miscounted the government members in attendance, and the opposition defeated an important clause in the bill, one dealing with the famous and perennial issue of the Crow's Nest Pass rates. There is an interesting footnote to that incident. Jack Pickersgill told me, many years later, that while he regretted the loss of the clause at the time, as matters turned out, it was a godsend; had the provision survived, it would have cost the federal treasury untold millions of dollars. So much for the omnipotence of governments and their conviction that oppositions can do nothing right. As Premier Alex Campbell of Prince Edward Island used to say, "Even a stopped clock is right twice a day!"

With the transport bill passed, Pickersgill made good his pledge; my reward of a seat on the Broadcasting Committee came through without delay. Now I was to learn of another parliamentary idiosyncrasy. Members mistrust those colleagues who are authorities in any particular field. The basis for this attitude is simple enough—concern over a possible conflict of interest; there is, however, more to it than that. Ministers are usually generalists, and most are uncomfortable when a member with specialized knowledge goes to work on their proposed policies and legislation. Public servants are even more uneasy and sensitive. Often, they are the real instigators of new, complex initiatives, and they have a proprietary interest in protecting their ideas from close scrutiny by those with practical experience in the fields under review.

This is especially true in broadcasting, where policy is a constant source of heated public debate. When I joined the Committee on Broadcasting, another of the periodic controversies was at its height. I had been partially responsible for this through my earlier participation as CAB President in the "Troika," a committee established by Pearson to make recommendations on broadcasting policy. The other members had been Andrew Stewart, Chairman of the Board of Broadcast Governors, and Alphonse Ouimet, President of the Canadian Broadcasting Corporation. The degree of disagreement among the three of us on fundamentals was only exceeded by the opposition of the policy makers and those who influenced them to all our views. By 1966, Judy LaMarsh, Pearson's third secretary of state in less than three years, was determinedly crafting a new policy to conform to her own preconceived and often faulty notions.

My personal relationship with Judy had always been excellent since the late 1950s, when we had been among the few then struggling to revive the Liberal Party. Despite our continuing friendship, Judy was inordinately suspicious of my motives where broadcasting was concerned. Given the gossip surrounding my political debut, she may even have felt threatened. Whatever her reasons, she employed her capacity for brutal frankness to inform me that she proposed to make my participation in the committee's work as ineffectual as possible.

Her declaration was yet another shock to my belief in an MP's ability to help shape and direct national affairs. The chairman of the committee, Bob Stanbury, was competent, hard-working and dedicated. In choosing him, however, Judy had run her own form of loyalty check. Stanbury was generally supportive of the LaMarsh objectives and could be relied upon to steer the committee in the right direction. As matters turned out, he need scarcely have bothered. Even while we were sitting, I was informed by an indiscreet and perhaps disgruntled official that the new legislation was in an advanced stage of drafting. Our deliberations were having no impact because the basic structure of the new policy had already been decided. Moreover, the CBC, through well-placed contacts, was privy to the full scope of the planning while the elected members had no such liaison. The entire exercise was a cynical charade, an insult to the committee and to the many witnesses who appeared before it.

All of this was possible at the time because of an inherent weakness in the parliamentary system. Unless a policy or issue was central to the government's concerns, cabinet scrutiny was casual and inadequate. When I complained about what had transpired in the Broadcasting Committee, several senior ministers confessed their ignorance of the whole affair. With other more important economic fish to fry, broadcasting had become largely "Judy's baby," as one minister put it, and she made the most of it.

During his time in cabinet before becoming prime minister, Pierre Trudeau was deeply conscious of this weakness. As a result, he beefed up the system of cabinet committees, attempted to strengthen the parliamentary committees, and introduced a system of checks and balances designed to reduce the ability of ministers to act almost unilaterally on important issues. These measures brought their own complications, but they did reduce the blatant ministerial horse trading and empire building of the Pearson era.

As a backbencher, I was the occasional beneficiary of such practices. When I was in desperate need of an allotment of funds for road work in my constituency, Jack Pickersgill convened an informal meeting of a few influential ministers in the government lobby. While I sat in silent awe, the ministers proceeded to make concessions to each other—a wharf here, a grant there—until Jack extracted the money I was seeking. The new Broadcasting Act evolved, it seems, in much the same way. No other minister's turf was being threatened and, since public flack was minimal except for the usual special interest groups, the minister responsible was given a pretty clear road. There was, of course, much that was good in the new legislation, and a more exhaustive study might not have produced anything better for the times. But the convoluted, secretive process offered little hope to MPs. In my case, it served only to increase my feeling of uselessness.

Oddly enough, Judy LaMarsh obtained no sustained satisfaction from her legislative victory. Despite our many arguments, we remained close personal friends, and she sought me out often to vent her frustrations. Judy, a strong supporter of public broadcasting, was nevertheless deeply mistrustful of the hierarchy of the CBC. Key appointments were about to be made at the top, and Judy had her own candidates for these pivotal positions. The Prime Minister had other ideas, and the LaMarsh nominees were rejected one by one. This was just as well since, when she tried the names out on me, I was astounded by many of her choices. They were all acquaintances of mine, and their talents, while impressive, did not equip them for the big jobs for which they were being touted. Judy was furious over Pearson's unwillingness to cooperate, and soon lost much of her interest in broadcasting. Instead, she concentrated on her responsibilities for the Centennial celebrations and discharged them very well.

Pearson was no better equipped than Judy to fill the key broadcasting posts. I advised him to name at least one person with experience in the field to either the presidency or vice-presidency of the corporation. Otherwise, I argued, two green newcomers, regardless of their ability, would be at the mercy of an incredibly well-entrenched

CBC establishment. The novices would be taken into the camp before they knew what hit them. Pearson was unimpressed. He wanted people who could take "a fresh look" at the CBC. His choices were George Davidson, a distinguished public servant, then Secretary of Treasury Board, and Laurent Picard, a professor, established mediator and trouble-shooter. Their credentials were impeccable on paper, but their lack of experience in broadcasting soon had the effect I had predicted. Davidson, in particular—as president, the more visible of the two—was soon voicing the familiar arguments and defences we had heard from his predecessors and, thanks to his long bureaucratic career, skilfully beefing up CBC budgets, even though Pearson and others had seen him as the man to keep spending under control.

I viewed the evolving events with mixed feelings. It was satisfying to be proven correct, but I was increasingly disturbed by what I was learning. I was familiar with the process of lobbying, but ill-prepared for the number of special interests constantly bearing down on government. Most revealing was the confidence, even cynicism, with which entrenched groups, both in government and outside, manoeuvred and contrived to lessen or offset the impact of virtually every new initiative on their activities. Most irritating for the backbencher anxious to contribute to the governing process was his almost total lack of real power, a situation made intolerable by a denial of access to important information. Government departments, agencies and crown corporations, as well as various business sectors, were linked to and participated in key decision making. MPs, however, even those who supported the government, were limited to what was said in caucus or at an occasional briefing, where impatient ministers seemed committed to disclose as little of significance as possible.

In later years, the system improved considerably, partly as a result of the Trudeau reforms, but also because many of the new MPs were ready to challenge the old methods and to remind ministers that their power depended on the support of backbenchers. Such challenges were uncommon before the 1960s. There were minor revolts, of course, such as the Walter Gordon-Mitchell Sharp split over Medicare when members openly chose sides. But most of the time, party discipline was rigid.

There were a number of reasons for the failure of caucus to rock the boat more frequently. One was the extraordinary loyalty of Liberal members to Mike Pearson. Plagued from the start by controversies, scandals and internal cabinet dissension, Pearson gained support in caucus with each new crisis. His self-effacement may have been contrived, as some suspected. Or maybe, as I concluded, he always saw something slightly absurd in the machinations and rituals of party politics, and rarely took them seriously. Whatever the reason, Pearson always managed to turn his darkest hour in caucus into a personal triumph. He never hesitated to acknowledge his need for caucus support or to assume personal responsibility for government set-backs. As a result, he invariably turned grumblings of discontent into a groundswell of sustaining sympathy. A backbencher's impulse to kick over the traces would be stilled by his unwillingness to add to Pearson's seemingly endless woes.

Not all of the docility was so selflessly motivated, of course. Pearson's inability to ever lift the Liberals beyond minority status may have served him better than he knew. Many members toed the line out of fear of triggering yet another cliff-hanger election. Their influence might be minimal on important national issues but, as government supporters, they felt themselves better placed to serve their constituencies than they would be in opposition. That argument carried considerable weight with me at the start. Of all the federal ridings in Canada, mine was in greater need than most of generous helpings of government largesse.

Three

The region comprising Burin-Burgeo has long been referred to as "the Forgotten Coast." My aim, as a newly elected member of Parliament, was to change that, but my determination was equalled only by my ignorance about how to go about it. My early experiences in Ottawa did nothing to help. Finding, much less manipulating, the levers of power proved far more difficult than I had anticipated.

When I entered politics, the fishery remained as much the mainstay of Burin-Burgeo as it had been when my grandfather came to the area from Scotland. Yet in Ottawa, the fishery was not a priority for either politicians or bureaucrats. Those charged with administering fishery policies were not among the more exalted mandarins, and such appeal as the industry had was centred on the west coast of Canada. Jimmy Sinclair, a former minister of fisheries and resident of British Columbia, had seen to that. His task had not been difficult since, by any yardstick, the salmon is a more exotic creature and a more lucrative asset than the lowly cod. Jack Pickersgill fought valiantly to right the balance. His dogged and successful effort to have unemployment insurance benefits extended to fishermen, over the objections of practically everyone in government and the fish trade, was among his more remarkable accomplishments. But the very importance of this move reflected the dire financial plight of the people I represented. If the phrase "benign neglect" had been coined at the time, it would have described the government's attitude exactly.

The government, however, was not entirely to blame. The paternalism of an outmoded mercantile system also affected the situation. There was evidence of it wherever I went during constituency visits. Often, a single merchant set prices to be paid to fishermen, established the rates and conditions on which essential credit was granted, and was the only source of fishery and household supplies. The result was, at best, a form of enlightened feudalism, at worst shameful exploitation. It produced a precarious and overly dependent lifestyle for fishermen and their families. Complicating the problem was the tendency of the government, when it did act, to make common cause with the trade. Precious few public dollars flowed to the fishermen except through the sticky fingers of the merchants. Consequently, the traditionally fierce independence of the fishermen was tempered by a sense of resignation, even fear. Many could scarcely call their lives their own.

With very few exceptions, I found in Ottawa a total unawareness of these conditions, and no disposition to learn. Nothing could empty the House of Commons more quickly than a debate on fisheries, even if someone was interested enough to launch one. I was told more than once that if I craved political advancement, I should not annoy busy ministers with fishery problems. As one old hand put it, "The fishery lacks political sex appeal."

Gradually, a few of us, including Richard Cashin—later the head of the Fishermen's Union in Newfoundland—began to make slight dents in the wall of political and bureaucratic indifference. Several years would pass, however, before government and Parliament would undergo a real change of heart. This would happen only after such issues as the Law of the Sea and various international economic upheavals highlighted the value of Canada's ocean resources. In the meantime, representing Canada's largest fishing district was no snap, to say the least.

Although I had had a long and close association with the fishery, it took that first autumn in Ottawa to teach me the complexities of the industry. It was, in fact, more than an industry; it was a unique way of life for thousands of people. I began to see why its many interlocking elements baffled the uninitiated and made the more familiar problems of farmers and other primary producers seem simple by comparison. At least when a farmer claimed a crop failure, it was relatively easy to test his contention. Harvesting the ocean was a different matter. A catch failure could be caused by anything from an act of God to human neglect and laziness. If two men were working the same fishing grounds, one could reap a bumper yield, while the other caught practically nothing despite a comparable effort. Foreign marketing was a dog-eat-dog affair; the most vulnerable exporter, hounded by creditors would be left with no choice but to force prices down for everyone. Demands for income stabilization were hard to meet, even when government was willing, because of the threat of retaliatory tariffs.

Adding to these problems was the always inflammatory issue of overfishing. Huge fleets of foreign vessels raped the stocks within sight of land while Canada adhered scrupulously to the letter of international law. Often, I had the difficult task of attempting to explain government policy, or the lack of it, in Newfoundland communities where the lights of dozens of foreign trawlers were visible offshore, illuminating the night sky like the reflected glow from a neighbouring town.

A case could be made for Canada's reluctance to act unilaterally to curb such abuses, arrange more orderly marketing and introduce a more effective price support system, but these reasons frequently became a convenient excuse. The East Coast fishery simply did not have the clout to force Canadian negotiators to take risks in the international arena. Their game plan and their concept of Canada's emerging role in the world called for patient, plodding tactics and the attainment of a broad consensus, even if this took years to achieve. It was all very rational, high-minded and widely endorsed. In the meantime, however, a key resource industry and the livelihoods of tens of thousands of Canadians were in genuine peril. It is hard to believe that any other important industrial or resource sector would have been permitted to reach such a precarious state without major government intervention, regardless of the risks and costs involved.

In the case of the fishery, my warnings and pleas and the strongly expressed concerns of others brought only spasmodic, temporary relief. The overall situation grew steadily worse. Far from triggering more decisive action, the deepening threat to almost every aspect of the industry produced a sense of resignation among government planners. Those who influenced spending were reluctant to provide funds for stopgap measures, or even for essential marine works. Official arguments were dispassionate and coldly logical. Without a basic rationalization of the industry and a settlement of international issues, those who controlled the purse strings saw no reason to throw good money after bad.

This was an attitude I would hear expressed very often, and not only in connection with the fishery. Today, as in the 1960s, there are dozens of Canadian industries and entire industrial sectors whose continuation could not be justified on straight economic grounds. If left to the harsh dictates of the marketplace, such industries would collapse. Yet most survive with large infusions of government help because the alternative of massive economic and social disruption is too horrendous for the politicians, and much of the public, to accept. I was often confronted by this problem during my public career. As will become evident, I found the task of dealing with it incredibly complex and agonizingly painful.

My principal concern as an inexperienced backbencher in those troubled times was naturally the plight of my constituents. As I sought to help, my education in the wondrous ways and workings of government took a quantum jump. I discovered how impotent the private MP could be in attempting to master the system, and how ill-equipped he was to carve a path through the almost impenetrable jungle of red tape. Of necessity, I had taken a crash course in fisheries during scores of meetings with my constituents, both labour and management, and I was not without ideas. But in Ottawa, I encountered baffling contradictions from a phalanx of officials wedded to their policies, skilled in the tactics of rigidity, and not particularly sensitive to the constituency problems of a lowly backbencher.

Had there been consistency and a common position in the bureaucratic approach, it would have been easier to devise arguments against it, to plan ways in which it might be modified. There was, however, no such coordination. As I attempted to interpret mutually exclusive policies and to avoid personal feuds among top officials and ministers, I became trapped in interdepartmental rivalries. In such a climate, wheeling and dealing were unavoidable, and once I accepted this, the last vestiges of my naïveté vanished. I was learning how the political game was played, and if that was the only way, I would play it the best I could. It was, after all, the only game in town.

Many who have no direct dealings with the federal government see it as a massive, well-oiled machine, its multiple mechanisms meshing smoothly and efficiently as they control the nation's business. The reality falls short of that concept. Once I was inside, I found government to be a maze of separate, often watertight, compartments. Direction and influence flowed up as well as down. Obscure, anonymous officials jealously guarded their piece of the action and, if prudent enough to avoid encroachment on the territory of others, were free to wield substantial power.

The relationship between cabinet and bureaucracy did not conform to the simple textbook model of elected ministers making policy and civil servants dutifully carrying it out. Many ministers were slavishly dependent on their officials, and some of the most outwardly obsequious officials showed, privately, the least regard for their ministers' talents. Others in high places were wedded to the precept that no ill would befall those who went by the book and carried out policy regardless of circumstances or special conditions.

The importance of private members waxed and waned with the government's mercurial assessments of its electoral security or peril. Paradoxically, when the polls were bad, an effective member of the opposition was often wooed more assiduously by a minister under fire than were the members of his own party. Then, as now, politics was largely a matter of personal relationships. The old adage holds true: "It's not what you know, but who you know." In politics, this could be embellished by adding that "what you know about who you know" can sometimes be helpful, as well.

There is seldom anything sinister in this intricate interplay of forces and personalities. It is merely traditional office politics elevated to a fine art. All such machinations tend to proliferate near the top, rarely affecting ordinary workers, those thousands of civil servants who perform their tasks routinely in all parts of the country, sparing not a thought for the huge government apparatus and complicated process of which they are a part.

As I sought to understand and get a handle on this unwieldy structure from my cubbyhole in the basement of Centre Block, I found myself doing battle with the bureaucracy on several fronts simultaneously. After weekends of constituency meetings, I was back in Ottawa to buttonhole ministers, track down elusive officials, and seek advice from more experienced members. The corridors of power were often blind alleys of frustration for a new parliamentarian with only a single secretary to help him.

Although voter concerns are always changing, a steady allotment of public works is still what butters political bread, especially in a rural fishing constituency. The member who provides a new wharf confirms his value to the district; if he cannot get the facility, he is demonstrably ineffective. Bob Winters, who then represented a Toronto riding, was a native of the Maritimes. He had also been Minister of Public Works under Louis St. Laurent, and was well aware of the political importance of highly visible federal facilities. Bob advised me to search through the voluminous Estimates for possible sources of funding for my needed projects. I soon struck paydirt in the most unlikely places.

Plans for a stretch of road in my constituency had been shelved for lack of funds. But because of an inadequate liaison between the various planners, there was still a hefty allocation in the Estimates for the construction of two bridges along the route the proposed road would have taken. Officials advised me solemnly that while the road project could not be reinstated, the money for the bridges was still available. I had learned by now not to look a gift horse in the mouth, and I gratefully welcomed the calling of tenders for the two bridges. Their construction would provide welcome jobs for some of my constituents and, I reasoned, with the costly plans in place, someone would get around to building the road sooner or later. As it turned out, I was right, but for a few years in my constituency, there was the incongruous sight of two magnificent bridges leading absolutely nowhere.

This was not my only early experience with the mysterious inanities of government budgeting. Public Works officials were granted the funds to build a fishing wharf at Sagona. When I visited the small community, the residents were in the process of leaving. The only ones remaining were a group of workmen planning to move out as soon as the job was done. With the community abandoned, the costly pier was a white elephant even before completion. Common sense dictated a halt to the project and diversion of funds to communities where marine works were needed desperately. Although I made the case forcefully to officials, no such accommodation was possible. The sacred Estimates had assigned the money to Sagona, and Sagona was where it must be spent.

In later years, as the budget process became more flexible and sophisticated, such incidents occurred less frequently. Yet even the most careful watchdog cannot catch them all, nor restrain completely those public servants who, if told to provide a mailboat on the landlocked prairies, would promptly carry out instructions.

Two other examples of my growing ingenuity provide evidence of the devious methods an MP must occasionally employ to meet the needs of his constituents. My home village of Swift Current on Placentia Bay needed a post office, but an insufficient volume of business was being done in the existing privately owned facility to meet the department's formula for new construction. I arranged with business associates to have a good deal of their mail dispatched through Swift Current. Revenues rose dramatically, if temporarily, and while officials never knew the source of the unexpected increase, the required volume was reached and Swift Current got a spanking new post office.

I used the same technique to have the antiquated telephone system replaced by a modern exchange. When there were phone calls I could delay, I waited until I returned home for weekends and placed the calls from Swift Current. The phone company recorded a sharp upturn in volume, and Swift Current obtained direct distance dialing well ahead of many larger communities.

I was beginning to take a certain pleasure in devising methods to circumvent some of the rigidities of the system. I was also more at home in Ottawa, although I still felt intimidated by the general atmosphere of the House of Commons, and the distinct coolness I encountered in many quarters. As I continued to feel my way, guidance came from a surprising source—John Diefenbaker. With his finely honed political sense, the Old Chief was well aware of my discomfort and disappointment with my parliamentary experiences. During a dull session of the Commons, Diefenbaker came to sit beside me at the far end of the back row, the place assigned to me as a junior member. He could understand my mood, he told me; he had gone through a similar experience many years before. "Parliament can be a cruel place," he said in that familiar sonorous tone, his observation all the more poignant because he was already embroiled in the bitter struggle that would soon cost him his party's leadership. He went on to reminisce quietly and with considerable humour about his unique career, making much of his love of Parliament. "You'll find there's no place like it," he predicted, "but take your time. A new member shouldn't open his mouth in this place for at least a year."

I took Dief's advice. My first speech in the House did not come until the late spring of 1967, Centennial Year, when I moved the Address in Reply to the Speech from the Throne. Members and the media were complimentary, and one of the first congratulatory notes I received was from John Diefenbaker, by then the private member for Prince Albert.

Despite my self-imposed silence in the Commons, the volume and complexity of my other duties had increased greatly. Earlier problems in the constituency had not abated; if anything, the fishery was getting worse. Unwilling or unable to cope with devastating foreign influences, government followed a natural tendency to seek untested but dramatic domestic solutions. The most controversial of these was the Resettlement Program, a plan to reshape the face of Newfoundland and alter a culture and lifestyle that had endured for centuries. It involved me in one of the most difficult and bitter experiences of my political career.

A basic weakness of the fishery was the curse of isolation. It contributed to economic and social stagnation, limited choices and opportunities, and sustained a tightly and narrowly controlled system. Roads were an obvious answer, and I was able to have many important highways constructed in my constituency during my years as a member. However, since many communities were on islands or extremely remote, there was no practical way to break their isolation.

By the 1960s, the controversial Resettlement Program had been devised by the Newfoundland government with Ottawa's help. The logic of the plan was sound. Moving people to larger centres would give them access to better services and more gainful employment, and would enhance their independence. But the program soon became mired in excessive and needless regulations.

The idea of relocating was not repugnant to many of those affected. Newfoundlanders have always been somewhat nomadic, and by the early 1960s, more families had moved on their own—without recompense—than would do so under the auspices of the government. Conflict arose because when governments stepped in, compulsion and regimentation were introduced for the first time into what had always been a matter of individual choice. Public planning was in many ways the antithesis of the very private decision of whether or not to move and where to move. For a new MP, the conflicts caused by the policy were a challenge. I became a principal spokesman for constituents in their dealings with remote governments, their struggles with dozens of incomprehensible forms, and the unresponsiveness of a frequently dehumanizing system.

As I travelled throughout the constituency in those days, often to places where Barbara and I had experienced such pleasure during the campaign, I could feel the palpable tension and emotional turmoil. Families were often divided—the young determined to go, their elders stubbornly opposed. There were strident charges that those who wished to leave were being bought off with public funds. There were even occasional fist fights and destruction of property.

The bureaucratic passion for tidiness had produced a mind-boggling array of regulations, but two were the source of greatest dissension. There had to be near unanimous agreement to resettle before anyone in the community could get financial assistance; this placed those reluctant to go under great pressure. Also, people could move only to designated areas called, in impersonal official language, "receiving centres." While the restrictions made some sense, they were not worth the rancour they aroused, and I resolved to have them modified. Despite my determination and pleadings, the system was slow to yield. I had to cope as best I could with continuing frustrations and painful human conflicts, all the while torn personally between logic and sentiment. I described this condition as the "Paradise syndrome" because of an incident I experienced in the small island community of that name.

Paradise, Placentia Bay, is no beauty spot. Years before, I had wired Barbara from there: "Am in Paradise. Don't bother to be good. It's not worth it!" The founders gave the harbour its exotic name because, like its Biblical namesake, it is extremely difficult to enter. Resettlement had brought real trouble to Paradise, and I was asked to arbitrate the dispute. The main spokesman for those opposed to relocation was an elderly gentleman, well-spoken and erudite, although he had never travelled far from his small village. In a soft, sad voice, he expressed the familiar arguments: a feared loss of old, treasured values, uncertainty over the people's ability to adjust to new surroundings, and a deep mistrust of the government's motivation. His was a moving appeal, the anguished thoughts of a splendid man confused by this unexpected and unwanted complication. Even as he spoke, however, a grim reminder of the other side of the conflict was taking place across the harbour.

Summoned by a distraught mother, I found her teenage son lying in delirious semi-consciousness on the kitchen couch. He had gashed his hand badly, and without medical attention, infection had set in. The taut, inflamed skin had split across the knuckles, and an angry redness reached well up the arm. It was an obvious case of blood poisoning. No suitable boat was available, and since I had come by plane, I offered to fly the young man out to hospital. As the old man helped to carry the patient to the wharf, I was struck by this dramatic illustration of the tragic contradictions inherent in the move to centralization: the old man, a worthy example of the virtues of a rural existence, and the youth, a victim of the hazards of isolation.

The young man recovered, but his close call hastened the abandonment of Paradise. By the end of the year, it was deserted. The family of the injured youth now live near St. John's and have no regrets. The old man moved reluctantly across the bay to Placentia, the nearest town to his village. He wrote me often, telling of his disorientation and loneliness, and within three years of the move, he was dead. As he had lost one Paradise, I hope that he found the real thing. If so, I suspect he still harbours a lingering wish to go home.

The impact of the Resettlement Program on Burin-Burgeo, and on all of rural Newfoundland, is still hotly debated. Academics have studied it interminably and, if anything, the passing years have lessened their objectivity. The empty villages with their dilapidated churches, rotting wharves, skeletons of houses, overgrown roads and neglected cemeteries lend themselves easily to the creation of myths. They are now portrayed by incurable romantics as once blissful, rustic havens, ravaged by mindless politicians in the most barbarous act since the Scottish clearances. In truth, life in these remote areas was seldom idyllic, although its pleasant side, to which we were exposed during the election campaign, remains fondly remembered.

My own attitude toward resettlement must remain ambivalent. In time, I managed to get the regulations modified, convinced as I was of their unnecessary harshness. The decision to go or stay was left to individual families who could resettle more or less where they wished. But by then, the wave of migration had subsided; only the acrimony and bitter debate remained. In retrospect, I believe much of it could have been avoided. Experience suggests that most of the affected communities were falling victim to progress before the program started; given more patience and tolerance, the problem of isolation would have corrected itself. This knowledge, however, does not ease my regret over the passing of a distinct era in Newfoundland's long history, the era into which I was born. Its attractions and hardships have influenced my life profoundly. They explain, in part, my lifelong preoccupation with politics and why, while I was still a boy, I had resolved to become some day the elected member for the south coast.

Four

While, arguably, the Trudeau era had its beginning with his election to Parliament, it was certainly a low-key start. No one within the Liberal hierarchy saw him as a potential prime minister. To most, including me, he was an unknown. The objective of Liberal strategists was to win the open support of Jean Marchand and to persuade him to run in the next election, which Prime Minister Pearson had originally planned for 1966. I and many others with close ties to the party were encouraged to woo Marchand at every opportunity. I cannot recall a single mention of Trudeau's name during all of this period.

Later, many Liberals would take credit for recruiting the future prime minister; no doubt some played a part. In the end, of course, by his own account, Marchand was primarily responsible for bringing both Trudeau and Gérard Pelletier on board. Marchand once gave me an amusing account of the meeting at which all three decided to seek election as Liberals. Marchand had all but succumbed to party pressures, but wanted his two close friends and allies in various Quebec labour causes to agree to enter federal politics with him. Neither was keen to oblige, and Trudeau in particular had strong reservations. While seeking to persuade him, Marchand surreptitiously poured Trudeau a stiff Scotch that put his abstemious friend somewhat under the weather. Many years later, I asked Trudeau about this incident, and he laughingly acknowledged its truth. It was, he added, the only occasion in his life when he had tasted hard liquor. How much, if at all, the drink affected Trudeau's decision will never be known. A much more intriguing question, in retrospect, is whether Trudeau would have been prepared, or even available, to run if Pearson had not been persuaded to move the election ahead to 1965. A year later, the restless, peripatetic Trudeau with his myriad, short-lived interests might well have been off on another adventure. Or, given his tenuous links to the Liberal Party, it might have been impossible to recruit him under any circumstances.

Trudeau was not on Pearson's mind as he struggled with conflicting party advice concerning the wisdom of calling an early vote. His reservations centred on the dubious appeal of a campaign with only one issue—the need for a majority government. I was among the many who argued against going to the electorate on such a platform, especially since the government had not received serious parliamentary obstruction and was less than three years into its mandate. The campaign manager, Walter Gordon, favoured an early vote and by Labour Day, 1965, he had won Pearson over. At the time the writ was issued, Marchand's candidacy remained uncertain, and neither Trudeau nor Pelletier were even being mentioned.

The first I heard of them was from Keith Davey, who was then the National Director of the Liberal Party. The campaign was already under way when I visited him at the Party's Ottawa headquarters. At least two of Davey's characteristics are constant: he is fascinated by well-known personalities, and he is addicted to the telephone. As usual, when I entered his office, he had the phone to his ear, and this time, he was spreading the word about three new "star candidates" from Quebec. I heard the details simultaneously in a series of asides. Davey's enthusiasm is often infectious but, on that occasion, I did not find it difficult to resist. Marchand's candidacy was good news, of course, but I knew scarcely anything about Pelletier and had never heard Trudeau's name before. To Davey, however, they were the kind of "name candidates" he was forever seeking. They would, he predicted, add colour and media interest to a lacklustre campaign. Despite my subdued reaction, I had had enough exposure to Davey to be cautious about dismissing his elation out of hand.

The 1965 campaign was the third on which I had worked with Davey. While his love of a good political fight led him to commit some major tactical errors, his political instincts could be uncannily sound. A disciple of Walter Gordon, Davey had helped him and a handful of other key Liberals in the breakthrough campaign of 1962, and in the rebuilding job that had preceded it. My main contribution to that effort had been to persuade Gordon and other party insiders of the importance of political broadcasting, and especially the effective use of television. Jack Pickersgill had been an early convert. Although never a "natural" for television, he had willingly accepted guidance, and had used the medium effectively in his Newfoundland campaign.

Once a campaign has been successfully waged, the most difficult business of cabinet making begins. Mike Pearson, with his wry, self-deprecating sense of humour, described the difficulty for me when, a few days after the Liberals had won the 1963 election, I asked him how he was progressing with the job of forming a cabinet. He smiled in the special way he had of conveying frustration. Things would be easier, he allowed jokingly, if he could find a potential Toronto minister of both Italian and German extraction who was a practising Anglican, popular with the business community, but sympathetic to labour and, he concluded with a chuckle, preferably left-handed. Pearson never disguised his dislike of the cabinet making process; nor did Pierre Trudeau. He was never comfortable with the responsibility of choosing the men and women to whom he, and only he, could offer and withdraw a place in the ministry.

Every leader I have met in the free world has expressed similar sentiments. Nowhere, however, is the job of cabinet making more difficult, and usually more haphazard, than in Canada. No Canadian prime minister gets the cabinet he wants. Leaders are limited by what the electors give—or do not give—them. This is perhaps the essence of democracy, but not when choices must be tempered by regional expectations and traditions, inevitable compromises, pressures and political expediencies, and the growing tendency of provinces and regions to deny any representation even to victorious parties.

While these regional near shut-outs have serious implications, they are not new to the cabinet making process. During his years as prime minister, Pearson retained respectable, if not spectacular, electoral support in British Columbia. On the Prairies, however, the corporal's guard of Liberal survivors gained automatic entry to the cabinet. And by the time Pearson retired, there were no Liberal members from Alberta or Saskatchewan, and only one from Manitoba.

After his 1968 victory, Trudeau had a choice of potential ministers in all of the western provinces except Saskatchewan, where only one Liberal, Otto Lang, was elected. But Trudeaumania spent itself at the Quebec border. Francophones in New Brunswick retained their traditional Liberal loyalty, but Prince Edward Island stuck with the Tories. Allan MacEachen, in Nova Scotia, and I, in Newfoundland, were the only elected Anglophone Liberals in Atlantic Canada. Since MacEachen was already in the cabinet, and since my status as the lone Newfoundland survivor virtually assured my appointment, we were probably among the most relaxed Liberal MPs as the Prime Minister pondered his choices.

I played no direct part in the process by which Trudeau arrived at his decision on the makeup of his first post-election cabinet. I learned most of the details later from various sources. Also, through my participation in several subsequent cabinet shuffles, not to mention a few crises, I came to know how Trudeau handled this particularly difficult aspect of his job. His method demonstrates the complexities of forming a cabinet and the sometimes more difficult business of shuffling its membership periodically to inject new blood and fresh ideas.

In 1968, and ever since, Trudeau played his cards close to his chest. Only a few close advisors, inside the caucus and out, were consulted. All were made well aware of the Prime Minister's abhorrence of leaks and his insistence on confidentiality. As an added precaution, however, Trudeau rarely revealed the whole of his thinking, even to the main players. An Ontario confidant might be asked for an assessment of certain members from that province. Or someone assured of being appointed would be asked his preferences and if he would like the portfolio the Prime Minister had in mind. But the names of others being considered would not be divulged, or if they were, several names would be given. Then, if leaks did occur, they were so contradictory that the media pundits usually wound up with egg on their faces.

In 1968, Trudeau's biggest difficulty in choosing a cabinet started before the election. Having decided to go directly from the leadership convention into an election, he recognized that party unity was a top priority. Trudeau was conciliatory to all his rivals for the leadership. Only runner-up Bob Winters decided to retire.

Winters' experience demonstrates how the new prime minister moved quickly to ease tensions and lessen bitterness born of disappointment. A few days after the convention, before the election call, Winters stopped by my Centre Block office and asked me to walk with him to the West Block where he had an appointment with Trudeau. What should he do, he asked me, if his recent rival, now prime minister, asked him to stay on? I urged him to do so, pointing out his strong support in the Party and his undoubted value in the election whenever it was called. Winters was reluctant. He knew that he had missed his big chance and he was bitter because he felt, with justification, that he had been let down by some in the party hierarchy. They had talked him into a return to politics and into seeking the leadership with promises of support which did not materialize. As we parted, he asked me to wait in my office where he would come and report, following his meeting with Trudeau.

When he did, it was all over. The Prime Minister, he said, had been very gracious and had offered to implement one of Winters' pet ideas—the creation of a single Department of Industry, Trade and Commerce and to name him Minister. Winters' mood had not changed, however, and he declined.

In July of 1968, I was sworn in as a member of the federal cabinet crafted by Pierre Trudeau in the wake of his remarkable election victory.

Ten years and ten months later, after his defeat on May 22, 1979, Trudeau handed in his resignation and with it, automatically, the resignations of his ministers. Apart from Trudeau himself, I was one of the few left who had been at Rideau Hall to help form the new government on that exciting and promising day more than a decade before. Even I did not actually witness the finale. A few days earlier, I had resigned my Commons seat to assume the leadership of the Newfoundland Liberal Party. While the transfer of power was under way in Ottawa, I was fighting, unsuccessfully as things turned out, a general election in my native province.

During my nearly eleven years in the federal cabinet, I held six portfolios, chaired several cabinet committees, participated in most federal-provincial conferences, dealt bilaterally with all the provinces on scores of issues, represented Canada on various international bodies such as NATO, attended two economic summit conferences and, in the process, travelled millions of miles. All this was in addition to the normal responsibilities of a cabinet minister and a member of the House of Commons.

Throughout these active years and since, many have asked me if my public career was worth it and if I truly enjoyed it. Frequently, I answer with a variation of the fairy-tale description of "The Little Girl With The Curl"—when it was good, it was very, very good; when it was bad, it was horrid!

One fact is most depressing in retrospect. Although good men and women in government, in Parliament, in bureaucracy and at comparable levels in the provinces were basically sincere and tried very hard, the principal issues today are not significantly different from those we faced in the heady, optimistic days of a new administration. If anything, many of the problems, such as inflation, have grown more serious, despite the best efforts of all concerned.

Since two of my portfolios exposed me to international affairs, I can testify that this situation is not peculiar to Canada. Other countries may have different problems, but solutions are equally elusive. Nor are the characters and abilities of the decision makers major factors, although some undoubtedly have a transitory impact. In the 1970s, most of the key political figures in Canada and elsewhere changed frequently, often with dramatic suddenness. Both at home and among his international peers, Trudeau remained one of the very few constants, and even he saw the string run out before his early and unexpected comeback.

Domestically, at the end of Trudeau's tenure, not a premier was in office who had been there ten years ago. Quebec, for example, had seen five premiers from three parties since Trudeau became prime minister. Political parties in power had changed at least once across the country, except in Ontario.

When I resigned from the House of Commons after thirteen and a half years, only about fifty members had been there as long or longer. In the same period, we in government faced three leaders of the official Conservative opposition and three leaders of the NDP. The turnover among those holding cabinet posts is far more frequent than some, particularly the media, often suggest. In a cabinet averaging thirty members, I served with well over twice that number of colleagues, and the shuffling of portfolios within cabinet was even more extensive.

The assumption of permanency within the ranks of senior civil servants is also faulty. Although many top bureaucrats merely move between departments, significant numbers leave the public service entirely for various reasons. Even the basic structure of senior government management undergoes periodic changes, and within departments, this process is seemingly unending.

Much has been said about the power exercised by those within the Prime Minister's and the Privy Council's offices. Yet even there, personnel changes are frequent, as are the divisions of responsibility. For example, Trudeau had four different principal secretaries, at least as many chief press officers and a wide variety of policy advisors. Again, a look at the record reveals, in all of those areas, an experience similar to that of other western industrialized countries.

In making these points, I am arguing neither for nor against the wisdom or advantages of frequent shifts in the pattern of leadership. I will leave such an assessment until later. My immediate purpose is to point out the intractability of most fundamental, long-standing problems and their stubborn resistance to new and different approaches, regardless of the skill and keenness of their advocates. Nor is there permanent improvement when new and radical ideologies are introduced or promoted. Despite my occasional despondency over the slow rate of progress and even, in some cases, apparent regression, I subscribe to Winston Churchill's belief that "democracy is the worst possible form of government—except for all of the others." I draw some comfort also from Churchill's often revealed irritation that the world's monumental imperfections display such resistance and longevity.

If these observations are correct, and if experience and history lend them credence, then the quality of leadership, the creativity of fresh ideas and the vigour applied to new approaches can only ameliorate the effects of important developments and events. They cannot, however, root out fundamental problems or ensure their permanent eradication.

I am referring of course, to Canada and western industrialized democracies, but my basic premise is, I believe, universally applicable. In some respects, it is more evident in non-democratic countries where public opinion and reaction rarely impede government planning and action. Those in authority—and they are not without talent, as much as we may disagree with their ideologies—are free to impose whatever possible solutions they can devise. Yet we continue to witness the general failure of their planning, a failure evident in the lack of freedom and low economic status of their citizens.

There are those who will disagree with my contention. They will quote reams of statistics to demonstrate the steady advancement of Canadians economically, socially, and across the whole range of measurable growth. The same yardsticks will produce roughly comparable results for most countries of the developed world. Superficially, such findings are correct, even though the rate of "progress" is now declining rapidly.

What the figures do not demonstrate are the methods by which these advances have been sustained. During my years in public life, my experience was that while we attempted to deal with the root causes of problems, we ended up, as a rule, adjusting to these problems, often entrenching them further while greatly inflating costs in the process. Having had a close relationship with business in all my portfolios, I can attest that much of the private sector is scarcely more creative.

One reason for this widespread tendency is the questionable assumption that a solution exists for every problem, if only we had the wit to find it. The public generally holds this view, as every politician knows. Competing politicians reinforce this public conception, and business frequently shows a marked ambivalence toward the policies and methods governments employ.

These attitudes have exacted a very high price. But more importantly, statistics cannot measure the intangible impact, the general public mood, the widespread sense of unease and uncertainty. My varied experiences and political instincts, however, tell me that what might be called "the Canadian state of mind" is less tranquil, assured and confident than it was ten, or even twenty, years ago. Hence, my belief that what passes for progress is often illusory or, at best, transient.

One further observation is important to my conclusions. The unpredictability of the future is universally acknowledged, yet everyone is preoccupied with attempting to foretell what is to be. I can recall hundreds of government forecasts that were proven erroneous by the passage of time. Business predictions often miss the mark by a country mile. And, of course, our personal lives usually demonstrate the folly of anticipating future developments.

Yet despite all of this, our society needs planning; in some respects, governments need it most of all. But although business can sometimes redirect its efforts, and individuals still show a commendable resilience, when government forecasts and anticipations are wrong, the policies and programs flowing from them have already achieved a life of their own, even when they are shown to be the wrong answer to a wrongly identified problem.

There is another great weakness in government planning and decision making. I have learned the truth of the old adage, "The unexpected must always be expected." There are problems, even crises, that simply cannot be anticipated. And while these problems are real, serious, and must be dealt with, governments often lack the flexibility and capacity to provide a positive response. Similarly, past experience is of little value in dealing with a development for which there is no precedent, as many aspects of the oil crisis have shown.

What is needed, therefore, is not a new team of managers; we are generally served well in Canada in both public and private sectors. We need a thorough re-examination of what is being managed. We need to reassess our objectives against a realistic test of attainability. This may be seen by some as too bleak a picture. But if the common goal is a better and more contented Canadian state of mind—not wholly free of uncertainty, of course—we must see ourselves, without illusions, for what we are today.

However it may be described, the Canadian economic system, with its large private sector orientation, ultimately determines the economic well-being and level of financial security of Canadians, whatever their jobs and sources of income. The majority may not understand its complexities, but they quickly sense when it turns sour and affects them directly. Such a feeling is widespread today. Without significant changes of direction and basic new approaches, I foresee a most difficult time ahead with which conventional wisdom simply will not be able to cope.

Five

If, in 1970, cabinet was having a difficult time introducing new programs and managing the financial affairs of the country, this could be largely attributed to two factors: the mounting costs of national defence and the uncontrollable surge in expenditures on health and welfare.

In the case of national defence, we managed to stem the tide by freezing the defence budget for a period of three years. In the case of health and welfare, John Munro was directed to head up a comprehensive study, the main objective of which was to see how the expenditures of over two billion dollars could be put to better use. This implied that John and his officials, as well as a cabinet committee, should try to determine what new initiatives in the social welfare field were desirable for the 1970s, and most importantly, how we could switch the emphasis from existing programs in order to find funds for new ones. There was no doubt in my mind that it was not the intention of cabinet to greatly increase at that time our total spending on welfare measures. Similarly, I was satisfied that there was general agreement that many costly programs could do with major revisions; some could be eliminated entirely. It was agreed that when this comprehensive exercise had been completed, the findings would be prepared in the form of a white paper, and that this would be given to the public for consideration before the government made its final decisions.

From the outset, the exercise was highly frustrating. To understand why, it is necessary first to understand something of the character, personality and motivation of John Munro, the Minister of Health and Welfare—although, in all fairness, the problems which arose did not occur wholly, or even largely, because of Munro's attitude. The main problem was essentially the high cost of an enlightened welfare system in relation to the total resources of government. It was taking far more than the government could afford, or would be able to afford in the foreseeable future, to establish a social framework acceptable to those who were preoccupied with the needs of the underprivileged and who saw government action and response as the main, if not only, solution to these problems. But having said that, I must also say that since John Munro was a prime advocate of government action in the social security field, he could be counted on to plan a review which would lay far more emphasis on what he considered to be necessary reforms than on the fact that there just weren't enough funds to pay for them.

This difficult undertaking also illustrated a fundamental flaw in the system of cabinet committees. Generally speaking, the membership of cabinet committees was determined by the prime minister on the basis of the interests and competencies of various ministers. For example, the Economic Policy Committee had a large representation of what might be called the business and financial wing of cabinet. The Social Policy Committee was weighted in favour of those who had either portfolios related to social affairs or a special interest in social security.

In the first year in particular, this composition created within the committee an unanimity of thoughts and objectives, without the necessary counterweight of opinions more concerned with the economic impact of social reform. Because of this combination of circumstances, the preparation of the white paper became, in that first year, largely a matter of proposing new government initiatives that would be superimposed on the existing structure without major changes to policies already in effect. This would have added considerably to government expenditures in the welfare field. Early submissions to the cabinet committee revealed that even minimum improvements would probably cost the Treasury an additional billion dollars annually. This result was inevitable; in addition to the considerations I have mentioned, the work of preparing the draft white paper was placed primarily in the hands of professionals in the social security field who, quite naturally, preferred the expansion of welfare measures to the more difficult job of rationalizing what was being done at present.

The field of social security is complex, particularly when there is an absence of guidelines. The committee found itself bogged down in all manner of considerations, as each issue discussed was discovered inevitably to have an effect on some other government program. For example, at the same time that Munro was working on a general social security paper, Bryce Mackasey was preparing major reforms to the unemployment insurance program. Also, it was clear that the White Paper on Taxation would have a considerable effect on the tax burden of low-income families. And there were other related considerations. The result was that John Munro experienced a good deal of frustration in moving his paper forward, and the timetable against which he was working had to be changed almost every week.

A further complication was largely of Munro's own making. He was quite open in discussing with the media and at various public appearances both the fact that the paper was being prepared and, more importantly, the various issues that were under consideration. One must make allowances for this situation, as it was necessary for Munro to discuss a number of proposals with the provinces because of their shared responsibility for welfare measures. There is no doubt, however, that because he believed so passionately in the need for reform, Munro was also seeking to build a base of public support for what he wanted to do, and in this way, to apply pressure so that cabinet would support his recommendations.

After the first year of committee deliberations on the proposed white paper, it was evident that insufficient progress was being made. As well, Prime Minister Trudeau felt the necessity to balance to some extent the representation of ministers on the Social Policy Committee. I was one of those assigned to that committee after the first twelve months, as part of this attempt at balance. It was for me a most unsatisfying experience. Even though I was quite prepared to take a strong stand in favour of total reform and moderation in terms of extra expenditures, I found my experience on the committee frustrating and largely futile. When various measures were brought forward and I found them objectionable, Munro would invariably respond by saying that the matter had been considered by the committee prior to my joining it, and he could not see how he could get anywhere if, at each meeting, new members, or those who had not been present on a previous occasion, insisted on discussing fundamental principles all over again.

Because the committee continued to be heavily weighted with advocates of social security measures, it was almost impossible for me to make any headway unless I was prepared to antagonize most of the other committee members, and to take the extra step of talking to the Prime Minister privately about what was going on. I also found that I was being cast more and more by Munro, Mackasey and one or two others in a reactionary role.

This, of course, was far from being the case. My main concern was that the problems of the poor could not be solved simply by giving them a few dollars more. The real difficulty was to find a means through which the causes of poverty could be attacked, and the cycle of poverty broken. On top of this, I was deeply conscious of the problem created for government by massive increases in various social security programs at a time when revenues were not accumulating fast enough to meet the demand. This, in my view, was the real lesson to be learned from the Pearson years, when such major measures as the Canada Assistance Plan, the Canada Pension Plan, Medicare, the Guaranteed Income Supplement and others were all introduced within a period of a few years without enough consideration being given to the overall impact of these programs on the economy. Consequently, what I argued for in the committee during its second year was a greater emphasis on the reorganization and rationalization of our whole approach to welfare, rather than on attempts to devise ways in which payments could be increased. Eric Kierans was wholly sympathetic to my point of view, and was even more outspoken in his criticisms of the welfare-oriented ministers and officials who demonstrated an incredible naïveté regarding the economic impact of what they were trying to do.

It can be said that the preparation of the White Paper on Social Security did not really disclose a split between the forces of the right and left within cabinet. Rather, the process revealed a division between those who favoured planning and a careful approach to additional expenditures and those who maintained that where a public need exists or is perceived to exist, it must be answered by government, even if this ultimately creates more serious problems.

This issue was resolved, at least in part, when we came to a detailed study of the 1971-72 Estimates. These were very sobering documents for the members of the Committee on Priorities and Planning. They showed that even allowing for substantial forecasting errors, there was very little in the way of additional funds that we could assign to new projects or to increase expenditures in the social security—or any other—field.

With this knowledge, the committee had no choice but to put in place a ceiling of something like one hundred and fifty million dollars as the total amount that could be added in 1971-72 to all forms of social security. When this information was conveyed to the Committee on Social Policy, it forced a more realistic approach to the preparation of the white paper. It also produced a tremendous dilemma for the committee, which had to decide how best to spend the allotted funds in the next fiscal year. The fact was that if an increase were recommended for old age pensioners, and this was unanimously agreed to be a priority, the increase would consume virtually all available funds. Nothing else could be done, at least not in 1971-72. It would have meant, for example, that expenditures for native Canadians would have to be frozen.

After many frustrating and sometimes contentious discussions, Allan MacEachen, chairman of the Social Policy Committee at the time, made a proposal that received general agreement. We would advise cabinet that the amount of funds assigned for social security was inadequate, if the money had to be applied across the whole spectrum of social security measures. The committee suggested that either money would be spent on services other than old age pensions and supplements, or the funds would be assigned to the elderly and everything else would have to remain more or less static. It was an interesting ploy. The government had already committed itself to increasing veterans' pensions and allowances, and it was now forced to take a new look at its budgetary assignments.

When the committee's recommendations were brought before cabinet, they produced an interesting debate and discussion which caused the Prime Minister to become quite irritated with Ben Benson, the Finance Minister, but more particularly with the officials in the Department of Finance. What Benson said, in essence, was that in light of the Social Policy Committee report, an increase in old age security payments should be done on a non-budgetary basis, that is, the funds should be provided out of loan funds, earmarked taxes and other sources. This way, they would not be a charge against the government's cash flow position. This disclosure revealed a major—even incredible—omission in the presentations made to us by Finance. Up to that time, we had been operating on figures that applied strictly to budgetary items but, as Benson's statements indicated, this did not give an accurate picture of the government's financial state. The Prime Minister became annoyed because, under the circumstances, the instructions of the Committee on Priorities and Planning to various ministers and committees looked ridiculous, indicating as they did no other alternative but the one hundred and fifty million dollar ceiling. Now Ben Benson was saying that old age security could be dealt with out of funds not previously included in the various considerations of cabinet and which most of us, including the Prime Minister, didn't know that we had.

The result of all this was a general agreement that we should move as early as possible to increase old age security, that we should increase veterans' pensions, and that the original one hundred and fifty million dollars should now be reassigned to other priority items. Even more importantly, the Department of Finance was instructed to revamp its methods so that whenever the cabinet or the Committee on Priorities and Planning was considering the general state of government finances, it would have access to both budgetary and non-budgetary figures.

Even with these extra considerations included, it was clear that there was no way in which major new expenditures in the social welfare field could be undertaken in the foreseeable future. At long last, explicit instructions were issued to the Social Policy Committee to prepare a white paper that would not commit the government to additional funds, but which would generate reforms through a reassignment of major expenditures. For example, a basic question was raised relating to the universality of certain programs, particularly family allowances. Munro and his associates were instructed to devise a formula whereby those at the lower end of the income scale could have their family allowances raised, the money being generated by eliminating family allowances at the top end of the income scale. There was also a general instruction that the universality of all programs would be examined carefully.

These events occurred in the late spring of 1970, and Munro returned to cabinet just before the summer recess with a redrafted submission which he wanted to release immediately for public discussion. There was a good deal of work before cabinet and its committees at the time, and the new papers presented by Munro did very little to calm our fears that we had not dealt with the matter in sufficient detail to commit ourselves. It was agreed, therefore, that Munro would spend the month of August rewriting the paper with a view to getting it before Parliament in the dying days of the session, and before a new session opened in early October. But the deadline simply could not be met, and the session ended without the paper being introduced. On that occasion, we dealt with some of the specific proposals in the Munro paper, and although he was quite competent in giving us reasons for his proposals, John did not succeed in stilling the fears of the majority that it would not be wise to present a white paper at this time; we still had not decided with any clarity what our general philosophy towards social security and the myriad of related issues should be.

One of the chief subjects for discussion was the Munro proposal to alter significantly the basis on which family allowances were paid. Instead of giving them to all families regardless of income, Munro proposed that they be doubled at the lower end of the scale, and phased out beginning with families earning seventy-five hundred dollars a year or more. This plan generated a good deal of discussion about the growing tendency to regard the large middle-income group as ripe for additional assessments used to help the poor. A number of us, including John Turner, Art Laing and Joe Greene, were concerned that our thinking was becoming unbalanced, and that a legitimate concern for the poor was causing us to bear down too heavily on the middle class. Art Laing pointed out that the Liberal Party had always drawn a significant part of its support from this middle-income group, and that the increasing number of moves to tax them more heavily or reduce their share of government benefits could have negative political consequences. Ben Benson revealed figures showing that the same group who would lose under the new family allowance plan were also due to be hit by other government programs. For example, many would be paying unemployment insurance premiums for the first time under Mackasey's new scheme. This included all teachers, civil servants and a great many others who had previously been exempt. Also, the benefits of the white paper started to peter out when this same income group was reached, and many of them would be paying slightly more if the new plan were implemented. To reduce or eliminate family allowances for this group would simply add to their disenchantment, aside from the fact that the total impact of our policies would make them poorer by a hundred dollars a year or more.

John Turner was amongst those who, with Ben Benson, emphasized that family allowances are paid to mothers directly. The money in many cases constituted a special nest egg, and mothers would be upset to lose such payments, although the overall position of the family might be improved by the cumulative effects of program changes. It was obvious, however, that if we were to give larger family allowances to the poor, and not at the expense of the Treasury, then some groups would have to lose their benefits.

I suggested that we should only increase the level of family allowances for those below the established poverty line as an alternative to paying double allowances to those earning up to seventy-five hundred dollars a year. If this were done, I suggested, we might go on paying the present rates of family allowances up to a much higher point on the income scale. Mitchell Sharp pointed out the problem that is created when there are different levels of tax exemption for children who are receiving family allowances and those who are not. There was, he said, something inconsistent about the current tax tables, if higher-income people could still take the full deduction of five hundred dollars annually. This meant, in effect, that wealthier people sometimes benefited more from our programs than did those on the lower end of the income scale. It was agreed that this whole question would have to be examined in detail, and much work would have to be done to come up with a formula that did not have within it an unfair bulge between those who would get double allowances and those who would lose them.

This whole discussion was most frustrating. It raised fundamental issues that were not seen in all their complexity by most of those demanding loudly and insistently that we improve our social security structure. Trudeau asked Munro to prepare additional data for us on the proposals advanced by ministers during the discussion. There seemed no doubt that we were getting ourselves committed to some changes, but it was equally clear that there was very little enthusiasm within cabinet for proceeding in the manner that Munro proposed. It seemed also that we had passed the point of no return as far as the publication of Munro's document was concerned, but I expected that when the time came to make the final decision, there would be general agreement that the paper should go forward as only one phase of a general review of social security. It would not be presented as the product of exhaustive study on the whole issue or as the total package of proposals that the government was prepared to implement as a reflection of its philosophy.

At the same meeting, there was a most enlightening and amazing discussion on the state of the Canada Pension Plan. It now appeared that virtually all of the forecasts regarding the financial aspects of the Plan were incredibly inaccurate. As things stood, there would be considerably more in the fund than the experts had anticipated. The issue had now become one of deciding what new initiatives it might be appropriate to take under the Canada Pension Plan, now that the reserves existed to finance such improvements. Munro's paper suggested that workers who were disabled should be treated as if they had reached retirement age, receiving the same benefits as if they had paid into the fund for the expected number of years. He also wanted wives of disabled persons to receive special payments out of the fund.

This proposition brought strong protests from some ministers, especially Joe Greene. Joe's argument was that the Pension Plan was precisely what its name implied—a program to provide workers with a pension by right at the time of retirement. He argued that changes that would allow the Plan to give special payments to wives of the disabled, or any significant departure from the normal pension and insurance principles, would lead to charges that the government was turning the Plan into a welfare program. Munro in particular, and Mackasey to some extent, disputed Joe's contention and maintained that it was entirely consistent with the intentions of the Plan to use the pension fund in the manner in which the white paper proposed. This had not been resolved completely, but I expected the decision to be not to alter the proposals in the white paper but to put them forward simply as ideas, and as with all of the other suggestions, to indicate clearly that we were prepared to change or withdraw them should a significant portion of the public object.

One of the most startling proposals to emerge from the white paper was one which, if carried through, would ensure that every widow in Canada received a pension if her husband had contributed to the Canada Pension Plan. Basically, the plan was to increase the present level of payments to each widow so that she would be guaranteed a minimum of eighty dollars a month plus twenty-five percent of her husband's annual earnings as determined under the formula that applied to the Canada Pension Plan. On questioning, Munro conceded that this measure would be made available to widows regardless of their financial status and other sources of income. The only exception would be if the widow went to work and had earnings of her own.

There were many contradictions inherent in this proposal; one thought of the case of the wealthy widow who had no need to go to work and could therefore collect legitimately under the Munro proposal. Yet the comparatively poor widow who had no choice but to take a job would jeopardize her pension and would lose most, if not all, of it. This measure was so intricate and involved that I was not entirely sure that Munro understood it fully or saw its implications. Certainly, it was inconsistent with the basic approach of the white paper which was to eliminate universality in matters of social welfare.

This, then, was the background against which the White Paper on Social Security was finally brought before cabinet in the early days of October. The Prime Minister began by inviting general comments on strategy and on the total content of the paper, rather than on specific items. Munro gave a very good summary of the general approach adopted in the paper but, not unnaturally, his presentation tended to favour the document and all of its contents. To give him credit, he did point out the areas of likely controversy and the areas in which different options had been set down for cabinet consideration.

The difficulty was, as it was so often, that the paper preceded any thorough discussion by cabinet of the philosophy we wished to adopt in relation to social security and a score of related issues. Some time ago, a decision had been made to set up, with assistance from experts, a special committee to explore not only the question of social security, but also the deeper and more difficult question of how various government policy alternatives might affect the shape and nature of Canadian society in the future. This more comprehensive study would deal with a host of issues, such as the possible effects of government policy on the urbanization of Canadian society and the relative merits of moving toward phasing out small communities or supporting their survival. Questions of this nature—and there were dozens of them—should have had a profound and direct effect on the social security measures we planned to undertake. Yet before that special committee had completed its work, we were discussing, and would undoubtedly invite the Canadian public to discuss, only one phase of a much larger issue.

Another reason for widespread cabinet unease as we began discussing John Munro's white paper was that Senator Davey Croll had, on his own and without either the advice or consent of cabinet, decided a year ago to mount a full scale Senate inquiry on the subject of poverty in Canada. This committee was holding public hearings all across Canada and obtaining a tremendous amount of publicity during the period when Munro was drafting his white paper. We had no way then of knowing what Croll's committee would recommend. Therefore, shortly after the government's white paper was published, it was entirely possible that the Senate report would appear and turn out to be in opposition to the government's proposals. This could be embarrassing, to say the least. But more importantly, it might be that the Senate committee, as a result of its public hearings, would have answers that were better than those in Munro's paper. Either way, the process became both involved and ridiculous.

A number of ministers expressed the view during the discussion that the government ought not to publish Munro's document as a white paper. Instead, some argued, we should proceed with the introduction of various improvements in the social security structure such as the increase in old age benefits which cabinet had already approved. This, it was argued, would be enough to meet any commitment that we had made publicly, and it would leave us time to consider overall policy ramifications in much more detail with the benefit of both the special committee study and the report of the Senate committee. Naturally, Munro opposed this proposal; he had already announced publicly on dozens of occasions that a white paper would be forthcoming.

Despite the course of events, I continued to argue as I had for more than a year in committee that what Munro was producing was in no way a new approach to social security. In essence, it simply committed the government to a perpetuation of most long-standing social security schemes, but with bigger expenditures than ever before. I also made the point which had struck me forcibly on many occasions that even though it required millions of dollars annually to increase payments to the old and underprivileged, the individuals concerned obtained only minimal benefits. In reality, all we were doing was helping them, to some extent, keep pace with increased costs brought about by inflation and other economic forces.

I argued further that what we were talking about primarily were normal increases to keep pace with the cost of living, and that, in my view, these would not be enough in future to keep the underprivileged even mildly contented. The formulas with which we were working did not take into account what I regarded as one of the major forces in society—that is, the revolution of rising expectations. I told my colleagues that, in my view, it was completely unreasonable to expect that those below the poverty line would be less anxious to obtain added benefits from our economic system than those in middle- and higher-income groups. For this reason, it was not simply a question of providing funds that would enable the deprived to go on living at the level at which they were, and which only made allowances for the shrinking value of the dollar. I said that we could expect that as levels of affluence continued to rise, the poverty line would rise also, and within a short time, the current minimum at which a family might be expected to live could increase to as much as six thousand dollars. I did not argue that this was unreasonable, merely that no government could be in a financial position to meet such rising expectations. Therefore, the real emphasis of our planning should be on ways and means in which more of those below the poverty line could be given the opportunities to earn more for themselves. I saw the Munro proposals as something of a mug's game that would do very little to help the poor increase their income. Nor would the proposals gain the government much credit, as they did not address the basic causes of deprivation and would, in the long run, leave the poor as far out of the mainstream as ever. In the end, they would consume enormous amounts of public funds that might well be used more effectively to attack the basic causes of poverty and to stimulate economic growth.

The Prime Minister agreed fundamentally with my proposition, as did quite a few other ministers. Even Bryce Mackasey did not like the white paper in its present form, and shared my view that it was too long, too repetitive and, for the most part, really no more than a review of existing problems and of the alternatives which had already been put forward for dealing with them. On this score, I was surprised and disappointed that the draft of the white paper covered almost a hundred typed pages before getting down to any firm recommendations.

Munro's fundamental argument in replying to my comments was that even if there was considerable economic stimulation and less unemployment, a very large portion of those receiving various forms of welfare would be unable to take advantage of enhanced opportunities. This, of course, was demonstrably true. There are always the aged, the severely disabled and others who, for one reason or another, cannot hope to be productive members of the work force. But although the Munro proposals introduced a degree of selectivity in payments to be made, there was still a tendency to spread the measures over a wide segment of the population, without facing the basic problem of limiting government assistance to those who needed it most urgently.

Six

On the first day of September, 1970, cabinet reconvened for its first full meeting since the August holiday. Although many of us had not seen each other for a month, there was little of the usual handshaking and back slapping or inquiries about how the holiday had been spent. This confirmed what I had felt for quite a while: that there was really very little sense of comradeship within cabinet. After more than two years, very few strong friendships had developed. Ministers are strong individualists and in cabinet, they are more like a board of directors than, for example, a group in some fraternal organization or service club. I do not know if this is true of all cabinets, but in my first one at least, each of us had a remarkable detachment from the activities and problems of other ministers except, of course, when some matter of policy affecting a particular department was being discussed.

Was this a good thing? In some respects, I think it was, since it enabled each of us to have his own private life without the kind of socializing that might result if we were closer to one another. On the other hand, neither I nor any of my colleagues could have any real confidence that we would go to bat for each other if any one of us got into difficulty. The only exception might be if the reputation of the whole government were at stake. I knew in 1970 that if I were to leave cabinet then, there were perhaps no more than one or two ministers with whom I would bother to get in touch with again on a social basis.

I felt that Prime Minister Trudeau was partly responsible for this state of affairs. When he arrived on that Tuesday for the opening of cabinet, he spoke scarcely a word of greeting to anyone, made no inquiries about the holidays, and simply plunged right into business as if we had never been away. By the same token, Trudeau rarely encouraged inquiries about his own travels or holidays, and it appeared that he felt no more warmth for any of us than we felt for each other. Yet there were times when one instinctively warmed to the man. He had a habit of self-deprecation that could be quite appealing and, every now and then, he would make some humorous comment about his position and the difficulties that it entailed. This tended to generate an instant sympathy and an anxiety on the listener's part to be of help. But soon after this rapport was established, Trudeau usually turned it off, and it was very difficult to get back on an intimate basis with him.

I suspect that unlike Mr. Pearson, who commanded a tremendous personal loyalty which served him well when he got into trouble, Trudeau would not have been able to generate the same kind of response from either cabinet or caucus. He controlled the situation because he was on top and this, I think, was the way he wanted it.

At that first cabinet meeting after the summer, there were a couple of incidents that did indicate, however, that Trudeau had a greater degree of sensitivity than he pretended. He made a couple of remarks regarding his vacation which suggested that he was upset by recent press criticism that he was taking too many holidays and was a playboy. It was also obvious that he was at least mildly irked by the speculative newspaper stories forecasting that Don Macdonald would become the new minister of national defence. On three occasions during the meeting when we were discussing a possible early recall of the House, the Prime Minister referred to Don as House Leader and added a comment to the effect that no change in that status had been made, and that it might not come for a considerable time. Incidentally, there were more than the usual number of cabinet leaks over the summer, and I awaited the inevitable cabinet row that would erupt over this issue before long.

As the reader will see, there was no shortage of issues or problems to be dealt with as the pace picked up after the holiday. First, we had to deal with the postal strike that plagued us that year, and Bud Drury advocated the immediate recall of Parliament and a legislated settlement. Bud was in an impossible position on this one. He was the watchdog on government economic policy and had considerable influence on its formulation. But he was also the chief spokesman for the government as an employer. If, in order to get a postal dispute settlement, he agreed to terms and conditions that did not fit the economic policy, he would be in great trouble in the future when other ministers, for whatever reason, wanted to subvert various guidelines.

Bud was an able man and very astute. I expected to hear at the meeting that most of us, including the Prime Minister, were reluctant to call Parliament together prematurely, and had serious reservations about legislating a settlement in the circumstances that existed. I had the feeling, therefore, that Bud had chosen to protect his position for the future. In other words, he would advocate rigid adherence to the guidelines so that his position would not be weakened in future situations. At the same time, he would not be surprised if government decided to breach the guidelines in order to achieve a settlement. In fact, he probably agreed privately with this approach.

Bryce Mackasey made several good interventions in the discussion. Although at times he could get carried away by emotion, it was obvious that he had a good grasp of labour problems and considerable sensitivity when it came to assessing the likely political consequences of our decisions in labour matters. While he was not always logical and temperate, his contribution on this occasion was very much to the point.

Allan MacEachen also made a useful contribution and showed once again that he was well ahead of most of cabinet in forecasting accurately what was likely to happen in the House of Commons. He pointed out the unique nature of the problem we were facing; that is, that we might call the House together to settle a strike only to find when the Commons met that the workers had decided to call off their rotating strikes, and we would be meeting to resolve a crisis that no longer existed. Another problem outlined by Allan and others was the difficulty of devising a formula for a legislative settlement. If we simply legislated on the conciliator's formula, we would be, for all practical purposes, removing the right to strike while imposing a final settlement along lines acceptable to us. It would be a unilateral use of the government's powers. If, on the other hand, we provided for binding arbitration in the legislation, there was the virtual certainty that the final settlement decided by the arbitrator would exceed the conciliator's recommendations, and might exceed the settlement we could get through further negotiation. It was clear that we were in an almost impossible position.

There were, I think, two main reasons for our dilemma. One was the basic nature of the legislation extending the right to strike to government employees. The postal dispute had made it clear that the normal laws of collective bargaining simply do not apply to dealings between the government and its employees. In some respects, the government had an excess of power in relation to the union; however, this was primarily political power and could only be exercised at great political risk. This, at least, was the consensus around the cabinet table. I think there was also unanimity in cabinet that the general legislation regarding public service bargaining had to be changed. But there did not seem to be any agreement concerning what the changes should be.

Jean Marchand, who had demonstrated throughout this affair a keen insight into labour matters, was surprisingly strong in advocating changes to strengthen the government's position. I did not think, however, that he was prepared to go as far as the removal of the right to strike. Even if the right to strike had been refused, post office employees were no more likely to abide by the law now than in the past when they had struck illegally. It was a difficult problem, and one which had to be dealt with quickly.

The second reason for our difficulties was undoubtedly the six-percent guideline. When this was introduced several months before, I warned John Young and the cabinet that no matter how many qualifications he introduced to emphasize that six percent was merely a guideline subject to variation, the only thing that would survive in the public's mind was the figure itself, and that would become entrenched beyond reason. This, of course, is what happened. Any settlement over six percent was publicized as a breach of guidelines and a failure of government policy. I felt reasonably certain at the time that this would be the outcome in the case of the postal strike. But although no final decision was taken on the first day of the session, pending the outcome of the mediator's efforts, I was willing to bet that the strike would be settled by negotiation and that the final contract would exceed the so-called guidelines.

There were also other developments. Speculation regarding cabinet changes narrowed to the point where it was now surprisingly accurate. This obviously irritated Trudeau, and it made it very awkward for those of us who had known all along the precise nature of the proposals, and who might now be suspected of leaking information as a result. But there was no way in which a blanket of secrecy could be maintained; as time went by, more and more people had to know, for various reasons, what was being planned.

After speaking briefly with Allan MacEachen, I concluded that he would take the House leadership without protest, even though he had reservations about it. I tried to reassure him and offered to work with him in any way I could.

At my department, I had a lengthy meeting with Jerry Stoner and George Scott. There was obviously a serious information leak concerning our plans for Toronto airport. Someone had been talking freely to reporters. This caused me considerable embarrassment; I had not yet seen the report, and already some of the contents had been leaked to the media. Quite frankly, I did not even know where to start in order to find the party responsible. With a wide range of other matters that had come up, the fall and winter promised a heavy schedule, but I got the impression that the new organization was starting to shape up, and I was hoping, as the new session convened, that we could move forward in an orderly and efficient way.

On Thursday, September 3, I was advised first thing of a special cabinet meeting called to deal with the postal dispute. Since Trudeau was on a three-day tour of eastern and northern Quebec, Mitchell Sharp presided over the meeting, and handled it extremely well. We were advised by Bud Drury that the mediator had been successful in getting from the union terms on which they would be prepared to settle the strike. The argument that followed concerned whether or not the proposals would destroy the credibility of the government's economic and anti-inflationary policy. For the same reason I mentioned before, Bud took a strong stand and was supported to some extent by Eric Kierans and Ben Benson. Frankly, I could not help thinking that all three were merely making noises and were primarily interested in protecting their future positions. Practically everyone else around the table favoured some form of negotiated settlement. Jean Marchand and I were among the most vocal in giving our support to Bryce Mackasey's logical argument that we had little alternative but to accept. Much of the rest of the discussion simply rehashed what had been said previously.

As a result of the meeting, Bud Drury was authorized to improve on the union offer if at all possible. It was learned later in the day that this effort had been unsuccessful, and a settlement was finally reached on the basis of the terms brought to us by the mediator.

On Labour Day, I returned to Ottawa early after a most pleasant weekend in Swift Current with the family. On the way back, I was greeted by the news of another oil spill on the east coast, about which there was very little reliable information. The next morning, however, the pieces began to fit together, although, as always, Transport officials initially played down the magnitude of the problem and sent optimistic reports. I had gone through this kind of experience before at the time of the *Arrow* incident and this time I resolved, after a meeting with the Deputy Minister and Dr. Pierre Camu, the marine administrator, that I would not waste any time in getting to the region to see for myself. This decision was reinforced by a call from Alex Campbell, the Premier of Prince Edward Island. Alex and I had developed a pleasant and useful rapport, and when he asked for my help, I wanted to respond as quickly as I could.

Our party left Ottawa at half past one and did not reach Prince Edward Island until five o'clock. Campbell was there to meet me, as were officials from the Armed Forces base. I had taken along a number of newsmen, but before talking to them, I obtained an up-to-date briefing from our chief officer on pollution matters, a man who impressed me more than anyone we had ever used in the pollution field before.

I had brought Dr. Camu and Dr. Patrick McTaggart-Cowan with me, and all three of us attended the briefing. While nothing could be known with certainty until a preliminary inquiry was held, I suspected that the investigation would disclose a good deal of neglect. The barge was owned by Irving Oil Limited, and this was a company with which we had had considerable trouble since the previous winter. We had traced to them a number of smaller pollution incidents, but nothing to equal this case. I was told by our district marine agent that the operator of the Canso Straits, an employee of ours, had actually recorded in his log on Sunday that the Irving barge would be the next to go. From all accounts, it was very heavily loaded, probably in excess of its rated capacity. In addition, the captain had elected to proceed on his way even though weather conditions were quite unfavourable, and high winds had been forecast.

I was appalled to learn from Dr. Camu that because barges were not self-propelled, they did not come under our inspection regulations. No one in the inspection service was authorized to look at barges and similar containers even though, as in this case, they could be carrying more than a million gallons of oil. Similarly, there was nothing to authorize the loch master, or anyone else, to prevent an overloaded barge from proceeding on its way. Obviously, such shortcomings in the legislation needed to be corrected and, if I tried to put a good face on a bad situation, this second spill coming on top of the *Arrow* incident would serve to ensure that my legislation in connection with shipping regulations would get on early in the fall session, with widespread support from all parts of the House.

It is quite unbelievable how, for so many years, shipping interests dominated marine law and all related fields. I was sure at the time of the barge incident that no one at Irving had made any effort to contact the Ministry of Transport until the company had checked out its legal position. I would not have been surprised to discover that they had no direct liability and no special responsibility to clean up the mess.

And it really was a mess. We flew over it by helicopter late on the day of the spill and, flying low and hovering over the spill area, I had the chance to see what oil can do in these circumstances. It had spread over a very wide area and my first reaction was, "In God's name, what can we possibly hope to do with it?"

Dr. McTaggart-Cowan proved most helpful, and upon our return to the Summerside base, we devised a strategy for attempting, at least, to cope with the spill. Basically, what we were trying to do was to ensure that we could contain within a boom any additional oil that might float to the surface from the barge, using peat moss to absorb oil on the surface of the water. Inevitably, however, the oil would have to come ashore somewhere in the Gulf. Therefore, reconnaissance was central to our strategy, and we had a mobile force of servicemen and others available who could be moved quickly to any site when it became evident that the oil was approaching the beaches.

In addition, we were assessing the particularly vulnerable areas around the shores of the Gulf where there might be fish plants or similar industries, or in the case of Prince Edward Island, coves containing oyster beds. At these locations, we planned to erect booms across the openings as a precautionary measure.

The whole appalling incident highlighted once again for me how woefully uninformed we were when we had to deal with situations of this kind. There simply was not the expertise anywhere in the world to deal with such occurrences, and I planned to advocate strongly that Canada take the lead in the necessary research. Although we had already done so to some extent, this was perhaps no credit to us; we had been obliged to dig into various questions as a result of the *Arrow* incident. Yet we had made substantial progress, and I became conscious of this fact when, just a few hours after the spill, we were able to assemble a good team and were aware of what steps ought to be taken. Everything now depended upon wind and weather conditions, and we could only hope that the measures we had taken would prove effective.

After the sudden need to respond to a crisis, I spent much of Wednesday, September 9, dealing with more routine departmental matters. Dr. McTaggart-Cowan, Dr. Shaffer, Jerry Stoner and Pierre Camu discussed with me the contents of the task force report on the clean-up of the *Arrow* oil spill. Obviously, Dr. McTaggart-Cowan in particular wanted to have the report published as soon as possible. It bore his strong personal mark, and I had noted over the past several months that he was not averse to publicity. In fact, he might, I conjectured, give us some problems once the report was published. The difficulty was that I had made it clear to him that if there was to be immediate publication, he was going to have to take a hard look at some of his recommendations. Since these involved other departments, I did not feel it proper to release the report quickly without consulting colleagues who might be involved in terms of suggested responsibilities for their departments.

In the end, it was decided that officials would examine the recommendations to see which would not create future controversy or conflict with other agencies, and would highlight those that might need special consideration. I decided that I might have to meet with the group on Thursday to try and resolve the matter.

There had been no significant change in the oil slick problem off Prince Edward Island. From all accounts, the task force was working well and moving ahead with the measures we had agreed on during my visit to Prince Edward Island. The slick had not reached shore yet, and we knew that we could be in for a prolonged period of waiting if wind directions continued to change, moving the slick back and forth along various sections of the shoreline. We had no option but to wait. Meanwhile, we had to turn our attention to other things.

In a full meeting of cabinet on Thursday morning, we had an animated discussion about the recognition of Communist China. It was always amusing to me on occasions such as this to observe the tremendous amount of time spent haggling over subtle differences in the meanings of words. In this case, we were looking at a proposed communiqué to be issued in the event that negotiations with China were satisfactorily completed. What made the lengthy argument over words somewhat ridiculous was that inevitably, should the agreement be completed, there would be all manner of press conferences and off-the-cuff statements by Mitchell Sharp, the Prime Minister and others. It would not then be possible for them to choose their words with the care that goes into a written document. The difficulty lay in the determination of the Chinese to assert in their communiqué their declared right to Formosa. The Canadian position held that in recognizing China, we did not attempt to define its geographic boundaries or any of its possessions; we simply recognized the government. In the proposed joint statement by China and Canada, the Chinese wanted to include the fact that they had pointed out to Canada that Taiwan was inside their territorial boundaries. Apparently, this was a much used diplomatic ploy which, as Mitchell Sharp explained, simply meant that we had heard the Chinese representations or assertions, but that we had not commented on them in one way or the other.

For myself, I grew slightly annoyed over the whole business; I felt that it was somewhat demeaning for us to woo China when, until then, the Chinese had not shown any real enthusiasm for mutual recognition. Mitchell Sharp said, however, that China definitely wanted to conclude a deal with Canada, had reversed its former position, and was eager to join the United Nations.

The Prime Minister showed himself to be very well informed on the whole issue, particularly as it related to the United Nations. I presumed that this was due to the time he spent there as parliamentary secretary. In any event, he stated the obvious when he pointed out that if we recognized Red China, consistency almost certainly required that we vote for its admission into the United Nations. Once again, there was an involved discussion about the various forms that resolutions take at the UN. Apparently, a vote was taken each year that settled nothing other than the fact that the delegates felt that the issue of China's admission was still important. It seemed that we had always supported this motion and would continue to do so. The bigger question of voting for China's admission would be left until we saw the outcome of the current talks with the Chinese.

Personally, I could not generate any enthusiasm for the discussions and did not participate in them to any significant extent. I had the feeling that many of my colleagues felt the same way, which suggested to me that there was no longer a serious political risk in taking this step. I wondered if there ever was, or if it was simply that public attitudes had changed markedly since the early days of the Pearson administration when the issue of Communist China generated such heated debate.

Nothing else of great significance was discussed in cabinet. The Prime Minister did make reference to his intention to select new parliamentary secretaries. This could mean that most of the members who had held these positions for the past two years would probably be dropped in favour of new nominees. I could understand the rationale behind Trudeau's thinking, but I had no doubt that the changes were going to raise a considerable row. Long-time members like Jimmie Walker, Russ Honey and Jim McNulty, all original supporters of Trudeau, would feel slighted, and undoubtedly the decision would create difficulties for them as they stood to lose both prestige and income. But if Trudeau was set on this course, I thought that it would be wise of him to drop all present parliamentary secretaries rather than to be selective. In this way, the move could be explained as an attempt to provide opportunities for more members to avail of the experience. It was a touchy issue and when it came up formally in cabinet the following week, one could be sure that there would be ministers who would question it. My guess was that they would not get very far; Trudeau had made it perfectly clear that he had decided on the question.

Later that day, in an afternoon meeting of the Committee on Economic Policy, Ron Basford brought forward proposals in connection with his consumer protection plan. I felt very bad about the discussion that followed; it seemed that at every point I was critical of Ron's proposals. I was not the only one, however. Bud Drury, Ben Benson and Eric Kierans were equally wary of some of the proposed new laws and regulations. The problem was not with Ron's objectives, but with the way he wanted to achieve them. For example, he proposed to prohibit anyone from being a director of companies that were either directly or indirectly competitive. I knew what he was getting at, but he could not define just what he meant by "competitive." Without a definition, there would be many difficulties in interpretation, and it was at this point that all of us raised objections. Another of Ron's plans involved trying to give a measure of protection to the small retailer who had to compete with national chains. Here, once again, Ron's aims were commendable, but his proposals were highly theoretical and, I feared, insufficient to accomplish his aims. At the same time, they would require the establishment of yet another extensive bureaucracy to police the private sector, and we would simply irritate a great many people without doing much good.

Ron Basford's difficulties in Consumer and Corporate Affairs clearly illustrated the problem which can arise when you set up an agency and staff it with eager and dedicated young people who do not have very much experience. They plunge in with great enthusiasm without analyzing the consequences of the laws and regulations they propose. It was something like the White Paper on Taxation all over again, where an undoubtedly brilliant group of people in the Department of Finance simply failed to see the problems inherent in some of their proposals, and revealed a complete lack of knowledge concerning political processes. Ironically, during the Thursday afternoon meeting, Ben Benson slipped me a note saying, "I hope all of this goes through, because if it does, it will cause everyone to forget the White Paper on Taxation."

When we were discussing the postal strike only a few days before, Jean Marchand, an astute politician in such matters, made a statement which fit the consumer problem, as well as many others. When Bud Drury made a point supporting his view that we should legislate the postal workers back to work, Jean Marchand replied, "What you say is perfectly logical, but it overlooks the fact that we are dealing with an illogical situation." This was true of so many of the decisions we had to make. Even when a course of action was clearly and demonstrably the most sensible, it was not always possible to introduce it; either it did not fit into the general pattern of Canadian life, or it would mean political suicide for a score of other reasons. This might have been a defect in the political process, but I was inclined to think it was probably a good thing—the only counterweight we had to the technocrats and bureaucrats whose worship of efficiency often resulted in personal hardship or restriction of individual rights.

My final meeting on what turned out to be a very busy day was with representatives of the Airline Pilots Association and others in connection with the hijacking problem. Mitchell Sharp convened the meeting, but of necessity most of the problem landed in my lap. I was sure that the pilots knew the difficulty of establishing satisfactory security measures at Canadian airports, but they had to make a noise to satisfy the members of their organization and to uphold their position in the international society to which they belonged. The main immediate request of the pilots was for detection devices at Canadian airports. I stressed that we were not opposed to the installation of these, but our assessment was that they were something less than one hundred percent effective. My own view, I expressed, was that a system of spot checks would be the best deterrent in Canada. In other words, we would adopt the system used by Customs and Immigration whereby all passengers knew that at any time their baggage could be searched. This was the route I proposed to follow when I met with other concerned parties in the future.

What was interesting was that although we had had only one hijacking in the history of Canadian aviation, this had now become a major problem simply because it had happened elsewhere. I conjectured that this was the result of mass media and our growing tendency to feel left out when we could not lay claim to a problem which was plaguing someone else. This may sound ironic, but the evidence suggests that it was so. As soon as some difficulty occurred anywhere, I was immediately asked by newsmen what we were going to do about the possibility of the same thing happening in Canada. This had become a standard news reporting technique. Newsmen would indicate, for example, that there was a jet aircraft pollution problem at Kennedy International Airport, and they invariably added words to the effect that Canada had not made any decision as to what it would do about its pollution problem. They failed to realize that Kennedy had a great deal more traffic than any airport in Canada, and that the two situations were not comparable in any significant way.

Friday was yet another day of seemingly endless meetings, all time-consuming and frequently useless. One of the annoying things about being head of a department was that you had to see so many people simply because someone asked you to, or because the parties concerned did not feel they had completed their representations unless they saw the Minister personally. It was quite annoying to have a busy schedule, then receive a call from an MP or another cabinet minister asking that you see some out-of-town visitor. The caller usually began by saying, "I know you can't do anything for him, but would you just give him a few minutes to state his case." Usually, the party had already seen the appropriate officials and everything possible was being done for him. Nevertheless, he had to see the Minister. I had four such meetings on September 11, and they consumed a great deal of time.

I also met with Dr. McTaggart-Cowan and others regarding the task force report on Operation Oil. Dr. McTaggart-Cowan, Jerry Stoner and other officials had worked out an arrangement regarding recommendations in the report, and I was now prepared to release it publicly within a week to ten days. I asked Bud Drury whether he thought the report should be published and he was most cooperative and helpful. He read the first volume and called to say that my judgement was right and that the report should be made public as soon as possible.

In the afternoon, I held a press conference to outline the new marine anti-pollution legislation. It said something about the press gallery membership and the media in general that most of the questioning had to do with the specific oil spill incident off Prince Edward Island. There were few questions about the proposed legislation, though this was much more important in the long run. I was looking forward to seeing how the shipping community would react, particularly to the plan to impose a levy on oil shipments in order to build a fund to pay for the clean-up of oil spills. But I was not particularly worried; the public was clearly on our side, and I doubted if I would have any problem in getting the legislation through the House quickly. If problems developed, it would probably be because some members would want to go further with this than I thought wise or practical at the time.

In the midst of this busy schedule, I was managing to have French lessons each day, and I felt that I was making progress. I knew, however, that if I were ever to become proficient, I would have to take time off to get a concentrated exposure to the language. And where would I find the time for this?

I spent the following weekend in Ottawa, and while it was pleasant to have two days alone with no appointments or commitments, I missed Barbara and the family very much. I did not want to make a regular practice of skipping weekend visits to Newfoundland. My plan had been to work on the speech that I would deliver at Memorial University's convocation the following month, the occasion on which I would receive an honorary degree. But Saturday turned out to be almost totally unproductive in this regard; in fact, I spent most of the afternoon asleep. On Sunday, however, I did manage to do an outline of what I wanted to say, as well as a good deal of polishing.

On Sunday evening, I went to the airport to greet Joe Smallwood who had come for the federal-provincial conference on the constitution. I drove him from the airport and spent four hours with him. Much of that time we were alone. For the first time, I was satisfied that he was genuine and sincere when he said that he planned to quit at the end of the year. Still, a long session with Joe could be quite painful; he had the habit of using in private the same repetition technique that he employed with the public, and even a simple statement or question could take as long as fifteen or twenty minutes.

The main topic of our discussion was, of course, the leadership, and while he emphasized his conviction that I should return to succeed him, he did not press this point as much as in the past. I felt that he now realized that I meant it when I said that I had virtually no interest in the position. Of course, he realized it for all the wrong reasons. His comments to me indicated that he felt that I had a passionate desire to become the next prime minister of Canada. This was, of course, the kind of ambition that he might have had if he were in my place, and he could not help but see the situation through his own eyes and on the basis of his own rationale. I told him frankly that I really did not have any great ambitions in this direction, but it was clear that he did not believe me. Nor, I suspected, would anyone else in Newfoundland.

Late in the evening, we were joined by Eric Jones, Joe's Finance Minister. It was clear from the discussion that Smallwood could not bring himself to simply quit and have the chips fall where they may. What he really wanted was to engineer his succession, and it was very interesting to see, from time to time during the meeting, how easily, even automatically, he slipped back into planning for the next election as if he would be leading the Liberal Party at that time. The scenario he had devised and which seemed to be his top alternative was to quit at the end of 1970 and have the Lieutenant-Governor call on Fred Rowe to succeed him. Fred Rowe would then call a convention at which he might or might not be a candidate for the leadership. I told Joe that I felt it was important to his plan that if Fred Rowe were to be the interim leader, then he should immediately disown any ambitions of running at the leadership convention. Joe disagreed and maintained that if Fred excluded himself from the race, he would be a "lame duck" leader, unable to exercise any control.

On reflection, I may have overstressed this point, and Fred Rowe's future actions might not have been as important as I had first thought. In any event, it was more or less academic because Fred would be asked as soon as he became premier what his future intentions were, and it would be only a matter of weeks before he would have to declare himself one way or the other.

Smallwood also brought up the matter of Andy Crosbie's involvement in the leadership race. Eric Jones, who was present for this part of the discussion, indicated that in his view, Andy would be totally unacceptable to hardcore Liberal Party members, and particularly to Joe's supporters. It was obvious that although Joe had initiated the plan to involve Andy Crosbie, he had now cooled to the idea and had accepted the view that his plan to install Crosbie as interim premier simply could not work.

During the course of the conversation, Joe went into considerable detail in outlining what he felt the Party's chances were in the next election. I did not know whether he was simply talking for effect, but his enthusiasm and optimism were remarkable and certainly did not square with the facts. He believed that the Party could win almost as many seats as in 1966. Also, some of the people he spoke of as candidates would not, in my view, be nearly as effective as he suggested. As always, his enormous capacity to rationalize continued to be one of Joe's great failings. What I have never been able to determine over all these years, however, is whether he genuinely believed the optimistic forecasts he made or whether he was simply wedded to the idea that, when talking to anyone about any subject, you have to put the best possible face on it.

Monday was a day for office work because, of course, the Prime Minister and many cabinet members were attending the constitutional conference. I had no part to play in this exercise at the moment and was therefore able to get a day more or less to myself to cope with the mounting number of departmental problems that had to be resolved quickly. In the afternoon, I spent some time at a meeting of the Economic Policy Committee. The subjects for discussion were a new international grains agreement and Ron Basford's involved paper proposing changes in the regulations governing product labelling. The wheat agreement discussion had an Alice-in-Wonderland air about it. Everyone accepted that the United States, and perhaps other countries, would not at this time accept an agreement containing firm prices, yet it was agreed that the Canadian position should be to push for such price inclusion. Here again, it is possible to see the shallow, even cynical, nature of so many international negotiations. What it boiled down to in this case, as in so many others, was that the subjective interests of individual countries continued to be the prime consideration; it was only when the interests of a number of countries happened to be the same that there was any point in seeking effective international cooperation. I pointed out to Jean-Luc Pepin that we would only get the price structure included in an international grains agreement if market conditions were good; in that case, the agreement would be relatively unimportant because in a strong market, sales would come automatically. He agreed with this position, but said that there were certain advantages to continuing talks with grain-producing countries. It really was a rather stupid and frustrating situation, one which gave the lie to all high-minded declarations about the growing willingness of the countries of the world to cooperate.

Early on Tuesday morning, Joe Smallwood called me and asked if I would have dinner alone with him in the evening. I agreed, and after a busy day with routine departmental matters, met him for dinner at six-thirty. He was in a subdued mood and reiterated most of the things he had said on Sunday evening, but with less emotion. I came away satisfied that he really wanted to retire and had probably made up his mind to do so at the end of the year. When he asked me bluntly what I felt he should do, I told him that he should take a page from Lester Pearson's book and retire gracefully without becoming embroiled in arguments over his succession. I could see that the logic of this proposition appealed to him, and we parted with his assurance that he would do as I suggested. But I was not sure; I could not help but wonder whether this resolve would hold when he became embroiled once again with the people in Newfoundland whose fortunes were so closely tied to his own, and who would be reluctant to see him go in any circumstances. Certainly, there were many who would want to take a hand in engineering the succession.

On Friday, we had our first look at a draft of the Throne Speech. The Prime Minister called a special meeting of the Priorities and Planning Committee, and afterwards, I felt that it was one of the more productive ones we had had recently. There were only a few ministers present, and since the agenda was not crowded, we had a good chance to discuss the contents of the Throne Speech, as well as our strategy for the coming session. The Speech as drafted had a good deal to recommend itself. The language was excellent and the package of legislative proposals impressive. My main criticism was that it did not pay enough attention to the unemployment situation or to the accomplishments of the government. Presented as it was, it would generate the criticism that it was an abstract document, philosophizing about Canadian goals and objectives but showing a callous disregard for those who were unemployed. There appeared to be unanimous agreement with my assessment, and I looked forward to seeing just how many of the proposed changes would find their way into the next draft, which we were scheduled to examine the following week.

As for our strategy for the new session, it was clear that despite our best efforts, we had far more legislation planned than we could get through. Here we were facing a classic dilemma; if we tried to railroad the measures through the House, we would be accused of trampling on the rights of Parliament. If, on the other hand, we adopted a leisurely pace and let the opposition set the timetable, we would wind up with many good laws still not passed when the session ended. There was considerable discussion at the meeting about our stand on the drug problem and the issue of abortion. On the latter issue, the consensus was that we could not get more lenient abortion laws through the House at this time, and would face another filibuster if we attempted to do so. Don Macdonald proposed that we should indicate at least our willingness to take time to discuss the subject, and I saw that this was a good idea. With regard to the drug problem, I suggested that we make reference to it in the Speech from the Throne without committing ourselves to a specific course of action. I pointed out that we had not received the final report of the LeDain Commission; this provided a good reason to withhold specific action until we had a chance to deal more thoroughly with the issue in cabinet.

Undoubtedly, the drug issue was going to be a difficult one to resolve. Not only was there a sharp division in the country; there was also one in cabinet itself. I was inclined to the view that we should legalize marijuana and make it available under the same conditions that controlled the sale of alcohol. There were difficulties in such a course, however; in order to make it work, we would have to get the full support and cooperation of the provinces. And I doubted very much that they were ready to go as far as we were.

On Monday, September 21, there was an important meeting of the Cabinet Economic Policy Committee. The main item on the agenda was the report of the National Energy Board on several applications for the export of additional quantities of natural gas to the United States. This issue was particularly important at the time because of increased interest in the broad question of what we should do about our energy resources. It was evident at the meeting that most of us were aware of the announced intentions of the NDP to make an issue out of the future export of energy resources to the United States. Whatever we decided, Joe Greene would be the main government spokesman on this issue, and it was obvious that he did not particularly relish the job. I concluded that he was beginning to realize that his outspoken, strongly nationalistic speech at Denver would come back to haunt him—especially as he faced the economic realities and political consequences which any policy decision that restricted gas exports south of the border would have in the West. The whole discussion illustrated once again the intrinsic difficulties which occur when important decisions must be made more or less jointly by a regulatory agency and government. The National Energy Board had sweeping powers and a unique degree of independence, and while it was true that it was up to the government to accept or reject any recommendation made by the Board, the government could not change the Board's report in any way. We were therefore faced with a situation where, when the report was made public as required by law, our total acceptance of its recommendations would open us to both accusations of rubber stamping Board decisions, and of supporting a policy of resource exports. On the other hand, if we rejected the report or departed significantly from its recommendations, we would be accused of interfering with an independent agency. As well, there were those who would charge us with trying to second-guess the Board on the basis of much less precise knowledge than the Board itself possessed.

Through all this discussion, I had mixed feelings about the competence of the National Energy Board. Yet the fact that the Board lived every day with the issues made it difficult to challenge members on important points without having access to the information they possessed. Dr. Robert Howland, the Chairman of the Board, was a deceptively mild man, but I could not escape the feeling sometimes that he was slightly contemptuous of many of us who questioned his and the Board's judgement. I wanted to look closely at the Board's recommendations, and I promised myself that I would not be compromised by the usual pat explanations that Board members offered. They could be entirely right, but I wanted to be sure.

One of the Board's decisions was to reject outright the application of Consolidated Pipelines for a permit to build and operate a line from

Alberta directly to the United States. It was clear from the comments of some of my colleagues that Consolidated had done a good job of lobbying. Not unnaturally, Bud Olson from Alberta and Art Laing, who had many acquaintances in the oil industry, were all for approving the report as it stood so that the additional exports could go forward. The most surprising interventions came from Bryce Mackasey. He was clearly grinding an axe for Consolidated and had been exceedingly well briefed. It was impossible to avoid the feeling that Bryce had discussed the matter in detail with Consolidated, and might even have indicated to some of the principals of that company the Board's findings. This tended to be supported by the fact that a Montreal director of Consolidated phoned my office, leaving word with my secretary indicating that he knew the matter was before cabinet, and advising me that he had heard that some ministers were opposed to Consolidated's position and that he hoped that I would do whatever I could for him. I did not talk to him, nor did I acknowledge the message.

One of the obvious faults with the National Energy Board's report was that it offered contradictory explanations to rationalize its decisions. This was evident to anyone who read the report in full, but a pertinent example will do here. The Board decided to recommend the export of additional gas, justifying this on the grounds that Canadian reserves were more than adequate to meet Canadian requirements, meaning that Canada's position was not jeopardized by additional exports. The Board went so far as to say that the total amount involved in the contracts could be replenished within two years of new discoveries. On the other hand, it rejected the Consolidated application on the grounds that reserves were insufficient to justify all of the exports involved in the total applications. I would have been surprised if those who opposed any exports at the time did not latch on to such an obvious discrepancy.

I had no doubt that the Board genuinely felt that it acted objectively in dealing with this complex matter. At the same time, I saw evidence of a tendency I had noted many times before and which was present in my own department: that is, those who were appointed to regulate a particular industry almost invariably took on some of the colourations of that industry. Despite their best efforts, they usually ended up agreeing with industry leaders. In my own department, I could see this happening with inspectors and others who dealt with the shipping community. Usually, they were inclined to side with ship owners and to feel that when I tried to press for greater recognition of the public interest, I was rocking the boat unnecessarily and that my proposals were naïve and impractical.

Jim Richardson and I both identified a major flaw in the National Energy Board's proposals. Although the Board cut down on the duration of the contracts and permits obtained by applicants, these nevertheless stretched over periods of fifteen to twenty years. That was a long way to look ahead, and it was impossible to anticipate what customers in the United States—or in Canada, for that matter—would be paying for gas at the end of the period. Despite this fact, the Board's recommendations were quite inadequate regarding the provisions made for getting a higher sale price if the American market improved dramatically. I felt that this was not only bad politically, but unsound from a business point of view, and I would press for provisions that would enable us to review the price structure periodically throughout the life of the contracts.

With Ben Benson in Europe, the job of chairing the Economic Policy Committee passed to Jean-Luc Pepin. As a chairman, Pepin seemed to have a pretty full grasp of the situation. Joe Greene was wisely reserving his position and, I speculated, genuinely wanted the advice of cabinet, even though he felt it necessary to recommend the adoption of the Board's report. We stayed on the subject most of the afternoon and finally decided at six-thirty to pick it up the following night.

Seven

I resumed my recording of events on Saturday, October 31, 1970. For a host of reasons, it was not possible for me to dictate these memoranda on a daily basis during the five weeks since September. There was the intensive preparatory work for the October 5 reopening of Parliament, a week in Europe, several complex problems involving my own ministry and, of course, the remarkable events that culminated in the proclamation of the War Measures Act.

Prior to the reopening of Parliament, we completed our discussions on the National Energy Board's report, and I was pleased that my own insistence on a clear price review formula was accepted by cabinet and included in Joe Greene's public announcement. General reaction to the decision to export additional gas to the United States was favourable, particularly in the West. There was the anticipated criticism from the NDP and other economic nationalists but, on the whole, I believe we came out of the encounter quite well. It was a bit surprising that the Ontario Liberal Association found, at its meeting in London in early October, a significant opposition among its members to any increase in energy sales to the Americans. I did not know if this was significant in terms of the future stance of the party, and we would not know with certainty until the national convention was held in October. There was no doubt, however, that, in Ontario in particular, due perhaps to the influence of Walter Gordon and others, there was a growing desire for a stronger assertion of national sovereignty.

I remained surprised by the influence that Walter Gordon continued to wield, particularly among Liberals in the Toronto area. Personally, I had never been impressed either by Walter's philosophy or intellectual capacity. From the time I met him in the late 1950s until the period about which I am writing, I had never been able to get close to the man or generate a strong liking for him. My experience with him during three election campaigns was not designed to enhance my belief in his political acumen. Indeed, I continued to feel that many of his decisions during these campaigns were disastrous for the Party and that, but for him, Mr. Pearson would have formed a majority government in 1963. Nevertheless, it was clear that Walter's campaign for greater Canadian control of the economy had a considerable number of followers, some of them in our own caucus but very few in cabinet.

As for the sovereignty issue, the NDP continued to push hard for a stronger nationalistic outlook while flexing its muscles in Ontario. This meant that Ontario Liberals would be looking for decisive action from the government, and this would make the November convention particularly interesting.

In the end, I felt satisfied with the conclusion of the gas export issue. The decisions of the National Energy Board were given a thorough airing in cabinet. The basic decisions of the Board were, I felt, sound under the circumstances, and the modifications with regard to pricing policy definitely improved the deal and made it more acceptable to the public. As for the reopening of the House, it was surprisingly quiet and uneventful. Like many of my colleagues, I had anticipated that the Tories would try to come in with a distinctive new look, but nothing of the sort materialized. Perhaps this was due to Stanfield's many problems during the summer with the so-called western revolt. And despite claims that there were no serious internal tensions, it might very well have been that the Conservative Party was widely split. Certainly, the western members did not go out of their way to show their support for Stanfield when questioned by newsmen shortly before the reopening of the House.

During this period, I continued to have doubts in Stanfield's ability to make it as a national leader. Given all of the developments that occurred over the summer, I was quite certain that he and his staff would have prepared a skilful attack on the government. Instead, it was close to pathetic to see how the question period dropped back almost immediately to the same dull routine to which we had become accustomed during the last session. The only noticeable change was in George Hees, whose questioning was much less frequent and much more subdued. Either he had decided that his previous tactics were doing nothing for his image, or—and I thought that this was more likely—some of the Conservative backbenchers insisted that he stop hogging the limelight so that more of them could get a chance to ask questions. In any event, it had become evident that there was no well-planned strategy behind the Tory questioning, and we were still very much in control of the House.

Prior to the opening of the House, cabinet had spent a great deal of time discussing the Speech from the Throne, mostly on the initiative of the Prime Minister. His idea was to use the Throne Speech as an effort to communicate something of the government's philosophical approach. There was no unanimity in cabinet about the wisdom of turning the Throne Speech into a dissertation on philosophical matters, but the view finally prevailed that the approach was worth trying. For my part, I favoured some form of declaration of principles but objected to early drafts of the Speech which tended to downplay current problems, particularly those related to unemployment and the high cost of living. This was a tendency I had noted in many documents coming from the Prime Minister's Office and, to some extent, from the Privy Council Office. It reinforced my feeling that while many on the Prime Minister's staff were undoubtedly capable, even brilliant, people, they tended to be out of touch with reality. This was, I suspected, a result of the fact that they moved in a relatively small circle and could not be said, by any stretch of the imagination, to have a natural grass-roots feeling about the country or an awareness of what ordinary people were thinking.

There were times when the Prime Minister also displayed this lack of awareness of what was going on in the country generally, and of the thoughts, attitudes, desires and aspirations of ordinary Canadians. This was another dimension of the perplexing and frustrating problem of trying to assess Trudeau's personal views and philosophy. Clearly, he had a good deal of compassion for the underprivileged and a basic sympathy with what might be considered general Canadian attitudes. On the other hand, his upbringing and experiences had not, except in the Quebec context, provided him with a lengthy or intensive exposure to everyday Canadian life. Because of this, I could not be certain that his instinctive compassion could be translated into a legitimate understanding of or sympathy with the goals of ordinary folk. There had been several occasions when, in conversation with Trudeau, I had made some quite casual statement relating to what a segment of the Canadian population thought about a particular issue. Generally, my assessments involved only what could be called common knowledge, conclusions which would be agreed on by most people who had had a fairly widespread and diverse exposure to the Canadian people. Yet, frequently, Trudeau did not share these assessments, and I was surprised when he did. Also contributing to his attitude was that he invariably applied a logical test to every proposition. In other words, while his first reaction might be to respond emotionally to a problem involving people, it did not take long for his analytical side to assert itself and compel him to conclude that an emotional reaction would not solve the problem, but only make it easier for those affected to bear. Time and time again, his private and public comments reinforced this view of his thinking process and his responses. Perhaps the best example was his attitude toward inflation: as he had said repeatedly, the easiest course that the government could take would increase employment in the short run, but in the long term, would merely fuel the fires of inflation. This would prove to be detrimental in the end.

What is true of the inflation issue applies equally to Trudeau's responses to new social measures that ministers brought forward from time to time. For example, he had been consistently unwilling to provide temporary relief for Canadian farmers. His argument had been that there must be a rationalization of farm policy even though this would probably involve difficult and unpopular policy decisions. He had taken the same view with regard to welfare; it had become evident that he lacked confidence in John Munro's ability to make hard decisions that would attack the root causes of poverty. Instead, Trudeau believed, as he told me privately, that Munro would only recommend more generous treatment of those who had need of social assistance, and that acceptance of the Munro proposals would only mean more of the same at increasing cost, without any permanent benefits.

The above observations, of course, merely recount my own attitudes and beliefs. However, in these and in other matters, Trudeau and I frequently thought along the same lines. This may be why he appeared to respect my opinions and to follow my recommendations. In other words, my interventions in cabinet served not to change his mind but to reinforce his own opinions.

Where the Prime Minister and I tended to part philosophical company was in the area of political judgement. For better or worse, I had always been a political animal, and because of my background, I tended on almost every occasion to assess the likely public reaction to our policies. When I did so, I had a much stronger tendency than did Trudeau to opt for solutions that would either enhance the government's position or at least not erode it. I believe that the true art of politics is not simply to act or even make important decisions; this is only part of the process. In my judgement, an effective politician is one who is able to forecast with reasonable accuracy, either intuitively or on the basis of experience, what the likely response to government decisions will be. This view is basic to my political philosophy. Good ideas in the political arena are pretty useless unless those who hold them are in the positions of power to carry them out. Therefore, for a government to act in such a way that it is thrown out of office in the next election is, in my view, a hollow form of political heroics. I have no use for those who seek power simply for its own sake, but for those who wish to retain office for the good they feel they can do, it is essential that, between elections, they take into account the degree of public acceptance their policies are likely to achieve. Otherwise, the odds are that the government will be defeated by those committed to the abandonment or reversal of such policies, and the objectives are lost.

I got the feeling that Trudeau, at least on his logical side, did not particularly care whether the policies he believed in were popular or not. If he was satisfied that a course of action was right, he seemed quite prepared to run the risk of unpopularity with the voters. On occasion, he said to me that there are worse things than being defeated.

At other times, he took a quite different approach, and this led me to believe that, like most of us, he suffered from basic conflicts in his own philosophy and in his approach to the problem-solving process. During the first months of 1970, there had been an evident increase in his concern for political considerations. This suggested very strongly that, as the election approached, he would be subject to the familiar virus that attacks all politicians faced with the prospect of being rejected by the voters.

I felt that Trudeau genuinely wanted to win the next election for a number of reasons. He had come to recognize, as we all had, that four years is insufficient time to carry out basic reforms and changes in long-established policies and methods of operation. And I am sure that he would have been very badly shaken if his toughening attitude in support of federalism could not be maintained throughout another term, and if it was reversed by another government with different views about Quebec. Whatever other objectives Trudeau might have had relating to the country as a whole, there can be no doubt that his basic motivation in entering politics and the influence that affected him most since assuming office had been the Quebec situation and his sincere conviction that, if any other party were to gain control in Canada at that time, it would be disastrous for the future of Quebec in Confederation. This provided him with a compelling reason to win the next election, and to win it handily. It was for this reason that, in recent months, he had sought my advice repeatedly, not only on the substance of government programs, but also on their likely political impact, and particularly on their possible effects on the next federal election.

There were, of course, less idealistic reasons for Trudeau's desire to win the next election. Despite the tensions of the office, a part of him thoroughly enjoyed the trappings of office and the exercise of power. He was not so cold and unimpressionable that he remained unaffected by public adulation and the superficial albeit important advantages of national leadership. With the mood of preparing for an election setting in, I foresaw during the next year a retention of the general thrust of our hard-line approach to problems, but with political considerations assuming greater importance in our deliberations.

A few months previously, I had told the Prime Minister that, in my judgement, it was important that we start immediately to plan our strategy for the next election. This would avoid the tendency as the date of the vote approached to revert to the kind of ad hoc decision making that had plagued the Pearson administration, and had led it to undertake important projects with long-term ramifications before thinking through the consequences of its actions. I suggested that what was needed was a strategy that would not make it inevitable for us to do an about-face on tough and unpopular reforms. Instead, we could soften their impact and time them in such a way that we would not head into an election period with a great deal of uncertainty in the country, and with unresolved, controversial issues still before the public. I saw increasing evidence that Trudeau was beginning to agree with this approach, and I surmised that as the weeks and months went by, I would be called on more frequently to provide input into policy discussions.

When Parliament reconvened in the fall of 1970, the kidnapping of James Cross overshadowed everything else. It began to preoccupy us in cabinet even before the new session was under way.

On Monday morning, October 5, I learned of Cross's kidnapping from a member of my staff who had heard it on the radio. At the time, I did not read any particular significance into the event. It was, I assumed, just another terrorist act, and Cross would be returned in short order after there had been enough publicity to satisfy what I thought was the abductors' main objective. It did not occur to me then that Cross was in any serious danger. The abduction would be regarded as another of the lawless acts we had been seeing regularly for some time in Quebec, acts attributed generally to the Front de Libération du Québec [FLQ]. It seems that mine was a fairly widespread initial reaction. On that first day, the media did not pay very much attention to the incident, and the reporting was generally low key.

On the following morning, there was a regular meeting of the Committee on Priorities and Planning. The Prime Minister introduced the kidnapping as the first item of business. For the first half hour, the discussion was quite casual, even lethargic. There was a measure of disinterest among the ministers present; certainly I did not get any sense of crisis or of special urgency. This may have been because the Prime Minister was quite subdued in his observations. He did not make any strong references to the FLQ, nor did he advance any views or suspicions that the Cross incident might form the basis of a general revolt or threat to law and order in Quebec. Like me, most ministers had not taken the abduction seriously; we viewed it as another escapade by the FLQ which would probably terminate without serious consequences once the abductors felt that they had adequately demonstrated their defiance of the law. We were not really prepared, therefore, for a thorough discussion of the affair, and, in the early stages of the meeting, the talk tended to drift. Our minds had not focused on the incident, and we were not ready to anticipate the events that might conceivably flow from the abduction.

So vague and generalized was the first part of the meeting, with various ministers simply debating general propositions such as whether a reward should be offered, that after about an hour the Prime Minister moved to close the discussion. He didn't see any purpose in continuing it, he said, and he assumed that the ministers were prepared to let the police handle it in the normal way. I intervened at this point. The Prime Minister, I thought, had misread the committee's view; I personally was definitely not prepared to leave the total initiative with the police. Mitchell Sharp echoed this view, as did one or two other ministers.

Trudeau promptly and, I suspect, happily, let the talk go on. It was my feeling that morning that the federal government should wait at least another day before making any response whatsoever. Having sent their communiqué, the kidnappers were probably somewhat scared and uncertain, I reasoned. If their actions were greeted by silence for an additional day, or even two, they might very well lose their nerve, free Cross and simply end the escapade.

With the benefit of hindsight, even though I wrote about the incident while Cross's whereabouts were still unknown, I am still inclined to believe that it might have been better if my suggestion had been followed. I continue to feel that what the FLQ was really looking for was recognition. It added to their stature, in their own eyes at least, to have all of the power and authority of the state focused on them and giving them an enormous amount of publicity. If there had been no immediate response from government, it is at least conceivable that they would have recognized the failure of one of their major objectives and lost interest.

At that first meeting, I expressed my hunch that the kidnapping could only be a bid for attention, that the kidnappers were not cold-blooded killers. After a time, the magnitude of their act would dawn on them, and they might want to retreat from the very serious position in which they found themselves actually confronting the state.

Mitchell Sharp, who as Foreign Affairs Minister obviously had a key role to play in the decision-making process, argued that since Cross was a British diplomat, we would be in a very difficult position if anything happened to him and we had made no effort to ensure his safe return. At no time in the discussion did any minister suggest that the demands of the kidnappers be met. The abductors in their communiqué had talked about the provision of safe passage to either Cuba or Algeria for those whom they wanted released. Our discussion, therefore, took the line of determining whether we should offer free transportation to the kidnappers themselves. I could not see the logic of this proposal. It was my judgement that the kidnappers would not take our word that their departure from the country was guaranteed, and I felt that they would react by stating that the offer was a hoax. They would suspect that they would be arrested the instant they appeared with Cross in order to take us up on the offer. There was even some talk at the meeting that such a reception might be quite justifiable under the circumstances. In any event, Mitchell Sharp continued to press his conviction that we had to make some form of offer in order to place on the record our concern for Cross, and thus avoid possible subsequent international criticism that we had cold-bloodedly ignored his safety.

Gordon Robertson, the Clerk of the Privy Council, also argued strongly for an immediate statement from the federal government, and brought forward proposals quite similar to Mitchell Sharp's statement. Our statement would have the effect of denying the kidnappers' demands, affirming the government's unwillingness to deal with them in any way, but offering them safe passage out of Canada if Cross were returned unharmed. Again, I challenged the logic of this proposal. At the moment, we were in no position to assure the kidnappers that they would be welcome in Cuba or Algeria. Also, I did not believe that the kidnappers would be so gullible as to present themselves to the authorities in order to obtain transportation, particularly since they would have to give up Cross in the process. Even if they were sent to Cuba or Algeria before Cross was released, how could they be sure that we would not then make a deal with one of those countries to send the kidnappers back? The discussion ended, and my point of view prevailed. The Prime Minister decided to wait and see, at least until the following day.

As soon as the meeting was over, however, I knew that both Robertson and Mitchell Sharp were not happy with the decision. Robertson, with whom I had an excellent rapport, told me that while he usually agreed with me, he felt I was wrong in this case. Mitchell Sharp joined the conversation and expressed the same view. Both said that they would prepare possible draft statements. It was clear from the events that followed that Robertson at least immediately discussed the matter with the Prime Minister privately.

The House opened at two o'clock to clean up some routine items of business from the old session. During this routine sitting, word was circulated to all ministers that there would be a full cabinet meeting following question period. At this meeting, much of the morning's discussion was rehashed, and both Robertson and Sharp produced draft statements.

There was no real unanimity among the ministers regarding strategy. In particular, there were wide differences of opinion on the question of whether or not a reward should be offered immediately. The argument against the reward was based on the feeling that to offer a reward at the time would increase Cross's jeopardy. If the kidnappers were aware that such a large sum had been offered for Cross, they would recognize that the heat was on and might conceivably kill him, bury his body and simply disappear. It was decided, therefore, that we would keep reviewing the wisdom of offering a reward, but would not make the decision immediately. I continued to argue that the waiting game was still the most advisable. But because all ministers were present, there tended to be a stronger feeling than in the morning that we should not rule out entirely the possibility of bargaining with the kidnappers.

It is interesting to recall the reaction of much of the press that day, particularly in the editorial columns. Most emphasized our responsibility to Cross, and suggested that we should yield to the terrorists in order to get him back. The same was suggested in cabinet. Therefore, even though the Prime Minister might have been quite prepared to take the tougher line of not responding in any way, he did not express his views, and cabinet decided on what was essentially a compromise. A statement would be issued, more or less along the lines proposed by Sharp, but also incorporating some of Robertson's ideas. The main argument in favour of such a statement was that a more or less noncommittal response could buy time during which the police might be able to track down the abductors. Consequently, the statement emphasized the necessity of establishing communication with the kidnappers so that substantive discussions could take place. These talks would determine what conditions the kidnappers might be prepared to accept in return for Cross's safe release.

There was no formal polling of cabinet to get the views of individual members as to just how far they might be prepared to go. I suspect that had this been done, the views expressed would have covered the whole spectrum from complete capitulation involving the release of the twenty-three prisoners, to the hardest line which, I suppose, I advocated more strongly than most. There was even some rationalization by certain ministers that getting the twenty-three terrorists out of the country would be a blessing in the sense that, once gone, they would never be able to return, and Canada would be well rid of them. This was not a view strongly expressed by any one minister, but merely the kind of casual comment uttered off-handedly on such occasions.

The events of the next few days tended to support my conviction that the exercise was basically futile. But it was useful in that it gave Mitchell Sharp what he was looking for; there was evidence for the record that we had gone as far as it was reasonable to expect of us in our attempts to recover Cross safe and sound.

On the following day, Wednesday, there was a formal ball scheduled at Government House as a prelude to the opening of that session of Parliament on Thursday. A regular cabinet meeting was held on Wednesday, and although Jean Marchand was not present, he personally indicated through the Prime Minister that he had some doubts about letting the ball proceed. There was general agreement, however, that any cancellation might be interpreted by the FLQ as a sign that it had succeeded in disrupting the normal course of events. It was agreed that those ministers who wanted to should attend; Mitchell Sharp, however, would stand by in the event that there was any communication from the kidnappers.

On Thursday, October 8, the House opened its new session as scheduled at eleven o'clock. Things went normally. I did not attend the formal ceremonies in the Senate, but returned to my office to deal with a heavy workload. There were many things I had to attend to before leaving for Europe on the following day. Nor did I return to the House in the afternoon to hear the speeches of the mover and seconder of the Address of Reply. I had planned to go, but due to a mistake in the announcement of the time, I arrived at the House when proceedings had already concluded.

On Friday, Prime Minister Trudeau led off the leaders' day speeches in the Commons. While he made some reference to the kidnapping, the issue did not really escalate further. As yet, there was no great sense of urgency or crisis evident in the House. For this reason, I decided, finally, that I would not cancel my proposed trip to Europe, and late on Friday evening, my wife and I and my special assistant, Eric Facey, flew to Montreal, and then on to Paris. I confess to a certain amount of misgiving both about making the trip and also about flying commercially to Europe. Earlier, because of the kidnapping, it had been decided that ministers should fly only on government planes, at least within Canada. The security on my trip was quite good, however, and we reached Paris without incident. For me, it was my first flight on the new Boeing 747 jumbo jet.

I was in Europe for the next six days, and my personal knowledge of events in Canada was limited to what I could learn from phone calls and cables, and to what I heard subsequently from my cabinet colleagues. The developments were also reviewed frequently at various cabinet meetings following my return.

I learned of the kidnapping of Pierre Laporte while still in Paris. I felt a terrible sense of frustration both because our earlier strategy seemed to be unsuccessful, and also because I was not present to take part in what I knew would be very difficult decisions for cabinet. I chose, however, to continue the trip, feeling that since events were uncertain, I might return for no good purpose. Also, Barbara had agreed to launch a ship in the United Kingdom on Wednesday, and any change in our plans would inconvenience a large number of people.

As to what went on in Ottawa during the next few days, the principal advocate of decisive action, apart from the Prime Minister, was Jean Marchand. Jean had gone to Quebec immediately following the kidnapping of Pierre Laporte. He returned to Ottawa greatly agitated by what he had seen and heard. The Bourassa government, in Jean's opinion, lacked the stability and unity to stand up to the kidnappers and to the FLQ in general. He also feared that there had been widespread FLQ infiltration of various important agencies in Quebec, the ramifications of which could be disastrous.

No doubt the statements he made subsequently regarding the infiltrations of the FLQ and the possibility of widespread acts of terror reflected his genuine and honest assessment of the situation. Probably, it will never be known with certainty just how accurate his judgement was. There can be no doubt, however, that among various groups with whom Marchand had contacts in Quebec, there was real concern, even conviction, that the province was on the brink of anarchy.

Jean Drapeau and Lucien Saulnier in Montreal were among the most vociferous advocates of extreme measures. This is not surprising, particularly in the case of Drapeau, a highly emotional man even in normal circumstances. Another strong influence on Marchand, and subsequently on others, was the intervention of Claude Ryan and various other well-known persons in Quebec. They called for negotiation with the kidnappers, and the meeting of their demands. A few days after my return, Marchand told me personally that Ryan had gone to various influential people in Quebec and had advocated the replacement of the Bourassa government with a provisional regime. This provisional group, Marchand said, was to have been lead by René Lévesque.

For purposes of clarity, it is not possible to keep this narrative in sequence. At this point, it should be recorded that several days after the proclamation of the War Measures Act, Claude Ryan published a statement in which he admitted discussing the possibility of a provisional government. He said, however, that he had talked only with others on his own newspaper, *Le Devoir*, and had not discussed such a contingency with anyone else. While this is at odds with Marchand's version, there can be no disputing Marchand's sincerity when he revealed the information to me. In any event, I was told by several ministers present at meetings during that critical week that Marchand had been most agitated in his declarations to cabinet.

Several weeks before the crisis, I had had lunch with Trudeau. I had told him that I was making good progress in terms of our negotiations regarding the new airport for the Montreal area. Trudeau replied that he was most impressed by Bourassa and felt that we were going to be able to work well with him. He did say, however, that he felt that Bourassa was somewhat confused and unsure of himself, and added that Bourassa phoned him almost every day on some question or other. I commented that Bourassa had phoned me on at least two occasions, and the Prime Minister replied that this tended to confirm his own judgement that the Quebec premier was looking for assistance and guidance.

This may have been at the back of Trudeau's mind as he debated what ought to be done about the Quebec situation. If, as seems likely, he lacked confidence in Bourassa's capacity to cope with a crisis situation, this would have made him receptive to the reports from various sources indicating that there was turmoil within the Quebec cabinet. Such turmoil could be aggravated seriously by the efforts of prestigious people like Claude Ryan who, the Prime Minister obviously believed, were proposing some form of interim government.

It had been clear for some time that there was no love lost between the Prime Minister and Claude Ryan. I had also noted during those two and a half years that Trudeau was strongly antagonistic to those who did not share his philosophical approach to federalism or his views on what needed to be done in Quebec. It was evident that among such people as Trudeau, Marchand, Pelletier and Marc Lalonde, there existed a common antagonism toward various other intellectual elements in Quebec who had been critical of Trudeau's policies and the government's efforts to defuse the Quebec situation. Often, in cabinet and in private meetings, Trudeau made no attempt to hide his scorn for those who, in his view, were inclined to take a soft line in Quebec. I have no doubt that when he referred during the crisis to the "bleeding hearts" in Quebec, Claude Ryan was one of those he had in mind. It is likely that, given this background of antagonism, the Prime Minister was exceedingly irked by Ryan's declaration, especially since it was supported by others such as René Lévesque and a number of union leaders. Their actions undoubtedly evoked a strong reaction in Trudeau, and may have been a key reason for his advocacy of the proclamation of the War Measures Act.

Another aside to these events casts some light on the Prime Minister's general stance. After the first meeting of the Priorities and Planning Committee where the Cross kidnapping was discussed, Bud

Drury and I had a private conversation. Both of us, I think, recognized from the beginning the futility of trying to negotiate with the kidnappers. Our common assessment was that the Prime Minister shared this view. Bud saw the dramatic events shaping up as a real test of power. He was sure the Prime Minister understood the situation in exactly that way, and was quite prepared to assert himself.

This was, of course, before the subsequent cabinet meeting at which a decision was made to make certain mild overtures to the kidnappers. With the benefit of hindsight, however, I am satisfied that from the very moment Cross was abducted, Trudeau saw the incident as an issue on which he could stand or fall, and through which he might be able to assert the federal position in a dramatic manner. Laporte's kidnapping added an important dimension to the crisis, and crystallized Trudeau's position. The Prime Minister saw that if he did not move decisively and immediately, his whole posture regarding Quebec and federalism would lose credibility.

Given this assessment, it is interesting to speculate as to whether or not the decision to proclaim the War Measures Act was influenced more by actual events transpiring at the time, or by a general feeling on the part of the Prime Minister and the Quebec ministers that the crunch had come: if they did not stand up and be counted, it would be the end of their vision of federalism.

During the period of my trip to Paris, the key meeting held in my absence was on the Thursday morning prior to the proclamation of the War Measures Act. There was a very heated discussion about the possibility of proclaiming the Act, and the Prime Minister, the Quebec ministers and some others were prepared to take immediate action. In fact, they were willing to introduce most of the extreme measures permitted under the statute. Joe Greene, John Turner and one or two others had grave doubts about the wisdom of proclaiming the Act at all. Primarily on their insistence, the decision was made that the measure would not be activated until a formal request for its proclamation had been made by the Quebec government and by the municipal administration of Montreal. Once this compromise had been agreed upon, the die was cast, and, of course, the rest is history.

The Prime Minister proclaimed the Act at four o'clock on Friday in line with a precise timetable, and with the concurrence of the province of Quebec and the city of Montreal. Since I was on an overnight flight from Europe, I did not learn of the proclamation of the War Measures Act until I arrived in Toronto. I was greeted with the news at the airport, and I immediately discussed its ramifications for the Ministry of Transport with my deputy, Jerry Stoner, on the phone from Toronto to Ottawa for the better part of an hour.

Since I was to receive an honorary degree and address the convocation at Memorial University of Newfoundland on the following day, I had to fly directly to St. John's, and had no opportunity for a first-hand briefing from the Prime Minister or any of my colleagues. The Saturday convocation went well, and it had been my intention to remain in Newfoundland until late Sunday evening. Very early on Sunday morning, however, I was awakened by my daughter, Heather, who advised me that Pierre Laporte's body had been found. I immediately made plans to return to Ottawa on the Ministry of Transport plane already waiting for me in St. John's, and I was back in the capital on Sunday morning.

Ottawa and, I suspect, the rest of the country was in something of a state of shock. The radio and television stations and networks were broadcasting whatever they could find out concerning the crisis, but during those early hours, there was a tremendous amount of repetition and a fair smattering of unconfirmed rumours and wholly false reports.

In this regard, the Canadian Broadcasting Corporation was a particularly bad offender. Among the other things reported in the early hours following Laporte's assassination, the CBC announced that Cross had also been killed, and that his body had been found. The confusion created by the CBC added additional fuel to the fires of those who had a strong antipathy toward the corporation. Particularly in Quebec, critics of the CBC were inclined to place much of the blame for the unrest on the great number of separatists who were said to be working for the corporation.

On Sunday morning, the Prime Minister called a special cabinet meeting to convene at noon. I and most of the others arrived in the meeting room a few minutes before him. When Trudeau entered, he showed only slight signs of strain; there was nothing particularly tense about his manner, and the meeting began almost perfunctorily. There was no emotional declaration from Trudeau, nothing calculated to set a mood or to condition us to take drastic action. The Prime Minister simply contributed a few words to open the discussion, and from that point on, acted more in the role of listener than leader of the debate.

The first item discussed was whether or not there should be any change in the government's attitude or strategy as a result of Laporte's murder. There was instant unanimity that, now more than ever, the hard line was essential. There was some mild discussion as to whether the offer of free exit from the country for Cross's kidnappers should stand. I questioned whether we could continue to offer immunity under such circumstances. I pointed out that we had, by proclamation of the War Measures Act, outlawed the entire FLQ organization. Furthermore, our whole posture had been that this was a conspiracy involving all elements of the FLQ; we had created a direct link between the kidnapping of Cross and the kidnapping and murder of Laporte. I suggested, therefore, that if we were to grant immunity to those who had kidnapped Cross pending his safe return, we would, in fact, be setting up a situation in which at least some of those who had contributed, if only indirectly, to Laporte's murder would have the opportunity to go free. Others argued that it seemed apparent that there were different cells within the FLQ, and that one group did not necessarily know what the others were doing. It was pointed out by some ministers also that the general tone of the communiqués from those holding Cross had been less violent than those of the cell that had kidnapped Laporte. Nevertheless, although the logic of my argument was generally accepted, it was felt that the offer of transportation out of Canada ought to be retained.

This view was reinforced when, during the meeting, Mitchell Sharp received a report indicating that another letter from Cross and his kidnappers had been received. This letter made it plain that Cross was still alive. In fact, the tone of Cross's own letter suggested that he was in no immediate danger of being killed.

At the time, an overriding concern for us was the need to show the public that we did not value one man's life over another. For example, Mitchell Sharp argued that a withdrawal of the amnesty offer following Laporte's death would suggest to the British that we were less concerned about Cross than we had been about Laporte. Conversely, if we now offered a reward for Cross's return, we would immediately be accused of having waited until after Laporte's death to make such an offer. Within Quebec in particular, there would have been widespread criticism that we had been less concerned for Laporte than we now were for Cross. Consideration was also given to the posting of a reward for Laporte's killers, but it was felt generally that any reward offer could jeopardize Cross's life still further.

My main contribution to the special meeting was an expression of my feeling that the main task that lay ahead of us was to cope with the inevitable claims that the government had acted irresponsibly, or had overreacted, in proclaiming the War Measures Act. In my judgement, the credibility issue would be the main one to surface once the original emotional response to events had subsided. I felt that this was particularly true in the case of the NDP; having gone out on a limb in criticizing the proclamation of the Act, its one defence would be to show that the measure had been unnecessary in the first place. I pointed out also that the news media, having gone along with us almost unanimously, would be asking us to prove our case. I felt strongly that someone should be at work documenting the various developments and supporting them with facts to the maximum extent possible.

The Prime Minister was surprisingly unresponsive to this suggestion. He did not argue against it specifically; on the other hand, he did not act to set up a task force to provide a rationale for the government's actions. Subsequent events made his reason for non-response very plain. It was his growing awareness, and perhaps concern, that very little in the way of concrete evidence was going to turn up.

I have the feeling that even as early as that Sunday, there was a suspicion in the Prime Minister's mind, as there was in the minds of many of us, that many of the claims made by spokesmen on the issue had been highly coloured and based on exaggerated rumour. For example, there had been reports that radio-controlled vehicles loaded with dynamite were to be placed strategically in Montreal, and their explosive cargoes set off by remote control. Nothing to confirm this report had been turned up by police. There had been no discovery of large stores of dynamite or weapons in the hands of the FLQ. Nor could evidence be publicly documented that would assert without question the existence of an organized plot.

When the War Measures Act was proclaimed, there was widespread hope within cabinet that the police sweeps authorized by the Act would, within a day or so, provide us with the kind of evidence that would justify the action we had taken. By Sunday, however, nothing significant had turned up; nor had the police captured Laporte's killers or tracked down Cross and his abductors. In other words, conditions on Sunday were not significantly different than they had been before the War Measures Act went into effect. There was no point, therefore, in trying to make a case for the War Measures Act based on hard evidence. This was the main reason for Trudeau's reluctance to initiate any kind of preparatory work on a general defence of our motives.

Like many others in cabinet, I was uneasy over this turn of events. We saw quite clearly what would happen in a day or two when we would be put on the defensive by charges that we had overreacted or, even worse, that we had acted for political reasons or from less than honourable motives.

There was another issue which generated considerable discussion and some controversy: this was the question of whether the Prime Minister should make another speech to the nation on Sunday night. The argument was that the excellent speech he had made on Friday explaining the reasons for the invocation of the War Measures Act had been made prior to Laporte's death; therefore, he should now bring his comments up-to-date and reinforce public support for our actions. I questioned the wisdom of such a move. In my judgement, Trudeau had achieved his goal completely on Friday and it was not necessary to stiffen public attitudes a second time. After the Friday performance, I asked, "What do you do for an encore?" The Prime Minister was inclined to agree, and little more was said on the matter.

Late on Sunday night, however, Trudeau did appear on television with a brief statement basically confined to references to Laporte's death. He expressed sympathy to the Laporte family, and generally but briefly reaffirmed the government's decision to hold fast. His statement contained substantially less than had been proposed earlier. On the following day, I told the Prime Minister in the House of Commons that I thought his Sunday speech was satisfactory. He responded that he had agreed with my opinion and had been inclined to not go on the air at all, but had been talked into a brief appearance by people in his own office. This points to a significant aspect of the whole affair; Trudeau's staff advisors felt from the beginning a need for the federal government to take and hold the initiative, and the Prime Minister, therefore, had to keep making statements showing both his control of the situation and the depth of his commitment. I did not argue strongly against this assertion; nevertheless, I felt that in circumstances such as these, there was a danger of overkill. I was pleased, therefore, that although the Prime Minister agreed to go on television, he confined his remarks to what was appropriate on such an occasion—an expression of sympathy and regret over Laporte's death.

There was virtual unanimity in cabinet at one point during that Sunday afternoon meeting. All of us were greatly upset, even alarmed, at the apparent inefficiency of the police forces in the emergency generally, but particularly following the proclamation of the War Measures Act. George McIlraith, who as solicitor general had responsibility for the RCMP, quite naturally came to the defence of the national police force. He did concede, however, in his oblique and somewhat mysterious way, that the Quebec police were perhaps something less than perfect. He claimed that there was an inadequate liaison between the two forces, and to some extent, between the police and the Armed Forces called in to deal with the emergency.

George seemed the most improbable man to have in charge of a national police force in such a crisis. He was overly secretive to the point where a number of ministers were upset by his unwillingness to tell even them all of the details. He also possessed an inordinate passion for precision, a tendency which made his explanations painfully long and confused. He never spoke in generalizations and qualified virtually every sentence he uttered. Not only was this annoying to ministers who are, in general, fundamentally doubtful of the efficiency of the police; it also meant that George's speeches antagonized his listeners simply because it took him so long to make a point. Moreover, each point was fenced in by enough ifs, ands and buts as to render it virtually meaningless. On several occasions, I detected Trudeau's impatience with George's plodding style. However, no criticism was voiced by him or by anyone else.

Yet George did not lack astuteness, and I know that he sensed the ministers' concern that so little had been accomplished by the police even after they were granted sweeping powers. At the Sunday meeting, therefore, he suggested a briefing for cabinet by top RCMP officials. In this way, we could get a general picture of terrorist activities from a police perspective, as well as an update of what had happened since the proclamation of the War Measures Act.

The meeting with the police was held on Sunday night with most cabinet members in attendance. The Prime Minister, however, was not present. From a police standpoint, it can only be described as a disaster. The officer in charge of intelligence relating to developments in Quebec read excerpts from a paper that was more than a year old. In many respects, it was less precise and complete than many accounts of terrorist and revolutionary activity in Quebec already published in the newspapers and elsewhere. A number of ministers, myself included, questioned the RCMP persistently on their operations. The responses were disquieting, to say the least. The commissioner of the RCMP conceded that the dragnet thrown out following the proclamation of the War Measures Act had produced nothing of any consequence. There had been no discovery of firearms or explosives. Reports of radio-controlled vehicles loaded with explosives had proven to be largely false. Another story about a woman in Hull having been brutally attacked by the FLQ appeared to have been a hoax.

The commissioner also revealed that even after Laporte had been kidnapped, the police had Paul Rose under surveillance but had lost track of him. He told us that within a couple of days of Cross's kidnapping, the RCMP had identified a partial fingerprint on one of the FLQ communiqués as belonging to Marc Carbonneau. He did not explain why, in light of this evidence, they had not announced that Carbonneau was wanted, or made any public declaration concerning this information which so clearly linked Carbonneau to the Cross kidnapping. The commissioner also said that a fingerprint identified as Rose's had been found on one of the communiqués sent in connection with the Laporte kidnapping. This was known even before Laporte's body was found. Yet again, there was no public indication that Rose was wanted. In fact, although they had had him under surveillance for some time, the RCMP did not pick him up because, as the commissioner explained it, they had hoped he would lead them to Laporte.

Towards the end of the meeting, the commissioner was asked if what he had been able to uncover both before and after the proclamation of the Act would be enough to support a claim that an insurrection was being planned. We were all shaken very badly by his reply—that, if asked that question, he would have to say that, up to that point at least, he had no such evidence. The implication of such a statement is obvious. If stated publicly in such a bare fashion, it would provide all the ammunition needed by our critics who had argued from the beginning that the invocation of the War Measures Act was unjustified. Seeing our startled reaction, the commissioner went on to say that, of course, he was referring solely to the police failure to uncover the large supplies of explosives, ammunition and firearms that were allegedly in the hands of the FLQ. He added that there was, in addition to the known thefts of dynamite and other explosives, and the known activities and writings of leaders of the FLQ, a general climate of unrest within Quebec. In the judgement of both himself and his officers, the total pattern was sufficient to justify the government's actions. At this point, I began to realize more than I had previously why Trudeau had not moved quickly to accept my suggestion that we try to prepare a rationale or defence of our actions. Clearly, he had been given the same type of background information by the RCMP, and had realized that in concrete terms, we did not have a compelling case to put forward.

It was at this meeting that Jean-Luc Pepin put forward what appeared to me, and to most present, the appropriate basis for a reply to those who we knew would be persistent in their demands for more information. Jean-Luc had done a great deal of research on the classic patterns of revolutionary developments over the years. In his methodical, professional style, he pointed out that what was happening in Quebec under the auspices of the FLQ fitted the scenario for revolution that had been employed in a great many countries, including Russia, down through the years. He cited chapter and verse from a number of history books he had brought with him. He showed that, basically, the plotters of revolution do not need to be in control of all of the elements that can lead to a breakdown of law and order. He cited examples from revolutions in other places where acts of terror had been committed as the first step in the revolutionary process. These had been followed by such incidents as kidnappings and political murders. These characteristics of revolution, he pointed out, were present in Quebec, and had been escalating for some time. Then he compared recent events in Quebec with those that had been part of early revolutionary movements. He cited examples where, on the heels of terror, public concern and unease had risen to alarming heights, again as in Quebec. As their next move, he continued, the revolutionaries moved to undermine confidence in elected governments and to create a widespread public impression that the governments were not in control of the situation. This, too, he maintained, was present in the Quebec situation. He then went on to illustrate that given the set of circumstances he had outlined in his examples, there had been, somewhat inevitably, meetings of radicals and students, and in Quebec during the previous week, such gatherings had been arranged, and the participants had voiced the classic denouncements of law and order. He then pointed out that, according to the classical pattern, the next step would have been for protestors to take to the streets. This would immediately set up a situation where violence, and perhaps excessive police retaliation, would undermine still further the public's faith in the capacity of established instruments of government and law to keep things under control. Thus, Pepin argued, the government was entirely justified in moving decisively when it did. There was clear evidence, he said, that street demonstrations were about to occur. He gave us examples of the mood of the student meetings held just prior to the weekend. Some of the leaders of the FLQ had sought, to some extent unsuccessfully, to arouse the protestors, and there was a report, published widely both in and out of Quebec, that a march on Ottawa was being planned for the following week.

Jean-Luc's lucid and orderly presentation of this argument gave us a good deal of comfort since we felt that it was the best response to employ during the coming days to rebut those who were already accusing us of overreacting.

We agreed at the meeting that the RCMP should prepare additional evidence in support of Pepin's statement, and the meeting broke up at ten o'clock. Subsequently, as we were leaving the cabinet room, it was evident to me that the ministers, generally, were very disturbed by the RCMP presentation and had had their confidence in the police force shaken severely.

In fairness, it should be recorded that the RCMP spokesmen present had been called in on very short notice. They were exceedingly busy and had not had sufficient time to prepare a thorough and up-to-date submission. There were some of us who accepted this explanation and who recognized that the police force was not as incompetent as some were inclined to believe. Nevertheless, it was quite an experience to confront those in whom we had placed so much trust, and to find that they did not have the type of straightforward, unqualified answers one would expect from people who exerted so much influence on the government when crucial decisions were being made.

It is important that I record, however, that there had been a certain tension between the government and the RCMP during the whole Trudeau administration to date. While I was Minister of Defence Production, the special Royal Commission on Security presented its report. Although I was not normally a member of the Cabinet Security Committee, I was called in to discuss the report because it expressed some criticisms of the security arrangements of the department I headed at the time.

At the meeting chaired by the Prime Minister, the RCMP vigorously denounced the Commission's report on security, and they were supported by the minister responsible, George McIlraith. I had the feeling that the spokesmen for the RCMP, including the commissioner and his deputy, were overly defensive.

They had an exaggerated idea of the force's competence and efficiency, and resented suggestions that in some way or other they were not doing their job effectively. That particular meeting did not result in any policy conclusions; it was concerned primarily with what portions of the commissioner's report could be made public. There was throughout the discussion, however, clear evidence that all of the ministers present except McIlraith were decidedly critical of the RCMP. At the very best, they had doubts about the force's capability to deal with new and emerging threats to law and order.

The same kind of evidence was clear to me on other occasions. In 1969, when the commissioner of the RCMP at the time was about to retire, I was returning from western Canada. I had agreed that my plane would pick up George McIlraith in Regina. During the flight from Regina to Ottawa, McIlraith showed me a letter of resignation which he said he was contemplating giving to the Prime Minister. I asked him the reason for his dissatisfaction. He told me that the Prime Minister was considering the appointment of a civilian from outside the force as the new commissioner of the RCMP. George totally disagreed with this approach and said that he would not remain in cabinet if Trudeau carried through with his plan. He told me that the appointment of a civilian to the top post would be exceedingly bad for the morale of the force. He also stated that the Prime Minister, and most of us in cabinet, underestimated the complexity of the job of the police force; we were therefore inclined to be overly critical and might conceivably support the idea of a civilian head.

As things turned out, George finally got a meeting with the Prime Minister on the subject. Apparently, he made his point because the new commissioner was appointed from within the ranks of the force. At the same time, however, the government did name a civilian as deputy commissioner with special responsibilities for intelligence matters. I asked George if the compromise was satisfactory to him, and he replied that it was.

Nevertheless, it had been evident from the beginning of the Trudeau administration that George was generally unhappy with what he saw as the government's lack of concern for security matters. Repeatedly, he told me privately of his concern for the status of certain people in the government whom he claimed were potential security risks. But on all such occasions, he added that he could not convince Trudeau to be as concerned about these matters as he himself was. He also told me on one occasion that he had asked the Prime Minister repeatedly to arrange for a security briefing by the RCMP to the full cabinet. While Trudeau had not refused to do so, he had never shown enough interest in the proposition to arrange such a session.

In early 1970, I asked George, who had previous experience as Minister of Public Works, how I could go about getting better office accommodations on Parliament Hill. I was having to meet a great many delegations and had an inadequate amount of space. George called me to his own Centre Block office and asked me if I thought that his space would be suitable for my purposes. I replied that it would, but I wondered why he was suggesting that I move in with him. He told me that he was very lonely and felt out of things, and that I should not be surprised if I heard that he was pulling out. Naturally, I attempted to talk him out of any such action. On that occasion as on others, he repeated his worry that he was really not getting anywhere with the Prime Minister and that important security matters were being overlooked by the government.

It was very difficult when talking with George to know whether what he said was as important or serious as he believed. George was a traditionalist in his attitude toward the functioning of government. He disliked the moves toward greater participation by caucus in government decisions, and had repeatedly expressed doubts about the wisdom of giving extra powers to parliamentary committees. When he put forward his objections, he generally coupled them with dire forecasts about what would likely happen to the system because of these changes. In this sense, George was essentially a reactionary and a politician from the old school. This, however, did not reflect on his basically Liberal philosophy on policy considerations. It was simply his approach to law and order issues and explains, in my judgement, why he had been basically uncritical of the RCMP's role, and why he was willing to accept their assessment of any situation, particularly the security issue.

Another small incident may help to illuminate the Prime Minister's and the government's attitude toward the whole question of security. On one occasion, we were discussing the future role of the RCMP. Gérard Pelletier dealt with citizenship matters, and hence, came into contact with the RCMP, which was the agency that checked out citizenship applications. Gérard expressed his unhappiness with the way the RCMP handled this particular task. In his view, the orientation of the force in this matter was quite wrong. There was also a similar criticism from Allan MacEachen who was then the minister responsible for immigration.

When the Cross case was first being discussed in the Committee on Priorities and Planning, I asked Trudeau why the RCMP had so little concrete evidence relating to the FLQ. I wondered why their intelligence was so incomplete, and why they had been able to obtain so few reliable leads after Cross had been kidnapped. In Trudeau's judgement, based on what he had seen, the RCMP had been spending most of their time trying to keep track of the so-called communist menace. In his words, they had been fighting communism to the point of preoccupation, and had not geared their operations or techniques to cope with the newly emerging threats to society posed by terrorist groups such as the FLQ in Quebec and elsewhere.

The foregoing discussion should indicate why, at the time of the Laporte crisis, the government was far from totally confident that the federal police force was capable of dealing decisively and quickly with the situation. I certainly shared this view, and nothing had happened since that initial, brief meeting on the day after Laporte's death to change my mind.

On the Monday following that dramatic Sunday, the House convened as scheduled at eleven o'clock. The debate on the Speech from the Throne was still in progress, and the rules provided for morning sessions four days a week during this period. One could feel a good deal of tension in the chamber as we reached the point where we were to vote on the proclamation of the War Measures Act. During the Sunday cabinet session, Allan MacEachen had indicated that based on discussions with leaders of other parties, he had come to the conclusion that the Tories were in a real quandary. The events of recent days, including the Prime Minister's televised speech on Friday evening and the massive support it had generated throughout the country, had made it clear to the Conservatives that opposition to the government's stand would be extremely unpopular. The Tory caucus was badly split, and in Allan's opinion, Stanfield would not be able to gain the support of all of his party members if he chose to oppose the resolution. All four Quebec members of the Conservative caucus had stated publicly their intention to vote with the government, and if necessary, against their own party. A number of western Tories were prepared to do the same.

MacEachen said we could, if we wished, cause Stanfield additional embarrassment. On the previous Friday, he had waffled badly in his response to the proclamation of the War Measures Act. He had given the impression that he opposed the measure, and that he would argue still further against its imposition in the form proposed by the government. On Sunday, when the news of Laporte's death consolidated public support still further, Stanfield was clearly on the horns of a dilemma. We could, said MacEachen, take a hard line in the House, or we could let Stanfield off the hook by indicating, as soon as the House opened, our intention to ask for endorsement of the Act, with a provision that the government would seek alternative, less sweeping legislation within a month. MacEachen doubted, as we all did, that this offer would win the support of the NDP. The assurance of alternative legislation would, however, provide Stanfield and his party with a rationale to vote for the Act without appearing to have done a complete reversal. In strictly political terms, there was a certain attraction in causing further embarrassment for the Tories, but no member of cabinet advocated such a course. Instead, there was immediate, unanimous agreement to accept Allan's alternative. We felt that we should do everything possible to be conciliatory in these difficult days.

This was not a narrow political judgement; all of us genuinely wanted to appear reasonable and to put the public interest ahead of other considerations, and most of us wanted to lift the imposition of the War Measures Act as soon as possible. We made a public commitment to do so in short order, knowing that the commitment to the House would serve as a spur requiring us to draft alternative legislation quickly. It would also avoid any temptation to keep the measure active if other incidents occurred. These might create a crisis atmosphere again and prompt us to take the easy way out by preserving the War Measures Act in force longer than we considered advisable.

When the House opened on Monday and Allan MacEachen made his announcement, the opposition's relief was obvious. Clearly, all impediments to passage of the measure had been eliminated. The vote itself was something of an anticlimax. The Speaker, as was customary, called for the ayes and nays. Under normal circumstances, that might have been the end of it; clearly, there had been a majority of voices raised in support. Undoubtedly, the NDP would have been happy if the issue had been passed "on division"—that is, without a recorded vote. For some reason, we had not considered in cabinet what we would do given such circumstances. Consequently, there was no agreed strategy to force a standing vote and isolate those who opposed the measure. Inevitably, however, there were both Liberals and Tories who wanted their votes recorded formally, and many more than the required number of members stood in their places in the prescribed way for the polling of individual members. Ironically, the NDP, who usually wanted a recorded vote on most measures, did not seek one in this case, and would have been happier if there had been no such poll of individual members. When the vote was taken, Tommy Douglas and David Lewis voted against the measure. This was no surprise but, unexpectedly, some NDP members refused to toe the party line and voted with the government. As much as anything else, this split revealed the agonizing that must have gone on over the weekend within the NDP.

On the next day, Tuesday, the regular morning meeting of the Priorities and Planning Committee was called for nine o'clock. This was earlier than usual because the House was still meeting at eleven. The session of the committee was held in a special room in the East Block where various members of the Prime Minister's staff and the Privy

Council Office had prepared a visual presentation. The Prime Minister started the discussion by expressing his desire to get the cabinet back to routine business as soon as possible. If the cabinet sessions were constantly preoccupied with the Quebec situation, he said, other important policy matters would be neglected, and we would, in effect, be playing into the hands of the FLQ. He then advanced a proposal that a special task force be set up under the guidance of his own office. The group would keep track of developments and devise an overall strategy for the government. The Prime Minister emphasized that it would not be the responsibility of the task force to make policy decisions. It would merely gather the necessary information and act as a liaison with designated officials in the Quebec government and the municipal government of Montreal. It would report to cabinet and to individual members regularly to indicate progress being made and to suggest possible government initiatives.

Before we moved to a discussion of this proposal, we were given a general assessment not only of the existing situation, but of possible developments that might occur under different sets of circumstances. The main participant in this exercise, taking us through the various options, was Buzz Nixon from the Prime Minister's Office, one of those little publicized officials who are given assignments related to long-term planning from a sociological point of view. He was a "think tank" type who was quite at home with the new jargon of the planners, and tended to advance unorthodox theories and concepts of the type Trudeau most enjoyed discussing. I should admit that such discussions have always appealed to me also.

Prior to the crisis, Nixon had brought forward to the Planning and Priorities Committee quite a number of papers on the subject of the various options open to government in terms of shaping Canada's future. I found these exceedingly interesting, and a good basis for the kind of philosophical discussion we did not have often enough at the cabinet level.

In setting out the government's options for dealing with the Quebec situation, Nixon made a series of charts and diagrams which sought to outline every conceivable eventuality. They covered the whole spectrum of possible developments ranging from the total collapse of the government of Quebec and the difficulties that would arise from this, to the opposite alternative where elected governments maintained control and moved to restore a high degree of normalcy both in Quebec and throughout Canada.

The list of possible disruptive events included in Nixon's diagrams was unsettling to say the least, but while it was useful to recognize that such developments were possible, Nixon had really drawn quite a long bow. We felt that we had to keep a proper perspective on events and not become too alarmist or lay too much emphasis on the possibility of a general breakdown.

As the exercise proceeded, I experienced a sense of unreality. If the projections and forecasts had been made public, most Canadians would have thought it incredible that specialists like Nixon would go through such an exercise. The public would have been inclined, I think, to conclude that there was a high degree of exaggeration.

Much more important and basic to the discussion was another phase of the Nixon presentation more directly concerned with the series of steps he and others felt ought to be taken to restore normalcy as soon as possible. Central to the plan was the necessity for both the federal and Quebec governments to demonstrate their firm control of events. A number of steps aimed at defusing the situation were proposed. The charts relating to this portion of the exercise were more acceptable because they stressed the importance of strengthening the economic base in Quebec, and the need to improve the confidence of the economic community. There had to be substantial evidence of ongoing industrial activity rather than uncertainty and fear. Insecurity would not only limit new investments, but might precipitate the withdrawal of existing industrial and business activities in Quebec. Nixon also provided a reasoned assessment of the long-term economic needs of both Quebec and the country in general, and a recommendation that special steps were needed immediately to curb unemployment and other causes of public unrest. During this meeting and throughout the crisis, it was impossible to tell just how seriously the Prime Minister took the various forecasts of possible events. Normally, I found him to be slightly bemused, if not completely cynical, with regard to those who tended to exaggerate the effects of government actions. On this occasion, however, he did nothing to de-emphasize the various possibilities listed by Nixon and others. It is impossible to say whether he believed the worst could happen, whether he was simply putting it forward as a possible scenario or whether, although he did not believe personally that the worst could happen, he felt it necessary to advance such possibilities, if for no other reason than to strengthen the government's resolve to remain firm and act decisively.

Following the presentation, a few of us made rather short comments. I chose not to express my doubts about the projected pattern the planners thought might emerge; however, because of the sense of unreality I experienced, I repeated my conviction that the priority problem was to develop a rationale we could make public to justify our decision to impose the War Measures Act. On this occasion, Trudeau showed greater agreement with me. Such a step was necessary, he said, and one of the assignments of the new task force would be to work toward that goal. In this exercise, they would take into account Pepin's

Jamieson at home in the district of Burin-Burgeo, also known as the "Forgotten Coast."

Jamieson wrote of fond memories of his district, as well as the challenge of representing it.

Jamieson meeting with some of his constituents

Jamieson relaxes while attending a soccer game in his district.

Jamieson's career in broadcasting served him well as a politician. He understood the dynamics of communication between politicians, media and the public.

On tour in the district of Burin-Burgeo during the 1971 Trudeau visit to Newfoundland.

Jamieson and Trudeau tour an industrial site in the district of Burin-Burgeo.

Jamieson with young constituents. He seemed to enjoy the fresh ideas of young people. During Trudeau's visit in 1971, Jamieson arranged for the youth from his area to meet the Prime Minister and Mrs. Trudeau.

Jamieson with Trudeau and cabinet colleagues in Ottawa. Although Jamieson became a relaxed and seasoned politician, he records that his first impulse was to quit and go home.

Don and Mrs. Jamieson, with Pierre Trudeau and Richard Nixon, attending the 10th anniversary of the opening of the St. Lawrence Seaway.

Canpress Photo Service (Chuck Mitchell)

Jamieson's several ministerial portfolios, most notably his term as Minister of External Affairs, led him into the international political arena.

Such exposure laid the groundwork for his last public post, as Canadian High Commissioner to Great Britain.

The Trudeau Cabinet, 1974.

earlier comments as being illustrative of what could have occurred in the unstable climate then existing in Quebec.

Here I added another point: in my judgement, as the public's emotional involvement declined, there would be mounting criticism of police action—or, more accurately, the lack of it—in coping with the kidnappers and the FLQ in general. Again, there was general agreement with my view. We all recognized, however, that it was out of the question for us to make any public statement that would serve to undermine public confidence at this critical time.

On the next day, Wednesday, little of consequence happened in government circles. Outside of direct government action, however, conflicts between the statements of various ministers began to surface. I had anticipated this all along and had been preoccupied from the day following Laporte's death with the need for a single explanation for our actions to which all of us could subscribe. This statement would constitute all that we would say in public to the media. Perhaps because of my background in journalism, I foresaw the inevitability of media pressure for more information on the background of the crisis. In the absence of a well-defined government position, different ministers would express divergent and conflicting views. In fact, this started immediately following Pierre Laporte's death.

Indeed, on the Friday before Laporte's body was found, when the matter was debated in the House, Jean Marchand had stated very emotionally a series of examples designed to bolster the government's case. Of these, perhaps the most dramatic was his claim that every level of the Quebec government and all of its important agencies had been infiltrated by the FLQ in the highest places. In addition, Marchand had talked about plans to blow up buildings and to carry out assassinations on an organized basis. In these and in a number of other ways, he had succeeded in creating an impression that the problem was urgent. At the Sunday cabinet meeting when I first discussed the possibility of preparing a common response to the anticipated enquiries, Bryce Mackasey made reference to Marchand's speech. He recommended that we all get copies of it to be used in any public statements we might make. I believe that Marchand had already realized by Sunday that he might have gone too far because he responded to Mackasey by saying that his speech was not designed to be read; the words were uttered for effect, he explained. Jean's English was not very precise, and it was difficult to determine from his comment to Mackasey exactly what he meant. What Jean seemed to be saying was that his speech on Friday would not look as good on paper as it had sounded when he made it. I suspect that by Sunday, he was a bit concerned that he might have gone too far in his utterances and in the examples he gave of potential terrorism. Still, there was no weakening in his conviction concerning the seriousness of the situation in Quebec.

By the middle of the week, John Turner, Bryce Mackasey and one or two other members of cabinet had made public statements principally to newsmen. These suggested quite specifically that the government had definite information concerning proposed terrorist activities that had not been made public, but when it was made public, would justify the government's action. This was a natural defence against those who had argued, and were still arguing, that we had overreacted. The implication was obvious; if the critics knew what the government knew, there would be no doubt concerning the wisdom of our action. A number of backbenchers, particularly those from Quebec but from other regions as well, had adopted this approach, and in the absence of an official government position, it had the effect of whetting the public's curiosity and of encouraging the media to ask still more questions.

Matters came to a head on Wednesday. Jean Marchand was interviewed by Jack Webster, an extremely aggressive and capable radio reporter from Vancouver. In this interview, Jean not only continued to suggest the existence of undisclosed factors; he also went as far as to claim that the Quebec organization known as Front d'Action Politique [FRAP] was aligned with the FLQ and was, as he put it, a front for the FLQ. Of course, FRAP was an organization of activists of every conceivable political stripe concerned primarily with civic matters and with various campaigns against poverty in Montreal.

By Thursday morning when cabinet met, the Marchand story had been given widespread national publicity. The Thursday meeting began with a general review of the Quebec situation and a presentation of the material shown to and discussed by the Committee on Priorities and Planning the previous day. Marchand was late for the meeting, but soon after he arrived, the matter of his statements to Webster came up. It was not raised by the Prime Minister as a special item; rather, it evolved from a general discussion of the intensified questioning of the approach the government had taken.

Marchand himself brought up the question of his own intervention. He admitted frankly that he should not have said that FRAP was a front for the FLQ, and said that he was proposing to make a statement of clarification. Nevertheless, he was prepared to stand by the rest of his statement to Webster. Obviously, this was the first time he had seen the Prime Minister following the interview. Trudeau was openly irritated by what Marchand had said, and told him flatly that when questions were asked in the House that morning, as they were bound to be, he did not propose to explain or defend what Marchand had siad, but would simply refer the questioners to Marchand. This new difficulty caused further discussion of the key question which I had emphasized for several days—the preparation of a government statement to which we could all adhere.

This time the Prime Minister showed even more interest and agreement than on the previous day, and he proceeded to articulate what he felt our position should be. He emphasized that we had been asked to act by the governments of the province of Quebec and the city of Montreal. Secondly, he said, we should call attention to the kidnappings of two very important people, a British diplomat and a Quebec cabinet minister. Also, we should point to the amount of evidence that made it clear that there was a general state of unrest in Quebec. Beyond this, he believed, the government should not go. He cautioned against throwing out hints to newsmen that might lead them to assume the existence of secret information.

At this point in the discussion, the ministers who had insisted earlier on getting the formal requests from the governments of Quebec and Montreal were prompt to remind everyone of their foresightedness. Without the letters, they said, and in the absence of any significant evidence turned up by the police, it would be very difficult for us to defend our actions.

With little discussion, cabinet approved the proposal to set up a special task force in the Prime Minister's Office. Gordon Robertson, Secretary to the Cabinet, and Marc Lalonde, Principal Secretary to the Prime Minister, would head the group, and Jim Davey would also have major responsibilities. The task force would have no policy making function, and would report directly to the Prime Minister and to cabinet. This dispelled most of our concerns about the proposal; still, I continued to be concerned that cabinet would not be directly involved with the crisis on a daily basis. I could, however, see the logic of Trudeau's position. He was anxious to get cabinet back to dealing with other policy questions and the running of the country in general. He feared what might occur if we continued to be preoccupied every day with the Quebec crisis.

The cabinet meeting was cut short by the meeting of the House at eleven o'clock. In the House, the Prime Minister did as he had indicated and denied that Marchand's statement represented the government's position. He left it to Jean to defend himself, and he did so, rather feebly, I thought, by falling back on the excuse that his English was less than perfect. When he had called FRAP a front for the FLQ, he explained, he had meant only that FRAP was giving moral support to an outlawed organization. This did not satisfy the opposition, of course, and as subsequent events showed, the Marchand statement was one of the most damaging in terms of the government's credibility with its critics.

The critics were a relatively small number of people in relation to the total population. Most of the public were clearly on our side and had no doubts about the wisdom or necessity of our approach. Nevertheless, the Prime Minister was becoming increasingly aware of the need to get something specific out to the public to defuse the critics' claim that we were hiding something. Yet it would be difficult to satisfy the critics by speaking frankly, since their main charge was that we had overreacted. Following the Friday meeting, Trudeau went further than on any previous occasion in the House to state the argument that had been developed in cabinet—that the request of the two levels of government in Quebec, plus the kidnappings and the general instability, formed the basis of our rationale.

It was at this time, about the end of the first week after Laporte's murder, that the story began to emerge concerning an intellectual group in Quebec, led by Claude Ryan, who had been advocating the formation of a parallel government, and what amounted to a new government, as an alternative to that of Premier Bourassa. It would include representatives of other parties and influential groups in Quebec. This report, which cabinet had been aware of even before Laporte's murder, was circulating around Ottawa during most of the week. Perhaps because of my journalistic background, I was sure that the story would surface sooner or later, and when it did, it would create quite a stir.

Although it has been charged that the story was leaked deliberately by members of cabinet, I myself saw no evidence of this. I do know that at the meeting on the previous Sunday, when we were given an assessment of the situation by the RCMP, Jean Marchand left before the session was over. As he was leaving, he came to where I was sitting and said that what we were hearing from the RCMP was not very helpful. Before long, he said, I would know that Claude Ryan had made a proposal to create an alternative government in Quebec. Jean told me at the time that it was his intention to make these facts known at some time during the coming week. If, therefore, there were ministers who spread the story, it is quite conceivable that Marchand was among them. I also suspected Bryce Mackasey of this. Mackasey had been interesting to watch during the entire crisis, a complex character, more cunning in his approach to politics than most ministers. Mackasey possessed two overwhelming characteristics: a compulsive need to maintain the approval of the Prime Minister, and an extreme sensitivity to press criticism. In his anxiety to get good publicity, Mackasey catered to certain reporters and columnists and gave them inside information that could not be attributed to him. In return, the reporters usually presented him in a good light.

This is, of course, a technique as old as journalism itself. I have no difficulty, when reading various columns and editorials, in picking out the best off-the-record sources for the writers. Invariably, a few days after a juicy tidbit is reported as coming from a highly placed unidentified source, there appears from the same pen a laudatory piece concerning a particular cabinet minister. It does not take a genius to put the two together. Furthermore, it is possible to identify the ministers who have this kind of relationship with a particular columnist. Using this technique, I found it not accidental that Bryce Mackasey's name kept cropping up in certain media with a remarkable degree of regularity and under the circumstances I have outlined. I had also been told by a number of reporters who were professional friends of mine that Mackasey was by far the best source of leaks in the entire cabinet.

Running a close second was John Munro. His staff were very skilful at planting stories that were both favourable to their minister and designed to advance various policy proposals he had coming before cabinet. However, Munro only employed this technique, as far as I know, in support of his own ministerial objectives. For example, there was the prize case of the leak to *Time* magazine of the LeDain Commission report on drug usage. There had been that summer a number of quite specific pieces in the newspapers relating to Munro's original ideas on what should be in his white paper on social policy. I doubted, however, that Munro would be in the least interested in releasing behind-the-scenes information on the Quebec situation.

During the furore flowing from the disclosures on Claude Ryan's activities, there was an interesting column by Ron Haggart of the *Toronto Telegram*, an obvious foe of the War Measures Act. The column itself contained nothing new concerning the Ryan incident. It did, however, make reference to the activities of Bernard Ostry. Ostry was one of those shadowy Ottawa figures who was said to have high level cabinet connections. The Haggart column suggested that Ostry's home was a meeting place for many cabinet ministers, and that at these meetings, many of the subsequent reports about events in Ottawa had their genesis. Ostry's wife was a member of the Economic Council of Canada. They seemed to be well off, although I personally had no knowledge of the sources of their incomes. At one point a year or so before, Ostry had been proposed for the job of dominion archivist. The Prime Minister put the name forward, but with no great enthusiasm, and since there were objections, the matter was dropped. Later, Ostry showed up in the Department of the Secretary of State. This particular post did not require order-in-council approval, and involved a decision which Gérard Pelletier could make on his own. Ostry was now a member of the bureaucracy working with Bob Stanbury on citizenship matters.

George McIlraith's objections to the Ostry appointment were interesting because on two or three subsequent occasions, he had expressed concern about the wisdom of having Ostry in the government service. With his usual secretiveness, George never gave me any clear reasons for his position, but when we had problems with young people in Vancouver who refused to vacate one of our hostels at the end of the season, George told me that part of the difficulty was Ostry's involvement in the hostel program. Ostry, he felt, had been inept in dealing with those who refused to leave.

In any event, the Haggart column told how the rumours concerning Claude Ryan's activities had originated with members of cabinet attending a party at the Ostrys. I cannot vouch for the accuracy of Haggart's claim that Ostry had connections with several cabinet members. Personally, I had never been impressed by Ostry. I had met him when I was a backbencher and he worked for the CBC. Mike Pearson had asked for recommendations concerning the possibility of televising parliamentary proceedings. When Ostry became aware of this, he spent a good deal of time lobbying me to get a recommendation that television be permitted in the House. After I entered cabinet, Ostry, who had by then moved to the CRTC, was appointed by the Prime Minister to the task force on information. When that group made its report, it was referred to a cabinet committee of which I was a member. I saw Ostry at a number of meetings, but beyond that I had no conversations with him. He showed up once in a while at meetings with either Gérard Pelletier or Bob Stanbury, and I had heard that he was quite close to Pelletier. Some believed that this accounted for his appointment in the Department of the Secretary of State. Since Pelletier was known to be quite close to Pierre Juneau, chairman of the CRTC, this would explain Ostry's move from the CBC to the CRTC, and on to Pelletier's department.

I found it interesting to observe at the time what seemed to be a strange group in Ottawa centred loosely around the broadcasting community. One of the prime figures seemed to be Stuart Griffiths of the television station CJOH. Griffiths had recently been given CRTC permission to proceed with a remarkably wide purchase of television and radio licenses that would make him the biggest single holder of licenses in Canada. Even before the hearing granting him this authority, Griffiths was boasting of assurances from Harry Boyle, vice-chairman of the CRTC, that the deal would go through. Another figure in this circle was Sydney Newman, an early producer with CBC Television who had recently returned from the United Kingdom to work at the CRTC. At one time, Newman and Juneau had been at the National Film Board together. Griffiths and Newman had been at the CBC at the same time, and had subsequently worked together in the United Kingdom. In fact, there was a complete circle linking the CRTC and Griffiths. And then Newman had become head of the National Film Board, an appointment sponsored by Pelletier. When I considered Ostry's positions, I could not help but speculate about the overall effect of such a combination of personalities and connections on government-financed media agencies, and on cultural and artistic matters.

Adding to the intrigue was the fact that Stuart Griffiths' right-hand man was Roy Faibish. During the Tory years, Faibish had been executive assistant to Alvin Hamilton, a commentator appearing regularly on CJOH. To complicate matters even more, Patrick Watson and Laurier La Pierre, the central figures in the dispute over the program "This Hour Has Seven Days," were also close to Faibish. For a time, both were employed by CJOH. The central question behind all this for me was whether there existed, centred in Ottawa, an influential group who exerted a strong but covert influence on broadcasting policy and on government decisions affecting the arts in general.

Two other regular contributors to CJOH were Douglas Fisher of the *Toronto Telegram* and Pauline Jewett, a former Liberal MP who was by now a professor at Carleton University. Pauline had been quite outspoken in her criticism of the government for invoking the War Measures Act, and there was no love lost between Douglas Fisher and the Prime Minister, or indeed, the Liberal government.

If, as Haggart suggested, connected and influential people were meeting regularly under the social auspices of Bernard Ostry, it might have been that a powerful segment of Ottawa society had been acting as a force outside the formal structure of government. Since I knew of no association between Trudeau and the group, I had no way of knowing if he was involved with any of the parties concerned. Even if Trudeau had tended to favour such gatherings, I suspect that his experiences during the Quebec crisis would have cooled his enthusiasm for such contacts. A great many intellectuals and liberals who had been his fans in the past had deserted him totally over the War Measures Act.

I must, however, return to the main thread of my narrative. The weekend following Laporte's murder was very quiet. None of the forecast violence or terror occurred in Montreal during the municipal elections. Earlier, Pelletier and others had expressed concern that the voter turnout might be low, and it would not have helped matters for Drapeau to achieve dominance if he did so on a token vote. As things turned out, voter turnout reached nearly record proportions. Drapeau not only won the office of mayor with a huge majority, but every one of his supporters was returned to council. The opposition was effectively eliminated. It is doubtful that the end result would have been different, even if Jean Marchand had not made his statement regarding the association between the FLQ and FRAP, the organization which had mounted the only alternative to Drapeau in the election. Nevertheless, because of the Marchand intervention, those who wished to were given an excuse to claim that federal intervention had been at the expense of opposition parties in Montreal, and had been designed to ensure Drapeau's re-election.

After the weekend, things returned to some semblance of normality in government circles. There was still tension and uncertainty; nothing had been heard from Cross's kidnappers. There was a universal hope that the Cross case would break so that all activity relating to the Quebec crisis could be concentrated on remedial measures without the constant necessity of evaluating the effects of our actions on Cross's welfare.

The Throne Speech debate petered out on Tuesday, and my bill amending the Canada Shipping Act in order to give us more powers to deal with oil pollution was the first order of business. I got it through the second reading with no difficulty.

Eight

For many years, but particularly from 1960 to 1970, the federal government, and indeed all levels of government, had greatly increased their overall expenditures in the social security field. Despite this, we were still facing a most serious problem and were criticized constantly for not doing enough for the deprived. In other words, the previous ten years of effort had turned out to be a more or less useless experiment, if the objective had been to change fundamentally the causes of poverty in Canada. Prime Minister Trudeau, on a number of occasions, acknowledged that he shared my view, as did, I believe, the majority of the cabinet. Yet we went on year after year assuming that if we simply spent more on social security, at some point we would have resolved the problem. John Munro conceded that my argument had merit, but argued nonetheless that it would take too long to devise a totally new approach to the persistent problem, and he was therefore prepared to advocate still greater federal expenditures and more tinkering with mechanisms already in place. When I reiterated my views on the subject at one cabinet meeting, I could sense Munro's annoyance that we were, in effect, threshing old straws. In a somewhat irrational way, I retorted that I probably knew more about welfare and poverty than anybody at the table, not merely because I had lived among it virtually all my life, but also because I had personal experience with various welfare measures and knew of their stultifying and demeaning effects. Although my comments were admittedly emotional, they did have an impact on the discussion, and John Munro subsequently reassured me in private that he did not feel that I was a reactionary and that he understood my views. He could not agree, however, that his paper was as bad as I maintained. All in all, such exchanges made for a depressing lack of real progress.

The week of November 15, 1970, was also a frustrating one for me, and in many respects, it represented the low point of the administration in terms of sound decision making. Following the cabinet meeting on Thursday, November 12, Ben Benson had to go to British Columbia for the weekend. This meant that he had to leave Ottawa while important decisions were still in the air regarding the special measures that we were trying to devise to combat both winter unemployment and to ease the economic situation in Quebec.

With Benson out of town and no cabinet committee meetings scheduled, it was left to officials, primarily Simon Reisman and the officials in Finance, to consolidate the various discussions that had taken place previously, and to prepare a more or less definitive paper on the specific proposals we would recommend to cabinet. By this time, I was resigned to the fact that, no matter how much further discussion took place, Benson and Reisman had hardened their position that the amount to be allocated for the next year in terms of special projects must not exceed three hundred million dollars, and that if we agreed to such a level of expenditure, we would also have to retain the three percent surtax scheduled for withdrawal at the end of 1970. As to the specific proposals that would make up the package, I saw little chance that the basic ideas presented at the initial meeting would change significantly.

I flew back to Newfoundland for the weekend and took Jack Pickersgill with me. He had a commitment to speak at the Chamber of Commerce in Gander, and the flight would give me an opportunity to discuss a number of important matters with him. We talked at great length about transportation policy generally, but the most pressing matter on his mind was the necessity of finding replacements for a number of members of the Canadian Transport Commission who had either died or were about to retire. I told him that I would do my best to speed up the appointment of replacements, but I pointed out that it was not easy to find suitable people at the salary levels we were permitted to pay. Although Jack is best known for his political skills, I could see that his years in the public service had also had a profound influence on him. Virtually all of his recommended replacements were already in the public service and were largely people who did not really possess the creativity and fresh outlook that I thought essential if the Canadian Transport Commission were to function effectively and to meet emerging challenges. I told Jack that, if possible, I would like to get some fresh faces on the Commission, preferably from outside the government structure. He did not raise any strong objections, primarily, I suspect, because he knew how difficult I would find it to get the people I wanted.

I told Jack that I was having trouble with getting the Prime Minister's Office to suggest appropriate replacements. For some time, I had been asking Marc Lalonde and others to suggest a good French-speaking nominee for the Commission, but they had not been able to come up with anyone. I found it interesting that, while the Prime Minister's Office was always insistent on knowing when vacancies occurred to which French Canadians might be appointed, in this case, they were less than helpful.

During the past two years, I had often expressed the view that we were becoming obsessed with inflation. I argued for a well thought out plan that would help turn the economy around if the impact of the anti-inflation fight became too severe. The Prime Minister and cabinet agreed that such a plan was necessary, but Benson and the Finance Department officials gave it lip service only. Now, when we needed something to provide economic stimulation, all they could produce was a frightful mixture of questionable measures, most of which flew in the face of the plans we had laid in the last two years.

I now had doubts about the effectiveness of government planning on the scale we had attempted. So many of the elements required for sound planning were largely beyond the government's control—provincial actions, the general public mood as exemplified by its reaction to the Quebec crisis, the inevitable pressures and influences of the political process, particularly as an election approached, the impact of the media on our supporters, if not on us, and, in economic terms, the course of events in the United States and throughout the world. Given this situation, departures from theoretical planning by government might well be the rule rather than the exception. And given the certainty that the unanticipated always happens, it is perhaps unwise for any government to lock itself into a particular stance such as we had done in the case of inflation.

I had no doubt that the planning we were doing, and had been doing, would be good for Canada in the long run. But to be really effective, long-term planning has to be adhered to firmly, and the consequences of it, which are generally predictable, must be lived with long enough for the policies to effect permanent improvements. This means accepting political unpopularity and the risk of defeat over something like the unemployment issue, for example. Perhaps this would be expecting too much of politicians and their supporters whose instinct for survival is very finely honed; if it is, no leader, no cabinet and no political party would have the nerve to persist in policies that are widely unpopular.

The fact is, of course, that long-term policies will always have their critics, and there will always be those ready to offer less painful answers.

The public, or at least large segments of it, is hardly likely to accept the hard road as long as there are those who can offer a less arduous route. Perhaps this provides the appropriate mix of checks and balances to ensure the health of our democratic system. There is no doubt, however, that the fact that governments have only a few years during which to make their policies work is an impediment to sound, long-range planning. Also, the advisory system of politics exerts a strong and not always positive influence on the planning process.

During one of the many discussions of Benson's budget, I posed a deliberately provocative question to Simon Reisman. As Deputy Minister of Finance, Reisman was highly opinionated and emphatic in his views. In the budget talks, he had insisted that the government had no choice but to keep the three percent sales tax and to introduce other proposed measures. Simon was also one of the primary architects of the anti-inflation program.

During one meeting, I asked him this question: "Simon, you are a permanent civil servant. Suppose as a result of policies you recommend, the government is thrown out. It would be defeated by another party committed to a reversal of the policies this government is following. Now, you show up some day at a meeting with the new prime minister and his cabinet. They tell you they want to shift policy. What would you tell them and what would you recommend? Obviously, it would have to be something different from what you now tell us is the only course we can follow."

Reisman conceded that this was a valid question, but naturally, he replied that he would have to say that he could suggest no significant changes in economic policy. This, of course, was nonsense. If another government wanted expansionary policies, I had not the slightest doubt that Simon Reisman and other officials would respond with policies quite different from those currently being proposed to us.

Although this was quite understandable, it illustrated a basic dilemma that governments face. There is no one approach to many problems, and we can only do what we think is best, either on a pragmatic basis depending wholly on the circumstances of the moment, or measured against long-range goals.

In the Priorities and Planning Committee, we were discussing at some length the role of the CBC. This item had not come up as a result of events in Quebec; rather, it had been planned for months, ever since it had been necessary in early summer to approve the CBC's budget, which had called for considerable increases in the corporation's expenditures for 1971-72. At that time, the Prime Minister had asked a small committee of which I was a member to examine the CBC's chief officials to determine whether or not their requests for additional financing were justified. I had been the principal questioner of Mr. Picard on that occasion because I was much more familiar than were the other ministers with broadcasting in general, and the CBC in particular.

At that time, I reached the conclusion, more or less concurred in by Mr. Picard, that the corporation did in fact need additional funds, but that this need arose because of various commitments the CBC had made throughout the years, particularly those made to meet the wage and working demands of its unions, some of which were quite indefensible. The CBC management was locked into a situation from which it would be extremely difficult to extricate itself. When this conclusion was conveyed to the Committee on Priorities and Planning early in the summer, it was decided that the additional expenditures would be approved. However, the corporation would be required to appear before the committee in the fall for a general discussion and review of its activities to see if there was anything we could do to reduce the steadily mounting expenditures.

This process explains why the item came up before the committee at a time when the CBC was under considerable fire: first of all because many were arguing that its French language section had been infiltrated by separatists; and secondly, because its handling of the Quebec crisis was considered inept and, in some cases, irresponsible.

The paper prepared by the CBC as the basis for the cabinet committee discussion was an incredibly inadequate document. It dealt only with the corporation's plans for expansion of services and spelled out, to some extent, the efforts of the corporation to institute new methods of financial control. On the overriding question of how directors and top management could exert a proper and legitimate level of control over the corporation's programming activities, however, the paper had nothing to say. Nor did it address the general philosophy of the corporation or the attitude of management concerning its programming responsibilities.

The Prime Minister allowed George Davidson, the president of the CBC, to go through a long and involved explanation of the difficulties of extending French language radio and television to small groups of French Canadians scattered throughout the country; he did the same thing in explaining television coverage to remote regions. It was clear, however, that Trudeau was annoyed because the corporation had treated the request for additional comment in a somewhat cavalier fashion. He quickly moved to focus the discussion on the role of the corporation and what it was appropriate for the CBC to do in terms of national issues and controversies. At issue were the age-old problems inherent in a state-financed broadcasting system. For more than a decade, I had been calling attention to these inherent problems in one way or another, and I confess to a certain amount of satisfaction as I saw cabinet finally coming to grips with issues which, when I had raised them initially, were generally dismissed as unimportant.

The crux of the whole issue was well stated by George Davidson when he said that there were really three policy options open to the CBC. The first of these, he said, was for the corporation to be, in essence, a carbon copy of private broadcasting with no special duties, and, hence, expected to perform in exactly the same way as the private licensee of a station or network. The second option he advanced was that the CBC could become the mouthpiece of the government in power, articulating and supporting government policies, and acting as an information outlet for the administration. The third option Davidson put forward was that the corporation had a responsibility to take positions. He was not at all clear as to how the corporation would arrive at such positions, nor could he indicate just who within the corporation should participate in the decision-making process. I disagreed with Davidson, although I had thought for many years that it would be exceedingly difficult to establish an appropriate role for the CBC as long as it was financed by public funds, and as long as it remained, at least nominally, a creature of the Canadian Parliament. I did say to Davidson, however, that I could not see that it was appropriate for the corporation to take only one position on issues about which Canadians might hold a variety of views. I also pointed out that the real difficulties in this area had arisen when the corporation departed from its original concept of neutrality and objectivity, and became itself an opinion-forming organization. I recalled that for many years, particularly in radio, the corporation had merely provided an outlet for a wide range of views. The CBC itself, however, did not employ opinion makers, nor did its producers have the same broad editorializing rights that later evolved. I pointed out that the new trend had emerged with television, and that as long as it continued, the corporation would find itself at odds not only with the government of the day, but frequently with Parliament or some segment of it. I also pointed out that there was what I described as intellectual incest within the corporation; virtually all of the creative people working for the CBC tended to share a common attitude toward most issues, and as a result, what emerged from the programming mix was not balanced reporting or objective observation, but rather a one-sided view of most major issues.

It was during this discussion that Trudeau introduced what I considered a bold proposition in terms of the government's relationship with the CBC. He pointed out that the government was engaged in an exhaustive and detailed effort to establish certain priorities for Canada and to devise a comprehensive program through which the country could be directed toward well-defined goals. He went on to say that when all of the factors were taken into account, it might become apparent to the government that one of the steps necessary for the maintenance of a stable society would be the discouragement of certain public expectations. He pointed out that the government was coming to the conclusion that the sum total of all the demands for change, improvement and reform far exceeded both the government's and the country's capacity to pay. Therefore, he maintained, one of the important steps that the government might have to take was the dampening of public enthusiasm for various new initiatives that were beyond our reach. Fostering such expectations would only lead to frustration and disappointment and would quite possibly sow the seeds of continued unrest and eventually, perhaps, revolution. He then made the case that there was something inconsistent in having the government reach such a viewpoint only to have an agency paid for by public funds and used by a variety of advocates make further demands.

The meeting with CBC officials was disturbing for several reasons. First, it revealed to me that although Picard had a good insight into the labour and operational problems of the CBC, he had not yet devised a formula for coping with them. Indeed, I think that it is fair to say that there was a degree of resignation in his attitude. He clearly recognized that he could not move quickly to instill greater efficiency, and it looked doubtful that the CBC would ever be as efficient as he believed it could be. Even more disturbing was the attitude of George Davidson. Four years previously, I had warned Mr. Pearson that it would be unwise to place an inexperienced man as head of the CBC, particularly if the managing head was also going to be someone with little detailed knowledge of broadcasting. I got little consolation from the all-too-apparent evidence that my prediction was correct. Davidson had bought the line of the long-entrenched officials of the CBC completely. The presentation he made to cabinet and the arguments he advanced in support of it could have been written by Al Ouimet, Ron Fraser or any one of a dozen others who had developed a remarkable skill for clouding the real issues surrounding the CBC, and making it impossible for the government to get a proper grip on the corporation's activities.

Unlike many others who were concerned about the CBC, I did not read anything sinister into the attitude of top management. Over the years, it had had to develop a corporate point of view toward its responsibilities, and in the face of persistent criticism that had always been directed at the corporation, it had devised a particular set of answers that seemed to have served it quite well in preserving the CBC from major onslaughts. Despite many changes, there was enough continuity in the CBC management for this line of reasoning and logic to have survived virtually intact for twenty years or more. Each new president and each new addition to the executive group very quickly assumed the same posture because, from the standpoint of the CBC itself, the arguments were entirely logical and defensible. If they were not, then more of those appointed to the Board of Directors—men and women with considerable talent and independence of thought—would have rejected the CBC's rationale and would have spoken out, publicly in some cases, against what was going on. But the truth of the matter is that there had been virtual unanimity at the top of the CBC's corporate structure for a long time, and unless the entire mandate of the CBC was to be changed, it was reasonable to expect the same type of arguments to be advanced once again.

Most of us around the table at the meeting with Davidson and Picard recognized this fact. What was disturbing was that we could not come up with a means through which the philosophy and approach of the CBC could be changed. Nor did we feel that, even in those areas where we saw the possibility of action, we would be able to implement new proposals without encountering a major political furore in intellectual circles throughout the country.

Trudeau went much further than I would have in suggesting to the CBC that there was, in fact, a strong case to be made for a closer relationship between the mandate and objectives of the corporation and those of the government. The logic of the Prime Minister's argument was irrefutable. However, I could see Davidson's fear that, if he were to admit that there were cases where the corporation should be aware of and directed by government policies and priorities, there would be a total break with the entrenched view that the corporation's role was to act independently. Yet even Davidson recognized that there was something inconsistent in having an organization paid for largely by the people of Canada often working to the detriment of government programs, initiatives and concepts approved by Parliament itself. This was an exceedingly difficult problem to resolve, but, in my judgement, it would become less important as time went by and as technology provided other outlets through which Canadians could get their news and commentary. Already, the advent of new methods had reduced the influence of the CBC as a national broadcasting service. But it was easy to see why French-speaking politicians, including Trudeau himself, appeared to be more concerned about this matter than were English-speaking leaders. In French Canada, there were few alternatives to the French language service of the CBC, certainly fewer than in English-speaking parts of the country with access to American stations and to specialized program sources.

At the meeting, Trudeau did little to conceal his irritation that the CBC's presentation was absolutely silent on the basic issues, and that Davidson and Picard attempted to confine their presentation to matters of economics and general efficiency. The committee agreed that Davidson should return to cabinet some time in the near future with a more comprehensive paper which, the Prime Minister indicated, should give a more detailed explanation of just how the corporation saw its mandate and how it believed it should proceed in carrying it out.

Pierre Juneau, the chairman of the Canadian Radio and Television Commission, put on an interesting performance at the cabinet committee meeting. He did not intervene in the discussion except when asked a direct question, and by the end of the meeting, it was difficult, if not impossible, to assess where he stood in relation to the two essentially opposite points of view expressed. I got the impression that Juneau was troubled by the current turn of events. As a French-speaking Canadian, he could see the dangers inherent in the structure of the CBC's French language operations. Yet all that he had said publicly, and all his input into the decisions of the CRTC, indicated that he supported maximum independence for the broadcasting structure, and certainly for the CBC. I believe that Juneau was discovering that it was one thing to have nicely defined theories about how Canada's broadcasting system should function, but it was something else to make the system conform to such theories. My own view was that, before too many years had passed, CBC television would be converted either by deliberate policy, the force of events, or some combination of both, into an essentially educational system. I was also reasonably certain that although there would continue to be pressures to keep government control over broadcasting, these would be eroded by the simple fact that various means of presenting television programs, such as closed circuit and videocassette, would make efforts at control less meaningful. Eventually, even the diehards would have to concede that the maintenance of a rigid regulatory structure was impossible.

In any event, I was happy that the important issue of Canadian broadcasting had finally been brought to the forefront of cabinet thinking. I had been in a difficult position on this question ever since entering cabinet. I had made up my mind at the outset that I would not try to play a major role in shaping broadcasting policy because, even though I was satisfied that I could think and act objectively on the issue, there were others who would regard my interventions as suspect. Therefore, I had only ventured opinions when they were asked for, and I had not raised on my own initiative matters relating to broadcasting that I felt should be the subject of top-level discussions. For example, even before the Trudeau government took office, Pierre Juneau had been instructed to prepare a recommendation to cabinet on the question of multiple ownership; he had not done so as yet, even though the CRTC had moved to approve a number of major sales. The most important of these was, of course, the approval of the sale of CFCF radio and television in Montreal, as well as all of the Thomson-owned stations in Ontario, to Stuart Griffiths and his company. In my opinion, this was a most unwise move, but I decided that I would not be the one to raise the issue in Parliament. And, as things turned out, it appeared that Griffiths might not be able to raise the necessary financing for his massive expansion plan.

By mid-December, when I next recorded events in and around government, the Committee on Government Operations was forced to come to grips with the problem of what to do about the uranium stockpile at Elliot Lake. This was partly a result of our earlier decision to prevent Dennison Mines from selling out to American interests. When we decided that Steve Roamen, the owner of Dennison Mines, could not complete the deal he had arranged with American buyers, we more or less committed ourselves to ensuring that, whatever happened, the mine would not close with the resultant loss of several hundred jobs. Joe Greene and some others maintained that even if we had not moved against the Dennison sale, we would still have faced the possible closure of the mine because of the state of the world uranium market. However, as we considered the question on December 17, others of us felt that our decision had greatly reinforced the responsibility of the government to take action that would avoid the unemployment crisis that faced us.

This whole exercise illustrated the tremendous complexity that develops when government takes decisive action in the private sector. Such action distorts the normal economic processes, no matter how commendable the objectives or how necessary the action. Joe Greene put forward the proposition that the government would have to put up thirty million dollars, beginning in 1971 and continuing for at least several years, in order to stockpile uranium against the day when market prospects would improve. There was exhaustive questioning of Joe Greene and his deputy, Jack Austin, and I think it is fair to say that none of us were overly optimistic that we would ever get a substantial portion of our money back. Even if we did, the money would be tied up for a considerable time in order to preserve a few hundred jobs. I am not depreciating the importance of this type of employment, but I found it ironic that in certain circumstances, we seemed to have no choice but to go far beyond what we would normally do in other circumstances. For example, I would not have had the ghost of a chance of getting a similar amount in order to ensure jobs for the workers who were laid off at the Argentia base. Indeed, simply to get an assured loan of less than twenty million dollars to build the wharf at Come By Chance took more than a year of negotiations and argument. Yet, with the uranium project, we decided to go ahead on the basis of very little discussion—simply because the Canadian ownership issue forced us into refusing Dennison the right to sell to an American buyer. The situation might have been more rational, of course, if we had had some clear-cut policy on the question of foreign takeovers. We seemed, however, to move from one ad hoc decision to another in a complex field, invariably at great cost to the Canadian people.

I had hoped that Herb Gray would soon devise a meaningful policy on the question of foreign ownership; otherwise, I could see nothing but trouble ahead if we continued to move either in response to pressure from economic nationalists, or because we were simply not sure what ill effects might result from another sale of an important natural resource to foreign interests. The meeting ended with an agreement to recommend to cabinet that we proceed with the stockpiling proposal. I had no doubt that the plan would get cabinet approval simply because no one knew of an alternative solution; we simply could not stand by and watch while an entire community was destroyed.

The cabinet meeting on December 17 was more or less routine, with many items on the agenda, none of which had any lasting importance. Briefly, Pierre Trudeau reported on his meetings with Edward Heath, the British prime minister. He told us that Heath was a tough customer who knew his own mind and seemed determined to stick by his decisions regarding Britain's sale of arms to South Africa and his government's plans to bring Britain into the European Common Market.

As usual, there was the inevitable questioning of our ability to close the House as scheduled for the Christmas recess. I cannot recall a single occasion when an adjournment for a holiday period—either Christmas, Easter or summer—was achieved smoothly and without some sort of last minute crisis. This time, the problem arose because both opposition parties refused to pass the CNR financial and guarantee bill. This hardy chestnut came up every year, giving the opposition an opportunity to blackmail the government: we had to get the measure through so that the railway and Air Canada could access monies needed for their operations.

This time there was a new twist to the old game; some of our own Liberal members were equally adamant in insisting that the CNR agree to changes in its pension plan before the measure was allowed to pass. In this meeting, I indicated to cabinet that I felt that we should take a chance and not try to force the bill through before Christmas. I had talked with Norman MacMillan of Canadian National, and learned from him that they could get by without legislation until the end of January, providing a clear route to a Friday adjournment for Christmas.

This most recent development served to emphasize the growing independence of many Liberal backbenchers and raised serious questions about the committee system. As well, it pointed to the difficulties which invariably arose when the long-established rules of Parliament were tinkered with. By giving the committees of the House much more extensive powers, the government had created a stick to beat its own back.

In the case of the CNR bill, virtually all of the Liberal members of the Transport Committee joined forces with the Tories in supporting what was essentially an NDP tactic recommending an income increase for CNR pensioners. When the report of the committee was brought forward in the fall of 1970 just after the opening of the session, I was faced by our own Liberal members with what amounted to an ultimatum. Unless I agreed that the report be concurred in by the House without debate, they would take the initiative themselves and embarrass the government by voting with the opposition. Under the circumstances, I had no choice but to agree to their demands. Thus, we had a situation where the entire House, including the government and its supporters, agreed that CNR pensions should be increased. Against this background, I saw no option other than to instruct the CNR to increase pension payments, and this, of course, raised a number of related issues. Was it proper for the government to instruct the CNR in an area which was clearly a management responsibility? And by agreeing with the report, the House was recommending substantial public expenditures while many authorities had serious doubts as to whether or not such actions were in keeping with the long-established rule that only the government could propose the expenditure of public funds.

I found both issues interesting—from an academic point of view at least. But the real crux of the problem was this: how could a government continue to function effectively if its own supporters could withdraw support on important issues? If they were to do so in the House proper, it would be tantamount to defeat and, in many cases, would constitute a demonstration of lack of confidence. But was it any less a defeat if the majority went against the government in a committee when money bills and related proposals were being considered? Both the House Leader, Allan MacEachen, and his predecessor, Don Macdonald, were most concerned about this development and the new wave of independence so prevalent in caucus. To be fair to them and to all of us in cabinet, we were not so much concerned with the new independent spirit of the members. In fact, we had encouraged it. But having done so, we came up against the intricate nature of the parliamentary system where, if one of the checks or balances is removed, the whole structure is suddenly endangered. I was sure that we would run into many more such issues in the future, and we would have to seriously consider how to get away from a system that demanded blind allegiance from its supporters, and how to give them a greater voice without running into a crisis every day of the week.

During this meeting, we also discussed the problem involved with the Lapalme drivers from Montreal. This was, of course, one of the ongoing difficulties created by the Post Office squabble of the previous spring, an issue which the government had dealt with poorly, and the one which prompted Trudeau to remove Eric Kierans from the Post Office. In fairness to Eric, the government had encouraged him to take the actions that resulted in his difficulties. Nevertheless, Eric, with his usual enthusiasm and lack of concern for the consequences, certainly did his part in dragging us into an unnecessary mess. The situation was not helped by the running feud that existed between Kierans and Mackasey, or by the failure of cabinet to retain solidarity on the issue.

Now several months after the actual strike of the Lapalme drivers and the deplorable circumstances which arose as a result, we still had strikers parading on Parliament Hill, and we were in a most difficult position in trying to resolve the controversy.

It also must be said, in order to keep matters in their proper perspective, that the CNTU and the workers did everything they could to compound the problem, losing any sympathy that the Prime Minister might have had for them. Jean Marchand was in a very difficult position. He had once headed the CNTU and still maintained strong connections with the Quebec labour movement. These connections were severely strained by the October crisis, but the tensions began even before that as a result of the Lapalme incident. I was not sure, therefore, how Marchand felt about resolving the problem. He and the Prime Minister agreed that Jean-Pierre Côté, who was now in charge of the Post Office, should try to devise a compromise that the Lapalme workers would be prepared to accept. Essentially, the likely offer would involve providing jobs for the strikers either in the Post Office or elsewhere in the public service. This would have to be, however, on a first-come, first-served basis, and the CNTU could no longer represent the workers. At the time, we questioned whether or not the workers were sufficiently devoted to the CNTU to accept the conditions.

Throughout the day, I was conscious, as on so many previous occasions, of how little I and most other English-speaking ministers knew about the relationships—past and present—between such people as Trudeau, Jean Marchand and key figures in Quebec labour and intellectual circles. Unlike the rest of the country where the past relationships and activities of political figures were fairly common knowledge, the Quebec scene had always seemed exceedingly vague. I also did not know how much the personal animosities that appeared to exist between Marchand, Trudeau and their former associates affected their decisions as members of the federal government and alienated them from those they were so close to in the past. None of the Quebec ministers—but especially Trudeau, Marchand and Pelletier—told the rest of us about events in Quebec and the in-fighting that must surely have been taking place. I had no hard evidence that Trudeau was sometimes guilty of petty acts of retribution against former friends and associates, but there were occasions when he made plain his disdain for some of them, engendering in me a suspicion that some very human characteristics might come into play when these people found themselves in conflict with the government.

Also on the agenda was a brief discussion of members' salaries and expenses. We now had the report prepared by the Beaupré Commission, and no one was happy with it. On the other hand, all members of the House, with the exception of Stanley Knowles, and possibly John Diefenbaker, were agitated that no action had been taken on the salary question. I anticipated many difficult hours devising a course which we could follow. There was no unanimity in cabinet regarding what should be done.

On Friday, December 19, the House closed as scheduled for the Christmas recess, but for cabinet members, there remained a few more days of work before the holidays. The pressure of committee meetings during the previous week had been tremendous, and it looked as though the next several days would be at least as busy. The Prime Minister indicated on Thursday his plans for a full cabinet meeting on the following Wednesday, the day before Christmas Eve. This meant that those of us who had long distances to travel would have to count on good weather to get home by the twenty-fifth. But Trudeau rarely displayed any sentiment for such festive occasions, and he was even a bit surprised that people like Paul Martin were most anxious to clue up on Tuesday.

In Friday's committee, we took a more or less final look at the Estimates for 1971-72. They represented a tremendous amount of detailed planning and reflected for the first time real results of the new planning methods introduced by the Trudeau government. I could see that we had made considerable progress in getting a better method with which to control expenditures and to look further ahead than we had in the past. I said in the meeting, however, as I had on previous occasions, that what worried me now was that we had committed virtually every cent of our projected revenues for the coming year, and we had no reserve for the inevitable special projects and emergencies that must arise. But despite this failing, I took some satisfaction from the work I and others had done to create a rational plan for our expenditures. When I looked back to the years previous to our administration, I could not help but be amazed at how unsophisticated the process of fiscal management had been. It was not hard to see how governments suddenly found themselves up against huge and unanticipated deficits as they went on committing new and sizeable outlays with no certain knowledge of where the extra funds would come from even after the

Estimates were prepared. At least, I thought, now we would get the bad news early, and if we had to commit ourselves to additional amounts, we would be able to see what these expenditures would do to our financial position.

On the same day, we introduced yet another feature—a system of monthly reporting by Treasury Board on potential new expenditures beyond those provided for in the Estimates. While cabinet might agree to a new program or additional spending, such outlays would not be authorized until after each monthly review. This would give us an extra opportunity to try to keep spending down. Yet, even with this arrangement, I expected the historical pattern to repeat itself, and that we would find ourselves in the new year needing hundreds of millions of dollars more than planned—and hundreds of millions more than the government could raise. Try as we might, we had not yet succeeded in taming the monster of government spending.

With Bud Drury out of town, I had to chair the Cabinet Committee on Government Operations on December 22, and I had no less than seventeen different items to deal with, some routine but others quite problematic. One of these was a proposal by John Munro that, instead of introducing legislation to ban cigarette advertising and otherwise restrict cigarette manufacturers, he would move by way of regulations under the Hazardous Products Act. I was very opposed to this. I could not help but feel that the government's entire approach to the question of cigarette advertising was more than a little hypocritical. But more importantly, I believed that if we moved to curb the promotion of a product which was in every sense legal, then we should not do so except through full debate in the House of Commons. Mitchell Sharp agreed with me fully, as did most of the other ministers with the exception of Ron Basford. As the minister responsible for the Hazardous Products Act, he wanted to make as much of an impression as possible with his new legislation, and with his whole effort toward consumer protection. I did not blame him for this, but I did think that his eagerness had blunted his judgement on the issue. The outcome of the discussion was a decision not to proceed by way of regulations, but to explore the possibility of getting the legislation into the House more quickly than usual. It became increasingly evident to me that there was a fundamental difference of approach between Munro and me, different enough to strain relations between us even though we had a good deal of affection for each other. My biggest complaint was that I found Munro's approach to important matters sloppy, and I felt that he was more interested in giving an impression of worthwhile progress rather than actually achieving it. Even when I made allowances for the complexity of some of the issues he had to deal with, I could not escape the fact that practically every project he brought forward was somehow controversial, not so much because of its content but because of his impatience.

I would be less than honest if I did not admit that his whole approach offended my sense of order. I resented the fact that he was quite prepared to use pressure tactics—including premature leaks to newsmen—in his often frantic efforts to get where he wanted to go. While I sympathized with his frustrations concerning the slowness of the system, I feared initiatives that were less than fully assessed. I could see how deeply governments enmeshed themselves in fantastic levels of spending by allowing their hearts or their political motivations to rule their heads. I also found John inordinately aware of and responsive to pressure groups, an entirely legitimate tendency, except that it ignored conflicting opinions that might be widely held. I felt that in controversial fields like drug use and other areas within John's jurisdiction, government had to move carefully even though most of its members were convinced of the need for reform.

In the Government Operations meeting, we put the finishing touches on the proposals dealing with the assistance scheme for Elliot Lake. As on the previous occasion, there was universal regret that such a step was necessary, but we could see no alternative. Then with uranium out of the way, at least temporarily, we were dragged into yet another controversy involving the possible takeover of another Canadian firm, Home Oil, by an American company. Joe Greene raised the issue once again, and I was as convinced as he was that there would be hell to pay if we stood by and allowed Home Oil to become foreign-controlled. When the issue had come up the previous August, we had decided that the best approach would be to sit back and hope that a Canadian buyer could be found. Now the situation was deteriorating rapidly, and Greene reported that the present owner, Bobbie Brown, might have no choice but to unload the company because of a lack of financial reserves. About all that we could decide was that Joe should keep a close watch on developments and alert the cabinet before any deal with a foreign interest was finalized. Here again, we had an example of just how difficult it was to resolve the foreign ownership issue, and I anticipated that after the Christmas break, we would have to come to grips with the issue once again.

On the last day before the holidays, there was a most interesting cabinet meeting. The main item of business was a discussion of the position that the Prime Minister should take at the upcoming Commonwealth conference in Singapore. Since Britain still intended to proceed with its plan to sell arms to South Africa, the question for Canada became the position it should take at the Commonwealth conference where, it was now being suggested, African and other black Commonwealth nations might pull out of the organization because of

Britain's actions. As the discussion got under way, two options were apparent. Canada could simply take the position that what Britain did was its own affair, and that Canada should not criticize its decision, but concentrate its efforts on persuading the African states not to withdraw. Such a stand would undoubtedly draw criticism. The second option involved siding with the African states and joining them in withdrawing from the Commonwealth should Britain remain stubbornly wedded to its plans. This would prompt tremendous criticism amongst the pro-British element in Canada and confirm their worst fears that the government wanted to scuttle the monarchy, using the arms issue as an excuse. It became obvious that it would be difficult for Trudeau and his government to escape unscathed.

It was through this type of issue that one got to know the Prime Minister better. Clearly, he had little emotional involvement, and his logical turn of mind allowed him to see both sides of the question free from bias. He would make no bones about his lack of patience with the type of unrestrained nationalism, even racism, being shown by many African states. He was somewhat contemptuous of the holier-than-thou attitude and emotional approach of many of the black leaders. He was deeply conscious of the inconsistency that would exist if Canada took the position that we had some right to dictate to Britain what it should do in foreign affairs or any other government activity, when we ourselves were asserting loudly that we wanted total independence, and that we would not tolerate any British intervention in our activities. It might be an oversimplification, but I drew from Trudeau's comments an impression that his view was that none of us were so pure or lacking in self-interest that we could afford to throw the first stone among our Commonwealth neighbours. Certainly, I did not expect the Prime Minister to declare himself for one side or the other, although it was generally agreed that such right as existed was on the side of the African states. Furthermore, to the extent that a government was obliged to reflect majority opinion on foreign affairs, we judged that the Canadian public would be more sympathetic to the viewpoint of the African states than to that of Britain. Undeniably, however, there were strong supporters of the British position among the Canadian public.

Trudeau did not anticipate a head-on collision at the Singapore conference. He told us that Heath had indicated that he would probably take a mildly conciliatory position without withdrawing his basic stand. To give the African states some option, he would make it plain that while the British government was disposed to sell arms to South Africa, no final decision would be reached until some time after the conference concluded.

It was, of course, difficult to anticipate in advance precisely what the role of a government leader should be upon occasions such as the

Commonwealth conference. A sizeable amount of flexibility was necessary so that the Prime Minister could respond to new developments and initiatives. In the last analysis, therefore, all we could advise Trudeau to do was to use his best judgement; we would be prepared to accept and support whatever he chose.

At the conclusion of the meeting, I had a rather unpleasant personal experience. Some time ago, John Turner had approached me to ask if I would authorize his use of a Jet Star aircraft for a trip he planned to take over the Christmas holidays so that he could attend various meetings in Asia and India. Normally, it was not our practice to send the Jet Stars overseas because of their somewhat limited range, and because of the demand for their use within Canada. Nevertheless, Turner was insistent, claiming that he could not get a military aircraft to take him, and that he needed special transportation both for security reasons and because he could not meet his various commitments by using a commercial plane. I continued to express my reluctance for several days while Turner kept up his demands and, at one point, even indicated his displeasure to one of my staff, adding that he was aware of how much I used the planes personally at times, not on government business, but primarily for my own convenience. These comments irked me considerably, all the more so since John did not say them to me personally. At the same time, however, I was anxious to avoid a major argument with him, so I instructed our flight services division to determine the feasibility of the proposed trip. When they came back with an opinion that the trip could be made without serious problems, I decided to let John make his own decision as to whether or not he wanted to proceed. I was not particularly surprised when he indicated that he did. But I was still uneasy about the risk involved in sending a relatively small plane across the Atlantic, as well as the possible political repercussions if such a trip were publicized. After the day's cabinet meetings, therefore, I decided that I should tell the Prime Minister both of John's request and of my decision to authorize it. Trudeau's reaction was most emphatic: he saw no reason why the aircraft should be used for such a purpose when there were plenty of commercial flights available. I told him that since it was my responsibility, I was prepared to proceed although, I admitted, I would be just as happy if John changed his mind. But I felt that I should not personally veto the request of a colleague or question his word that the use of the plane was essential. I must say that Trudeau was quite reasonable about my position and said that he would not interfere unless I wanted him to. I replied that I did not, and we left it more or less at that. Trudeau did suggest, however, that I might want to get advice from Gordon Robertson as to the precedent for such a trip and from Bud Drury as to the political ramifications of John's request. It so happened that both of these men were in the room at the time. Gordon was obviously edgy about the whole situation, but said that there was some precedent for it as ministers had taken planes for overseas business trips on one or two previous occasions. Bud Drury recognized my dilemma and agreed that the most I could do was to advise John of the Prime Minister's and my own reservations, and then leave him to proceed as he wished.

As soon as I returned to my office, I phoned John and advised him of what the Prime Minister had said, and told him that I thought he should explain to Trudeau why the plane was necessary. He responded that he did not know when he would get an opportunity to discuss the matter with the Prime Minister before leaving. This was obviously an excuse; he could have picked up the phone then and there and called him. In any event, he told me that he understood that I had done the appropriate thing, and that it was now up to him to choose. I left it at that, with little doubt that John would forego talking to the Prime Minister and would proceed with the flight as planned. This, then, was how I came to the end of what had been a very full day and a very full year. I would be glad indeed of the change and the rest afforded by the Christmas holidays.

Nine

This section of the memoir covering the beginning of 1971 was written during three separate sessions, two in February and the last on Sunday, March 7, 1971.

I will not attempt to outline in sequence the events that occurred during the early weeks of 1971. After the Christmas and New Year holidays, the House reconvened on January 11. By that time, the Prime Minister had left for the Commonwealth conference in Singapore with stops en route in India and elsewhere. When the Prime Minister was absent, the mood of the House was very different, and the same was true of cabinet meetings. This was due in part, I think, to Trudeau's particular personality and to the strange manner in which he dominated both the House and cabinet by his presence. But in a more general way, the absence of any prime minister tends to slow the pace of activity. No matter how good the acting prime minister may be, there is a feeling that no one is really in charge, and that major decisions must of necessity await the prime minister's return. In this sense, at least, a Canadian prime minister wields tremendous influence. I cannot imagine any decision of cabinet being upheld without his concurrence, even though it is entirely legal within our system for cabinet to act without him. An unwritten law prevails that only routine decisions are taken during any prime minister's absence.

This did not mean that cabinet was idle during January. There were several meetings, including a few special ones on the economic situation, particularly unemployment. Indeed, there was a total preoccupation with this issue, and for this reason, this portion of my writings is largely a general account of various developments centred around unemployment.

It came as no surprise to us that the Conservatives decided to launch a major assault on our policies as a result of increased unemployment. A few of us had forecast such a development months before when the decision to maintain a hard line against inflation was confirmed by cabinet. As one who was never too happy with our strategy on this issue, I think I was more prepared than most for the backlash that developed with the release of the winter unemployment statistics.

What our government had had for most of 1970 was really the worst of both worlds. As early as March, Ben Benson, the Bank of Canada and others began relaxing the various fiscal and monetary controls applied earlier to combat inflation. At the same time, we could say little of our efforts publicly, for fear of convincing everyone that inflation was no longer a threat. So, in an effort that turned out to be useless, we had to keep on attacking labour unions and others in an effort to curb their demands, while simultaneously pursuing policies designed to stimulate the economy. In retrospect, it is surprising just how much the behind-the-scenes attitude of the government changed during 1970, and how much of the change was apparent publicly. Yet we were tagged with the anti-inflation label and with the fairly widespread public conviction that we were callous and unconcerned about the effects of our policy in human terms.

Ironically, as the January meetings of cabinet showed, we were not in much of a position to take credit for curbing inflation. If we pointed to efforts in this regard, it would simply confirm Stanfield's accusations that we were indifferent to the impact of our actions on the unemployment situation.

Events of recent weeks showed that when a government finds itself in this position, whether by accident or design, it is pointless to argue logically against the inevitable and highly emotional criticism. Ben Benson had tried for weeks to defend our policies, and there was a good deal of common sense on his side. But he wasn't getting to first base with most of his critics, and the round had clearly gone to the opposition. Even Bryce Mackasey was clobbered for a speech he made on unemployment. Early on the day on which he spoke, there was a special meeting of cabinet to discuss our tactics in the debate. Someone suggested that Bryce open the debate for the government and he agreed, although he had planned that his parliamentary secretary, Ray Perrault, would speak for the Department of Labour. Bryce was ill-prepared, but he waded in with what was essentially an attack on the Tories and their track record during the unemployment crisis in the early 1960s. He also talked of the improvements we had made in services for the unemployed, but the whole business was a disaster, universally panned by the media and by opposition critics.

This came as a great shock to Bryce who was more concerned than most with his image and who followed this image in the press constantly. After the criticisms began to appear, he met me in the lobby, visibly shaken and wondering what he could do to recoup his losses. I downgraded the importance of the incident, saying that any minister who tried to defend the government in the present climate could expect the same reaction. But Bryce immediately began organizing a comeback. He appeared on several TV shows in the next few days and did as well as could be expected in rebutting the critics. In the end, he seemed to recover from the encounter without permanent injury.

Ben Benson was not so lucky. In cabinet and in public, he continued to insist that he had followed the right policies and, in fact, the only policies open to the government in the past couple of years. He was right, of course, if inflation was the menace that he, his advisors and the Bank of Canada insisted that it was. While the Prime Minister held the same view and was consistent about stating it publicly, it was not clear whether he arrived at this view under the advice of Benson and company, or whether he arrived at the same conclusion independently and then encouraged government financial agencies to apply pressure to the inflation issue. During the latter part of 1970, I had the impression that Trudeau was not happy with the performance of the Finance Department. But there seemed little choice but to continue supporting the general thrust of what was being done, since we had no encouragement to do otherwise from either Finance, the Bank of Canada or the Prices and Incomes Commission.

Despite this fact, however, Benson, now more than ever, continued to give the impression of a man who had no time for his critics, dismissing their suggestions as impractical. This was due, I think, as much to the White Paper on Tax Reform as it was to the unemployment issue. Business critics of the white paper were now smelling blood because of the general economic situation, and were intensifying their efforts to have general changes made.

In the latter part of January before Trudeau's return, there was a distinct feeling of unease in cabinet. We recognized that there was nothing we could do in the short run to ease the winter's unemployment. Both Benson and Reisman made it plain that things would get worse in February and March in terms of actual unemployment, even though the seasonally adjusted totals would decline from their 1970 high. Most ministers accepted this inevitability, even though some of us expressed strong reservations about the overall policy that had brought us to this position. But what was even more disturbing to virtually everyone in cabinet was that Finance officials were forecasting that even with the best possible economic performance in 1971, the prospect for the next winter was that unemployment would not be down by more than a single percentage point or so. Given the inevitable increase in the size of the work force, we would have at least as many unemployed the following year, even though the percentage might be somewhat lower.

As those facts began to emerge, Mitchell Sharp, as acting prime minister, suggested a special cabinet meeting for further discussion of the issue. Benson wanted the meeting deferred until Trudeau's return. But Sharp guessed, rightly I think, that the ministers wanted a full airing of the problem as soon as possible. The outcome of the discussion was not very satisfactory. The Finance people, especially Reisman, paraded out the usual arguments about good economic performance and insisted that the corner had been turned. But even when this point was conceded, it did not alter the fact that unemployment figures would not show a dramatic decrease in the foreseeable future. Essentially, the discussion revolved around a basic question: was a five or five and a half percent unemployment rate acceptable in a modern society if there were good social programs to ease the burden of those who were not working? It was pointed out that the average rate of unemployment in Canada during the 1960s was just a percentage point and a half below the current rate.

The discussion also revealed just how unsatisfactory our methods of measuring unemployment were. Even fourteen year olds who claimed that they were seeking work were included in the statistics although, since the school-leaving age was sixteen, such youths could hardly be considered unemployed. The statistics also failed to differentiate between those who were unemployed and in need, and the seasonal workers who made good incomes for the year, but were out of work because of winter conditions and were drawing unemployment insurance. My own province of Newfoundland provided a good example of this situation. Workers there might not be overly prosperous, but thousands had adjusted to a lifestyle that anticipated regular winter unemployment. And some, at least, preferred it that way. The statistics made no distinctions, either, between heads of households who were out of work, and other family members who might supplement the income of a main breadwinner who was employed. In many ways, the raw figures did not discriminate between unemployment and actual need.

It was useless to state this publicly while emotions ran so high, as it would only fuel the argument that government lacked heart and concern for the people. But there was no doubt that, given the complex circumstances under which we were operating, we needed much more sophisticated data than anyone was able to provide at the time.

The discussions regarding the economy continued in the same vein throughout January. The Tories made some progress out of Stanfield's cross-country tour to publicize unemployment, and out of their tactics in the House. Of late, Stanfield had been giving indications that he was not so pure and decent as he often appeared. He was beginning to reveal characteristics I had heard about from those who knew him from Nova Scotian politics. In the running debate on the economy, he had cultivated the image of sweet reasonableness and righteous indignation. Yet he allowed backbenchers like John Lundrigan to do the gut-level fighting and to employ rough political tactics. Ever since he had been named unemployment critic, Lundrigan had seized the opportunity for national publicity and was playing it for all its worth. This was blunderbuss rather than skilled political performance, but it was somewhat effective, and more importantly, it left Stanfield's personal image unsullied. I suspected that Lundrigan would soon find out that in Parliament, the limelight fades quickly for the hatchet man. I could not recall one who had made it to the front ranks of any party.

Throughout this period, I had been interested in watching the ongoing spectacle of the Newfoundland Tories jockeying for position. Until now, Jim McGrath had been the senior opposition member for Newfoundland. Now that Lundrigan was grabbing most of the headlines, McGrath found it difficult to avoid playing second fiddle. Peddle was all but out of it. Ironically, I suspected that the one with the greatest staying power would be Jack Marshall, a man who did his homework and engaged in none of the theatrical conduct that the other Tories from Newfoundland did. As for Walter Carter, he simply could not make an impression, even though it was obvious that he, too, was anxious to avoid being overshadowed by Lundrigan. Frank Moores, of course, had written himself off federally, whatever happened to him as provincial party leader.

All of the Newfoundland Tories, with the exception of Marshall, were wedded totally to the old-fashioned adversary concept of politics. They appeared to see their role strictly as that of opposition, and were combative and belligerent in virtually every exchange. While such tactics do work at times, I had a hunch that public reaction to this type of politics was changing, even in Newfoundland.

The unemployment situation drew a great deal of attention away from the news reports of Trudeau's participation in the Commonwealth conference in Singapore. Unfortunately, most of the publicity he received was devoted to his off-the-cuff antics, his being kissed by a monkey or riding an elephant. Almost any visitor to the area in question would probably do most of the same things without drawing very much attention. But there continued to be a fascination with Trudeau, and everything he did was noteworthy. And, of course, the opposition was obsessed with him mainly because they simply did not know how to handle him. They latched on to each new exploit, each new evidence of unorthodoxy, and by constant references to it, they drew even more attention to him.

I had come to accept the lack of ritual or special routine whenever Trudeau returned from a trip. Upon his return from the Far East, we resumed meetings of the Priorities and Planning Committee which he chaired. Trudeau entered the cabinet room as if he had never been away. There was no ritualistic shaking of hands, no formal words of welcome, nothing but a brief remark or two about the fact that he did not have much of a tan, and then we returned to business as usual.

The meetings of the Priorities and Planning Committee were the most interesting for me. On this occasion, we had papers prepared by Finance on the general economic situation and outlook. Unlike most of the other papers, these had a philosophical base, and they raised questions about the various possibilities open to Canada in the future if different options were exercised. The papers, which were well-reasoned and well-written, drew compliments from the Prime Minister. They posed such questions as the possible effects of a changed public value system on the economic climate and discussed regional economic policy and the desirability or undesirability of more population centralization at the expense, for instance, of the Atlantic provinces.

Yet despite the excellence of the papers and the variety of opinions they explored, they concluded generally in support of the status quo. There were no recommendations for dramatic shifts in the general thrust of government or private policy. The papers virtually dismissed the theory that there had been anything more than superficial changes in the makeup of the affluent society. Basically, they maintained that people would continue to buy consumer goods and support the traditional market-oriented economy.

This was where I basically disgreed with all government economic forecasters. For example, at this meeting, charts were produced tracing the fluctuations of Canadian and American economies over the past decade. Finance argued that patterns established years ago were simply repeating themselves, that the same cycle repeats itself endlessly. And while I knew that this was basically true, I was sure that new elements at work in our society—the youth revolution and higher standards of education, to name but two—were having effects that most conventional economists in the government and in the Bank of Canada did not even know about, let alone understand.

I tried to make this point again at the meeting, and I think the Prime Minister, and probably Bud Drury, understood what I was getting at. But, generally speaking, I found most ministers and officials to be interested in short-term goals within the conventional and comforting reassurances of precedent. In other words, if a set of circumstances brought a particular result before, one had only to recreate the circumstances and the same result would follow. Nowhere more than at this very top level of decision making was the generation gap, as well as conflict with new schools of thought, more evident.

I had little knowledge of where the Prime Minister stood in all of this. At meetings, he said very little that would provide a clue to his inner thoughts. His comments and questions were totally dispassionate. If he had any emotional involvement with the key questions, he rarely showed it. Either he was totally cynical about our chances of changing the human condition significantly, or he was simply attempting to draw out various points of view. It was evident that he welcomed and enjoyed my persistent assaults on the dogmatic, assured assertions of the Finance officials. Yet he remained personally uninvolved, aloof from the issues.

During my early acquaintance with Trudeau, I used to think, perhaps because of the persistent published commentary about his superior ability to think logically and to get to the bottom of any matter, that he had a scenario in mind as to how he wanted matters to turn out. I had the feeling that he would let cabinet and committee discussions roam over a wide range of choices, even though he knew from the beginning what he wanted to achieve. Now, I was not so certain.

Increasingly, I had the impression that, although Trudeau and his senior staff might have some general principles with regard to the direction Canada should take socially and economically, he had no overall blueprint. Indeed, there were times when he displayed a surprising lack of knowledge of fundamental pieces of information that were familiar to most businessmen and economists. And from the beginning of his administration, he had never articulated for cabinet any sweeping concept that might guide our thinking.

The one exception was the Quebec issue, on which he had very strong views. But in terms of both day-to-day issues and matters of long-term policy, I do not recall him ever leading cabinet discussions as most men with strong views would be inclined to do. His technique was to rely on position papers prepared by experts, often after consultation with ministers, and then to achieve in the subsequent discussion a consensus or policy. It was ironic in such circumstances to read so frequently of Trudeau's alleged dictatorial attitude. The real situation was quite the opposite, and I, for one, wished for more direction, more of a firm philosophy from the man who was, in the classic sense, "the source and arbiter of all public policy."

For many reasons, it was extremely difficult for the Prime Minister or any of us to argue seriously with the underlying principles of Benson's economic approach. The Finance arguments were persuasive, and the strategy plausible. Also, the whole field, as I noted earlier, was filled with uncertainties when it came to forecasting. For better or for worse, Louis Rasminsky and Simon Reisman, our chief advisors on fiscal and monetary policy, were adamant in recommending the policy we were now following. If anything, I suspected that they would have liked to be even tougher. Ben Benson appeared to agree out of conviction, although the influence of his officials was undoubtedly strong. If the government as a whole went counter to the expert advice it was getting, it would mean repudiating Benson and would almost certainly lead to Rasminsky's resignation.

Another factor troubling me, and probably other ministers, was that the economic forecasts of the past couple of years had been right, within a tolerable margin of error. Yet the feeling was inescapable that this occurred as much by accident as by design. For example, the consumer price index declined as hoped for. But the supermarket price was a major contributor to this decline—something which the government could take no credit for. Perhaps most frustrating for those of us who had to make decisions was the tremendous conflict we heard on every side concerning how the economy should be managed. Even the theories of John Kenneth Galbraith were now being challenged by those who were his disciples only a year before, and so much of the advice we got from the private sector was so self-seeking and subjective that it was virtually useless.

Despite all our consultations in January and after the Prime Minister's return, at the end of February our policies remained virtually unchanged. The only exception was the growing conviction that, regardless of the merits of economic orthodoxy, we could not go through another winter with the same levels of unemployment. An actual increase in the number of unemployed would be even more disastrous, especially on the eve of an election. There would be mounting pressure to introduce measures that would bring some relief.

Another change to arise from our recent experience was a growing feeling that we should look seriously at a system of wage and price controls. The Prices and Incomes Commission had worked on a number of alternatives for cabinet consideration. However, the imposition of controls could not be undertaken without a major cabinet fight. Mitchell Sharp and Bud Drury were opposed to it, as was, I conjectured, Ben Benson. I was wary of such a step also, and doubtful that such controls would work.

Throughout this time, we had also been trying to get some action on what had become known in cabinet as the "Jamieson kitty." For months, I had argued that while advance financial planning was essential, it was too rigid in its present form. We locked up every cent in advance, allowing no reserve for pump priming when it became necessary, or for those occasions when we would want to generate employment for political purposes. I had contended that we should have a reserve of at least three or four hundred million available for emergencies. Everyone had agreed to this in principle, yet no specific steps had been taken to see where the money might be found. After his return, the Prime Minister assigned me the task of finding such a reserve, partly by reducing planned expenditures in departments that had no urgency and by postponing others that were low on employment potential and political sex appeal.

Jim Davey had been working with me on this project, and in addition to locating funds, we had been trying to devise a list of pre-election projects that could be instituted across the country with the money saved. In this regard, Art Laing in Public Works had proved very difficult. Traditionally, Public Works had been one of the government's main sources of political leverage. But since Laing took over, trying to get him to spring loose for politically desirable projects was like pulling teeth. Laing's frugality might be commendable if it extended to the West or British Columbia, but it was a case of whatever British Columbia wanted, it got. Many ministers had become quite angry over Art's attitude. On Newfoundland matters, he gave me nothing but trouble.

Recently, I had privately told Trudeau that we had to get Art out of Public Works, and he agreed. He asked me to come up with a replacement but, so far, I had not come up with a name. The past summer when a few of us, including Sharp, Macdonald, Drury and myself, were discussing cabinet changes with the Prime Minister, it was proposed that both McIlraith and Laing should be replaced. McIlraith had since resigned, but Laing had stayed on. The suggestion for Laing was that he should become ambassador to Japan. But Art did not sound like a man getting ready to retire, and it looked as though the Prime Minister would have to encourage him.

McIlraith's resignation, however, came as no surprise. Although it was typical of George that his letter of resignation was correct in every respect and gave no hint of dissatisfaction, I knew from personal conversations with him that he was not too happy in cabinet. Very much of the old school, he was incensed by what he regarded as interference from young activists in the Prime Minister's Office. This, coupled with his failing health, was enough to prompt him to quit, something he had been contemplating for over a year.

McIlraith's successor, Jean-Pierre Goyer, was an unknown entity. The previous summer, when cabinet appointees were being considered, both Trudeau and Marchand expressed reservations about Goyer, claiming that he was unreliable and not pulling his weight in terms of Quebec policies. Consequently, he was passed over at the time. During the Quebec crisis, the Prime Minister gave him a position on the special task force established to deal with the problem. Apparently, he did quite well—well enough to ensure his appointment as McIlraith's replacement. Since his appointment, Goyer remained subdued in cabinet, apparently feeling his way. But in the House, his answers were long and often argumentative, and already he had been in trouble in the press. As I observed him, I speculated that he might turn out to be controversial in a highly sensitive position.

As for the general direction of government policy, the Committee on Priorities and Planning resumed regular meetings following the Prime Minister's return in February. In addition to several discussions on the economic situation, the main topic had been a review of our progress on priority problems defined a year and a half previously.

I had mixed feelings about our approach to planning. While it helped to have a concise list of major problems and the mechanisms for moving toward solutions, the difficulty was that planning tended to be overtaken by events or by other planning in different sectors of the government machine. For example, while I was coming up with a comprehensive paper on pollution control, Michael Pitfield in the Prime Minister's Office produced a structure for the new Department of the Environment. Thus, my work and the work of others was largely wasted.

In the financial field, we devoted an enormous amount of work on planning the Estimates. But then a crisis would develop, and the system had to be ignored as we proceeded with the worst kind of ad hoc decisions. Such was the case with the budget of December, 1970.

Out of two or three sessions on priority problems, we were able to somewhat revise our previous list of matters requiring urgent attention. This list did not include all problem areas by any means, only those which were not addressed by any existing federal mechanisms or programs. The key issues in this category included the future of youth and women in our society, the impact of policies on the estimated geographic spread of the population, and several others. Among them was the very special problem of national unity, the one for which the Trudeau himself had assumed personal responsibility.

A further difficulty in our planning process related to our legislative program. I agreed with the system in place because it gave us a chance to see in advance what ministers were planning, thereby preventing more activist colleagues from bringing into the House measures which were either not well thought out or at odds with other government objectives. Nevertheless, the process was painfully slow. In order to be passed, a proposal had to go through interdepartmental study, consideration by cabinet committee and then by cabinet itself, be drafted into legislation and then be reconsidered by cabinet. This often took a year or more; especially important measures took even longer. Since simple, non-controversial measures tended to get through the system faster while matters of substance bogged down, often the legislation for the order paper was either in short supply or inconsequential.

We had laboured mightily over this problem, but its many dimensions made it a difficult one to solve. And the greatest consultative process we had introduced—with the public, special interest groups and caucus—only slowed things down even more. Coupled with this was the bottleneck that could be created within the committee system when the opposition chose to dig in its heels.

During February, the Priorities and Planning Committee had been looking for a possible legislative program for the 1971-72 session, probably the last one before the next election. There were a lot of measures somewhere in the machine in various stages of processing. But there was very little political appeal in most of them, and it would be difficult to draft a Speech from the Throne based on what could be counted on to come forward. After a quick perusal of the items, Trudeau appointed an ad hoc committee of ministers to review the legislative list from a political viewpoint. It took little time to agree that the list contained few items with widespread appeal. As well, some proposed bills would be better left until after an election. We agreed to meet again to see what items now in preparation could be added to the list. Essentially, it was our view that we had to decide what program to put before the electorate, what components of the package eventually decided on should go into the pre-election legislative list, and what should be kept for the election platform.

It had also become evident that before long, cabinet would have to make some decisions on a number of unresolved issues such as the drug question, abortion, national ownership, the Status of Women Report and a variety of other pertinent issues. Obviously, these and a few others, including the pervasive one of national unity, would be the election issues, not the grab bag of items thrown up routinely by regular process.

Thus we began to shape our plan for the election. In addition to work on the legislative list, we now had my assignment to identify high visibility projects and find the money to pay for them. I had begun to observe a discernible change in Trudeau's mood and attitude, a growing consciousness of the approaching election and a recognition of what I had been voicing for months—that we must start now to prepare for the election, and we must weigh our actions and decisions with this in mind.

In February, John Munro sought once again to find a means through which to bring in his measures against cigarette advertising, an issue that had been in front of us for over a year. The issue remained as contentious as before, the key problem being whether to extend the ban to all media, or to restrict it to radio and television. Either decision was bound to produce a backlash from the media. Munro preferred a ban only on television and radio advertising. I called this approach a fraud and said that if we were going to ban cigarette advertising, we should have the courage to go all the way or not move at all. And although I genuinely believed that Munro's approach was hypocritical, I suspected that he felt that I was taking this stand because of a subconscious bias left over from my long association with broadcasting.

It gave me some satisfaction that the Prime Minister and others agreed with my views on cigarette advertising. Trudeau said that we had enough unresolved issues on our plate right now without inviting another prolonged debate. But the odds were better than even that the issue would resurface before long; Munro was nothing if not tenacious.

As we began to think in terms of election strategy, the big question hanging over our heads in all our planning was what should be done about tax reform. Following last year's hearing on the white paper by House and Senate committees, it was agreed in cabinet that the government would be prepared to accept most of the recommendations of the House committee. In fact, Ben Benson consulted frequently with the Liberal members while the report was being prepared. It was essentially a Liberal majority report. The other parties either voted against the recommendations or abstained.

The tremendous effort of preparing and drafting the recommendations into legislation got underway in the fall of 1970. Benson was overly optimistic about the speed with which this complex work could be done. I was not, nor were many of the rest of us. My main concern was that the huge piece of legislation would not get into the House until May, and there would be no chance that it could be passed unless the House sat all summer. That, to me, was a most unpleasant prospect. All members would be surly, and we would have problems maintaining a quorum, especially since every last clause had to be debated in the Committee of the Whole House.

Also, of course, there would be a question period every day with a chance for the opposition to score. While all of this was going on, we would have the added burden of trying to work out the next session's program with the House open. This was bad enough in July when the House was closed. With the House open, it could be a disaster that would seriously inhibit our ability to plan skilfully and carefully for the upcoming election.

There also loomed the possibility that a total stalemate would force us into an election in the fall of 1971. I did not see tax reform as the key issue in such an election. And no matter how much the economy improved, it would not be that good; the opposition would be able to raise the bogey that next winter would be worse than this one, and that we were trying to get the election over with before the roof fell in.

I made all of these points repeatedly throughout January and February, yet Ben still thought he could meet the deadline of an April budget. If he did, then in my view we would have gone into this major issue ill-prepared. There was also the fact that Ben had to get an agreement from all the provinces that they would pass comparative legislation. Otherwise, the measures could not come into force as planned until January, 1972. The time frame was simply too short for the effective and orderly handling of this basic issue. Yet we agreed that preparation and drafting should proceed as quickly as possible. If we hinted at delays in implementation, hard-pressed officials would slack off. Trudeau had said at the most recent meeting on the subject that we should at least get a package together for cabinet examination, and then decide on the strategy.

At the same meeting, we discussed what we would do if the session continued through the summer. The Prime Minister wondered if we could have a normal break later in the fall, starting the new session in December, perhaps. I said that I thought this impossible. We might get by with a November opening if the present session went into September because of the tax reform debate. But I felt that keeping the House closed later than that would give the opposition a field day complaining that we were afraid to meet the House. As most ministers agreed, it was decided that we would plan for a fall session and leave open for the time being the question of strategy regarding summer sittings.

Subsequently, Michael Pitfield told me that the Prime Minister was very much concerned about the entire handling of the tax reform question, and that cabinet would have tough decisions to make when the work of officials got back to them. Before it got back, however, it had to be considered by the special cabinet committee of which I was a member. Until this time, we had had only one meeting, and it confirmed my worst fears. On the basic question of what to do about the tax structure for small business, the proposals brought forward had to be rejected out of hand as too complex and theoretical. We had no option but to return to the drawing board. We planned to spend the whole March 13 weekend trying to make some real progress. Once again, I was sanguine about our chances.

Benson's problem was both serious and obvious. Without some resolution of the tax reform issue, business uncertainty would continue with possibly harmful economic consequences. On the other hand, if final proposals were brought forward and proved generally unacceptable to business and to large segments of the public, the opposition would have a ready issue, and business, too, might rise in revolt.

Actually, this possibility did not bother me as much as the very definite prospect that our total efforts in tax, welfare, unemployment insurance, finance, family allowance and other fields would have a detrimental effect on middle-income workers. Not only would this be bad politically, but I felt that this group was already being hit too hard now that we were applying the Robin Hood principle so far down the scale. I hoped that Ben was not fooling himself by thinking that his proposals would have a smooth passage through cabinet. Other ministers, I was sure, would balk at any combination that significantly hurt the large group of middle-income taxpayers.

I could see that it would be a rough spring. But then we had had a trying winter, with everyone's nerves a bit on edge. There was the furore over the proposed hiring of Francophones in the public service. I doubt that this did much harm except to the opposition, who lost ground in Quebec because of their stand. But I detected a deeply rooted unrest in the public service and elsewhere over our bilingualism policies. I feared that if opposition parties saw that they had no chance in Quebec, they would encourage a backlash in the rest of the country. Some Tory MPs were making cautious noises along these lines already. Stanfield, of course, would remain above the battle, but not only could he not control some of the western Tories; it might suit his purposes not to do so. We had to be very careful with the bilingualism issue, or we could throw away all the gains of the past three years, gains which might not be permanent in any event. Reports from Quebec were disquieting. The Parti Québécois was by no means a spent force, and it was clear that the ministers from Quebec, including Trudeau, had doubts about the strength and effectiveness of the Bourassa government.

On February 18, we had a meeting of political cabinet—that is, all the ministers plus officials from the Liberal Federation. We assessed the party's position in various regions, with Jean Marchand reporting on Quebec. His biggest concern was that there was no way for the federal Liberal Party to have an open confrontation with the separatists. He doubted if René Lévesque would take on the Prime Minister by running candidates in a federal election. Therefore, even if the Liberals scored heavily as was likely, the PQ would remain more or less unscathed. Marchand felt that we would have to provoke a contest with the separatists to resolve the issue. He felt that the Conservatives were all but dead in Quebec and that the Créditistes, surviving mainly because of Réal Caouette, would decline next time round. Marchand, incidentally, was the only minister to speak about the wisdom of holding an election that year. I did not think, however, that he was serious; in cabinet and in caucus, he was strongly opposed to such an idea.

There was, of course, a general review of the party's position. It was felt that British Columbia looked at least as good as it had in 1968. And there was potential for improvement on the Prairies. Don Macdonald forecast the loss of some seats in Ontario, probably in Toronto. He said that a number of our older members and some new ones would not run again, and that there was a danger of splitting the vote with the NDP in some areas, leaving room for a Tory win. At the same time, Don and other Ontario ministers were agreed that things were looking up for the provincial Liberals in Ontario.

I shared the view that the Liberals would pick up seats in the Atlantic provinces. With Regan elected in Nova Scotia, our prospects there were decidedly better. Prince Edward Island looked promising as well, and New Brunswick was not likely to be worse than last time. As for Newfoundland, a lot depended on how Joe Smallwood performed in the provincial election, but I believed that we could get back two seats in addition to my own.

It was now obvious that Smallwood was going to run again; indeed, he had been running since the start of the year. As usual, I had lunch with him on Christmas Eve. Despite his familiar pleas for me to return, he left no doubt that he would be disappointed if I did so. Since then, his every move had been geared to an election. He was indulging in his usual overkill, with a development conference on a lavish scale covered in its entirety on television. Promises were being made on every hand, and every community was slated to get something.

In all this, Joe was counting on me to get him some special assistance for roads. I knew that I would probably be able to do this, although every nickel of federal money was committed and more would have to be found, a consequence of too rigid advance planning. Before the start of the Newfoundland development conference in February, I arranged for Joe and a number of his ministers to come to Ottawa for talks with federal ministers and their officials. It was a good session and helped to pave the way for the conference.

At that time, the probable outcome of the Newfoundland election was anyone's guess. I had arranged to have an opinion from Martin Goldfarb, a very good researcher and public opinion analyst. Martin had since told me that he thought Joe could make it if he got some new faces and ran a good campaign. I had also suggested that the Warren Reynolds Advertising Agency handle the campaign. If Joe listened to their advice, I felt that they could help him considerably. The question was, of course, would he listen?

The roughest two months of the government's life had gone by incredibly quickly. In addition to the major issues I have written about, there were scores of others. We had another death sentence case to deal with—this time with no jury recommendation for mercy. That made it tougher, but there was little, if any, inclination in cabinet to let the hanging go ahead, and the eventual decision was to commute the sentence. All of us realized, however, that since the five-year test period would end in 1972, we would soon have to formulate a new policy. Throughout the discussion on capital punishment, I continued to be amazed that so many Canadians still wanted to see the death penalty enforced; this said something abut human nature but, at the time, I did not know what. Another puzzle to me was that so many Roman Catholics, who were dead set against abortion, were equally strong in their support of capital punishment. I wanted to, but could not, understand how they squared their stand on the death sentence with their belief in the sanctity of all human life.

Predictably, it was the Quebec crisis that really brought out the pro-hanging advocates. This was yet another reason why we had to carefully consider what to do when the Temporary Measures Act ran out at the end of April. So far, we had decided only that John Turner would propose permanent legislation for cabinet consideration. Once we had a document before us, we would have hard decisions to make in a few weeks.

It was ironic in light of all the important events of the year that the most talk had been about the Prime Minister's alleged obscenity in the House of Commons. The facts of this are well-known, and there is no need for me to record them here. I sat behind the Prime Minister, and therefore did not see what he did. On previous occasions, I had seen him engage in byplay of various kinds. In fact, we had all done the same thing on occasion. It was simply the mood of the House and the fact that the Tories smelled blood over the unemployment issue which caused the incident to be blown out of all proportion.

The media, also, deserve some responsibility for this. There were few in the press gallery who really liked Trudeau, and most would welcome any chance to put him down. Yet they were fascinated by him. As well, the almost unreasonably bad publicity for the Prime Minister and the government since the new year was quite a reversal for the press, following their all-out support of the government during the Quebec crisis. Now, with the crisis over, they felt compelled to demonstrate their objectivity, and how better to do it than to clobber Trudeau and the rest of us on the issue of unemployment?

Now Trudeau had made news again by getting married to a twenty-two year old. How could the press keep up with this totally unorthodox man? And what must the opposition have thought as time after time they were knocked out of the headlines by Trudeau's exploits?

In his decision to marry, as in so many of his other decisions, Trudeau gave us no advance indication of his plans. Or did he? On the morning of his wedding day, he and I arrived for cabinet almost simultaneously. He had been in Toronto the previous evening for a big Liberal Party function. I had been in London, Ontario, and had arrived back in Ottawa fifteen minutes after he did. When we met on Thursday morning, I asked him if he was as tired as I was. He replied by asking me what the expression was that I used so often. "It's a mug's game," I told him. We agreed that the expression was appropriate. Then he told me that he was going skiing. As other members assembled, Eric Kierans and others began kidding Trudeau about his Toronto speech on women's rights. Several of us said that our wives would now be impossible to live with. At this, he replied, "You fellows had better stop, or you'll talk me out of getting married." We thought that he was joking. Little did we know what was to happen shortly.

Ten

I wrote again on Monday, March 8, a day on which the most important activity for me was attending another cabinet committee meeting on tax reform. It was now clear that Ben Benson was in quite a predicament as to how to proceed on this very important measure. On Monday night, we talked at some length about the way in which the proposed changes to the tax structure would affect small business, a group that was one of the most vocal and had the most support from other spokesmen appearing before the House of Commons Committee on Tax Reform. In our attempts to change the long-standing arrangement which had given certain benefits to the so-called small businessmen of this country, we were dealing with a highly emotional issue. As I described it at Monday's meeting, being in favour of small business in this country was like supporting motherhood. You could always generate a great deal of sympathy and emotional support by talking about small businessmen as the backbone of the country and the foundation of the free enterprise system. The irony of this was, of course, that a great deal of the argument in support of small business originated from large and influential big business interests. They could avoid appearing subjective by talking about the big tax issues that really concerned them, all the while appearing to champion the little fellow.

Nevertheless, there was unanimous feeling within the committee that it would be impossible for us to implement the original idea—to tax all profits, big or small, at the full rate of fifty percent. Until now, all business has enjoyed a lower rate on the first thirty-five thousand dollars of profit. Therefore, what we were really talking about was not just a concession to small business, but one that extended to every incorporated business in the country.

The committee did not have much difficulty in agreeing that large corporations should not be entitled to this special deduction on their profits, or in agreeing that we should make some concessions to the legitimate small businessman. The troubling question that arose was: just what constitutes a small business? As in all of these meetings, officials from Finance and National Revenue complicated matters enormously. Since they understood the tax system from what might be called a professional standpoint, they responded to requests for an explanation of any proposal by plunging into complexities that were exceedingly difficult for the layperson to understand. Repeatedly during such meetings, I had to bring officials up short, and to ask them to give specific and straightforward explanations of how their proposals would actually change what a taxpayer already had in the way of concessions and payments. We went through a large number of possible arrangements that could be set up to define what a small business really was, and as on so many occasions in the past, I was struck by two facts relating to officials. The first was that officials, so deeply immersed in the internal complexities of the tax system, developed a viewpoint that made it impossible for them to create systems which could be easily understood by anyone outside the bureaucracy. Also, having seen the most ingenious abuses of the tax system, they tended to be vindictive in their approach; they possessed an overriding concern with plugging every loophole in the tax system. I suspected, too, that among a great many officials there was a measure of envy; they could see others attain wealth through means which they considered dubious at best, while they themselves had little opportunity to take advantage of what had been—for the most part—legitimate activities which certain taxpayers could take advantage of.

In any event, the glaring lack of sensitivity on the part of bureaucrats made it all the more necessary for interested ministers to ensure that, in the process of closing loopholes which had been exploited, we did not take away necessary concessions and arrangements from the vast majority who operated legitimately.

Ben Benson frequently revealed a basic empathy with his officials' views, views which I can only describe as punitive. He also appeared to have a deep-seated resentment of those who had a larger-than-average measure of financial security, and of most types of business people who managed to exploit the system successfully. In some cases, I detected a streak of meanness in Ben's approach. For example, he was preoccupied with the so-called fringe benefits most businessmen enjoy. Yet he was no different from the rest of us when it came to taking advantage either of his position, or of windfalls that might come his way. Although he sounded off frequently about the evils of expense account exploitation, he himself was quite prepared to accept free passes on Air Canada and CP Air for his wife's trips to Europe and other destinations. I had no doubt that these indirect benefits would not show up on Benson's tax returns. And while I had no argument with his taking advantage of such benefits which I considered entirely legitimate, it did make something of a mockery of his righteous indignation when examples were cited of businessmen who did likewise.

The result of this long and frustrating meeting was a decision to offer a special lower tax rate to small businesses, defined as those who would have less than four hundred thousand dollars in undistributed profits when the new scheme went into effect. Like all the other measures in the tax reform package, this one had many strings attached and was difficult to explain.

Perhaps the central issue that emerged from this particular reform was the basic one which maintained that a dollar of earnings was the same regardless of how the dollar was raised—echoing the familiar saying, "a buck is a buck is a buck." I continued to quarrel with this contention, perhaps because my own background was essentially in small business, and I remembered vividly how hard I had to work in order to get that business in a profitable position. An executive or high-priced worker in any firm usually punches in not more than forty hours a week; he has job security and all of the fringe benefits that that entails. He does not have to worry about bank overdrafts, sales decline, increased competition, or the hazards inherent in running a business. But most small businessmen, especially those starting up, work twelve to fourteen hours a day. Their families frequently help without any remuneration, and, of course, the small businessman rarely knows from one year to the next whether his enterprise will profit or even survive. I believe that, in some way or other, the person who assumes such risks and who, by doing so, often provides employment for others, is entitled to some form of special consideration in return for the extra effort he puts in as compared to the average salaried worker.

I was aware even as I asserted it that this was an emotional argument, one that would be difficult to accept and implement as a principle on which to base a tax system. Nevertheless, I felt that this case and others made it impossible to have a tax system which was in every respect equitable. The many complexities generated by our effort at tax reform had made me question whether the exercise was worthwhile, or whether we would not have been better off to simply concentrate on some of the obvious abuses present in the system and on efforts to lessen the burden on taxpayers on the lower end of the scale.

As I left the meeting, I was also greatly disturbed by the tenacity with which Ben Benson and the officials were sticking to the original plan to have the entire tax reform package introduced during the current session of Parliament with a view to implementing it on the first day of January, 1972. For the life of me, I failed to see how this could be accomplished. I knew that both Benson and the Prime Minister felt that the first task was to get the entire package completed, and that if we were to do this, we could not give the officials any indication that we might be changing our minds with regard to the timetable. Any hint of this would seriously slow the process of drafting the laws, and our ability to make wise decisions with regard to introduction would become even less clear than it already was. Nevertheless, as I have noted, such projects had a tendency to develop a momentum of their own; often, we found that by the time cabinet was in a position to make a decision, members had become captives of events, and plans had to go forward whether anyone had any enthusiasm for them or not.

Perhaps I was unduly concerned about this matter, and it might be that I was more reactionary than I thought. Yet, when I reviewed the occasions over the previous two and a half years when cabinet had made important decisions under pressure, and the difficulty that such decisions had created for us, I was not reassured. At the very least, I felt that my presence in cabinet and my caution could be useful in slowing down ill-advised initiatives by ministers who, in their zeal for change and reform, would not take time to anticipate reactions to what they proposed to do.

Although I was a member of the cabinet Committee on Social Policy, I did not always attend its meetings because so many of them were concerned with routine matters, and because the general makeup of the committee was such that, almost inevitably, I found myself in conflict with most of its members. This was especially true with John Munro and Bryce Mackasey, both of whom possessed a tendency to become very emotional and, in the case of Mackasey in particular, very antagonistic when their proposals were questioned. On the morning of March 9, however, I glanced at the agenda for the day's meeting and noted that John Munro had brought forward proposals dealing with the drug issue, and particularly with our attitude toward marijuana. Because I recognized the major importance, both politically and socially, of any decision that might result, I decided to attend the meeting and was very glad I did.

With the tenacity for which he was noted, John Munro had brought back to the committee his original proposal to have marijuana taken out of the Criminal Code and placed under the Food and Drug Act. I had never opposed this idea, but had always maintained that any such action should form part of a general government policy on the drug problem and should result in a significant change in the way in which marijuana users were treated. It will be recalled that when the first volume of the

LeDain report was tabled, Munro got himself in difficulty with the Prime Minister and John Turner by announcing publicly that the switch of jurisdiction would be undertaken. At the time, Turner insisted that any such step would be carefully considered in advance and should, as I myself believed, form part of a general policy. Munro was obliged to back down, but as with every measure where he was thwarted the first time, he found ways to reintroduce it, usually with a great element of surprise to his colleagues.

I could not understand why Munro took this initiative at the time. During the committee discussion, it became apparent that the only significant effect of the proposed move would be that marijuana users might possibly feel that their offence was less serious if convicted under the Food and Drug Act, rather than under the Criminal Code. John Turner and I disagreed with this contention, and no matter how objective I tried to be, I could not find any lack of logic in my position. It seemed to me that all the general public would be concerned about was whether a conviction would be recorded or not. An even stronger objection to the Munro initiative was that, with such a complex issue, a move in the direction Munro suggested would appear as a significant step toward legalizing marijuana. Many people would oppose the move on those grounds alone.

At the same time, most young people who were in favour of a more liberal approach to the use of marijuana would quickly recognize that what we were doing was not much more than window dressing. Therefore, we would get the worst of both worlds. Jean-Pierre Goyer, the new solicitor general, who had responsibility for the RCMP, was ambivalent in his approach to the Munro proposals. His concern was with the criminal record aspect of marijuana convictions, and he tended to feel that a move from the Criminal Code to the Food and Drug Act would be an appropriate step if something were done to ensure that the criminal record of a marijuana user brought before the courts could be erased under the new plan which John Turner was proposing. Goyer agreed with the rest of us that, without this provision, the Munro proposal was useless. John Turner pointed out that, as Justice Minister, he was opposed to the elimination of criminal records for a particular category of offences. His wish was that nothing be done until the bill regarding all criminal records had been dealt with, and the same standard would apply across the board. In the end, Munro was asked to take his paper back for re-examination.

I found this whole discussion very frustrating. The officials with John Munro, many of them doctors and experts in the field, told us that all their assessments had led them to the view that marijuana was less harmful than either tobacco or alcohol. If such was the case, there was a good deal of hypocrisy in Munro's approach, but even more, perhaps, in the stand taken by Turner and myself. If we were really honest, we would either legalize marijuana as tobacco and alcohol had been legalized, or ban these other two on the grounds of their harmfulness to the general public. Yet the double standard continued to apply, and all we were doing was attempting to convey to those who wanted a more liberal approach that we were sympathetic. At the same time, we would do nothing of significance because we feared the reactions of the large number of people who feared any relaxation of the drug laws, and who considered marijuana as dangerous a drug as any.

Herein lay the weakness of Munro's case on this issue and on many others. He was always prepared to compromise in ways which gave the public impression that he was progressive; at the same time, he displayed a real lack of courage in coming to grips with basic problems. He had shown the same attitude and approach with regard to cigarette advertising, although he knew that watered-down measures really pleased no one and offended some.

I found it difficult to believe, but some of my colleagues were telling me that Munro was tremendously ambitious, and was working toward the possibility of eventually becoming prime minister. Although I doubted that this would ever happen, it did provide a rationale for the general approach that Munro adopted toward his responsibilities, and explained his emphasis on publicity and his need to appear as both a reformer and a compassionate man with great concern for the disaffected in our society. Although I had no doubt that the latter was true, it became increasingly obvious that Munro's concern for the disadvantaged was tempered by strong ambition. All of his planning was geared toward the ultimate objective of leadership.

In the afternoon, Trudeau returned to the House following his brief honeymoon, and it was one of the more pleasant occasions in the chamber. All parties wished him good luck, and the congratulatory speeches carried a great deal of sincerity. Trudeau's response was generous, and he was sincerely moved when he coupled his thanks to members with an expression of regret over the death of our Saskatchewan member, Ab Douglas. All of us were genuinely shocked to hear of Ab's death. He was a thoroughly likeable man and a conscientious member, and his death was all the more of a jolt because he looked the picture of health. There had not even been a suggestion that he was seriously ill.

Following the question period, we had a meeting of the Priorities and Planning Committee, with the main item on the agenda being the knotty problem of what to do about members' salaries. Allan MacEachen, the House Leader, had been trying to achieve some form of consensus within our own caucus and among the members of the House generally. He had not had a great deal of luck. The Liberal caucus was split, although the majority clearly wanted immediate action and were prepared to run the risk of the political consequences.

This was especially true for the Quebec caucus, which was virtually unanimous in demanding the maximum raise and other improvements immediately. Members from Ontario took much the same view, but among them were strong dissenters who felt that a generous raise at that time would be detrimental politically. With one or two exceptions, British Columbia members were by far the most adamant in declaring themselves opposed to a pay increase and had gone so far as to indicate a willingness to speak against it in the House.

As for the other parties, the word was that most of the Tories with the exception of John Diefenbaker would support an income improvement, and most agreed that it would be best to do it right away instead of making it an election issue. Word out of the NDP camp was confusing. Obviously, Stanley Knowles would oppose a settlement of any consequence, and there were probably others who would take the same view. Meanwhile, rumour had it that the Creditists were of two minds on the matter. Representing mostly rural ridings, they worried about political impact; at the same time, like most other members, they were having problems themselves financially and would dearly love to have their incomes improved.

Cabinet itself was divided on the salary question. The Prime Minister began in the afternoon by indicating that he saw nothing wrong with a system of accountable expenses for members as recommended by Beaupré. His initial position was that if we were to go to a system through which members could collect all of their expenses provided they submitted evidence that the monies had been spent, he would be willing to support such a move immediately. On the other hand, there was strong opposition in the committee to the principle of accountability. Mitchell Sharp was particularly opposed, feeling that the current fixed sum idea was more consistent with the proper role of a member of Parliament. John Turner strongly supported this view, and added that a system of accountable expenses would create classes of members—that is, those who took full advantage of the expense system, and those who did not.

Although Trudeau appeared to have been influenced by the arguments against accountability, he was reluctant to move away from the Beaupré recommendations. Allan MacEachen produced a formula which provided members with a tax-free increase, and to meet the accountability provision, he suggested that cabinet could estimate approximate expenses fairly accurately, and could allocate the proposed funds under different headings. Each one of the headings would be allocated a certain sum, and the total paid to members without further accountability requirements.

I found it interesting that the officials in the Prime Minister's Office, particularly Jim Davey and Michael Pitfield, felt that part of the problem with caucus unrest had been created by the pay issue. They felt that members were grossly underpaid, and that government should give them a substantial increase. This, of course, might have been possible if all parties would agree not to become righteously indignant for political purposes, and it made it all the more important to have some sort of agreement with opposition parties before any measure was introduced.

Ben Benson advanced a proposal which had the attraction of simplicity. He suggested that, since there had been no increases at all since 1963, we should take raises in both basic salary and allowances, and add a four percent increase for each year since 1963. He felt that four percent was entirely defensible. Objections, however, were raised on the grounds that we would be criticized for a four percent increase because we had not given the same level of increase to pensioners and others. Such inequities, it was argued, would provide a ready-made issue for people like Stanley Knowles.

The underlying problem in all of this was, of course, a fear of the political reaction in the country. No one disputed any more the need for a raise for MPs, yet there never seemed to be a time when it was appropriate to do it. In the end, the discussion led to no conclusions except that Allan MacEachen should do additional work in gauging the position of other parties, and in working out his expense formula in more detail.

There were other pay increases to consider—those for federal judges and senior civil servants. Once again, it was agreed that, given the present rates in the private sector, we could not hope to get good people to accept positions on the bench or to retain top level civil servants if we did not come reasonably close to matching what such people would obtain in the private sector. Nevertheless, we recognized that if we increased the salaries of senior civil servants, this would further aggravate the problem with members of Parliament who would feel that they were the only group not receiving sympathetic attention. It was decided, therefore, to postpone any decision regarding the other two groups until we had decided what to do about members.

The day did not end with even these discussions. That night, there was a special cabinet committee meeting called to deal with the issue of Home Oil, a problem that had hung around since the previous summer. The company was likely to be sold to American interests, and control of the last large oil producer in Canada would have slipped through our fingers. The issue had generated a tremendous amount of highly emotional commentary from all parties, especially the NDP and economic nationalist groups.

There were very few ministers who were enthusiastic about government acquisition of Home Oil at this time. Until Herb Gray presented his paper on foreign ownership, we would lack any clear-cut policy for dealing with such situations. Also, the eccentricities of Bobbie Brown, the principal shareholder, had made the Home Oil situation one of the most complex I had ever encountered. Brown had put together a personal empire in a most ingenious way, and in order to get control of it, we would have to pay a considerably higher price for the shares that carried control than they were worth on the open market. And although Brown was compelled to sell to repay heavy bank loans, he nevertheless insisted that any deal must ensure that he remain chief executive officer of the company, with all the benefits and authority the position entailed. The potential American buyer, the Ashland Oil Company, had agreed to Brown's conditions and had offered him substantially higher than market price for control; apparently, through an interlocking arrangement with their existing companies, they had an excellent chance of working out a profitable merger. The government as a buyer would not have the same opportunity, but short of nationalizing Home Oil or setting the price arbitrarily by law, it would have to meet the Ashland offer if it wished to avoid infringing on Brown's basic civil rights.

If one was thinking strictly in terms of market value, the deal was essentially a bad one from the government's point of view. As well, the government's actions in this case would be taken as a precedent and might conceivably have a detrimental effect on further foreign investment in the country, or on what actions oil companies in Canada would be likely to take in the future.

All of these issues were thoroughly thrashed out during the evening meeting which lasted four hours. The most vocal opponent of government purchase of Home Oil was Eric Kierans. Kierans had fought against this project ever since it first surfaced the previous August, and he was now no less adamant than he had been then. In fact, the evening meeting was one of the very few occasions during the two and a half years of our government when tempers were genuinely strained around the cabinet table, and when harsh words flew between Joe Greene and Eric Kierans.

Kierans raised many objections to the purchase, but his major objection was that the government would be acting in an unethical way if it were to purchase Brown's shares in the involved financial structure supporting Home Oil without offering the same higher-than-market price to all of the minority shareholders. The nature of the deal was already fairly common knowledge around Ottawa and had been reported at length in the financial pages of various newspapers. What it amounted to basically was that Brown controlled Home Oil through a holding company known as Cygnus Corporation. Under the proposed deal, the government would not touch the Home Oil stock directly, but would attain control by buying all of Brown's shares in Cygnus. However, in addition to Brown's shares, there were many more held by shareholders in both the United States and Canada, as well as thousands of shareholders of Home Oil itself. Kierans' argument was that once the government acquired control of Cygnus stock, all other shareholders would be affected by the general market reaction to the government's decision. Therefore, he maintained, minority shareholders would have a legitimate complaint against the government if, as was very likely, all the remaining stock decreased in value. It was clear also that Kierans had no regard for Brown and felt that the government would have nothing but trouble with him when it became the owner and had to fulfil its commitment to retain Brown as chief executive officer.

Joe Greene, who had, I think, tried to present the problem objectively, really resented Kierans' emphatic opposition. He said that because the decision had been made last August not to buy Home Oil, a desision based largely on Kierans' advice, it would now cost the government more to complete the deal than it would have the previous summer. This Kierans disputed, maintaining that the basic ingredients were virtually unchanged. Indeed, Greene presented something of a puzzle in the whole matter. Immediately after his return to cabinet after a long absence caused by two heart attacks, Joe was relatively low-key and for a time took little part in major cabinet discussions. However, the previous spring he had begun to emerge as a most active cabinet minister and politician, starting with a nationalistic and strongly anti-American speech he made in Denver, Colorado. The widespread response was favourable, and since that time, Joe had been taking advantage of every opportunity to speak. He had worked to polish his image and to become a key government spokesman on the complex and controversial issue of foreign ownership. There had been, of course, much contradictory comment in his public utterances.

It was difficult to say whether Joe was a genuine economic nationalist in the Walter Gordon mould or whether his primary motive was to achieve a measure of national publicity and notoriety. All of this raised some intriguing questions about his plans for the future. Before he had his heart attack, Joe was undoubtedly still thinking of himself as a future prime minister. He had made a good impression at the leadership convention that chose Trudeau and was widely liked within the party circles that made leadership decisions. However, it was generally felt that two heart attacks meant more or less the end of the line for Greene, and that he might well choose to take a position on the bench, or perhaps a Senate post, before the next election. Indeed, this was discussed thoroughly in cabinet when there was still doubt that he would recover sufficiently to resume full ministerial responsibilities. And now here he was, assuming a key role in a major issue.

As for myself, my response to the issue was that I did not believe that we could sit idly by and allow Home Oil to be picked up by an American company. I felt that, even though the public at large did not understand the intricacies of the deal, public comment had somehow generated a feeling that Home Oil was our last chance to retain some Canadian control of the oil industry. We would give our critics a ready-made issue if we did not take steps to have the government purchase the company and thereby keep it Canadian. I did, however, state my feeling that, once we had completed the purchase, we should consider what we would do with the company; in my view, our purchase was strictly a holding action, and we should consider at once whether or not we would be prepared to sell the first time a Canadian buyer came along who was willing to ensure that company ownership would remain in Canada. I also said that if Home Oil were turned over to a Crown corporation such as Eldorado during the interim period, instructions should be issued that the company was not to undertake new and costly initiatives that could burden the Treasury, but should be directed to carry on as at present until we had decided on the ultimate disposition of the property. I did not rule out the possibility that it might prove advantageous to the government to use the acquisition of Home Oil as a building block around which we could develop a significant government interest in the oil business, as the British and French had done. I emphasized, however, that we should not make any such decision at that time, and reiterated my wish that we make it clear to Parliament and to the public the interim nature of any decision.

Don Macdonald was in favour of buying the company, and while he agreed generally with my views that such a step would be a holding operation, from that point on our views differed. I favoured immediate disposal as soon as a buyer could be found; Don was more supportive of government involvement, and felt that an effort should be made to establish a rational basis for the government to stay in the oil business. He suggested, for example, that it might be possible to arrange some sort of connection between Home Oil, once it was government owned, and Panarctic, already substantially, although not completely, owned by the government.

Art Laing was essentially opposed to purchasing the company. With his many connections in the oil industry in western Canada, he was no doubt reflecting the views of many oil company executives who did not want the government in the oil business under any circumstances. Art felt that we were buying ourselves a large package of trouble because, as he put it, it was not our job as a government to get directly into business, particularly in something as complex as oil. He maintained that we should let Brown do whatever he wished. As an aside, he pointed out that Brown was very popular in western Canada, and that we should avoid any action that would appear to be pressuring him or limiting in any way his civil rights. Basically, Laing felt that we did not need ownership of large companies to achieve control and carry out national objectives because we had adequate regulatory power which we could use to ensure that any industry performed in the best interests of Canada.

Bud Olson, the minister representing Alberta, also had reservations about the purchase and, I suspect, was aware of the opinions of Alberta oil companies with regard to the principle of government involvement. Nevertheless, Bud was not as vehement in his objections as Art Laing. He simply suggested that, if the decision was to purchase the company, we should make it very clear that this was not a precedent, and that we were still withholding general policy decisions pending the preparation of Herb Gray's paper on foreign ownership. Gray himself indicated his support for the idea of buying the company but pointed out that it was unfortunate that the decision had to be made prior to the finalization of his efforts to formulate a cohesive policy for action in all cases of potential American takeovers. The debate waged on, with Kierans remaining emphatically opposed until the end.

Although Bud Drury, as chairman, did not express an opinion, I had no doubt that his views closely paralleled my own, and that essentially, he believed that, under the circumstances, it would be difficult, if not impossible, for the government to refrain from any action designed to keep the company Canadian. Joe Greene, of course, was in favour of the purchase, and merely repeated all the arguments that he had presented earlier with his paper.

It was almost one o'clock in the morning before the meeting broke up with the decision that we would recommend to full cabinet on Thursday that Joe Greene and his officials be authorized to start negotiations with Brown on the basis of a proposal which would commit the government to an immediate expenditure of up to twenty-four million dollars. I cannot say that it was a happy choice for us, but it was certainly a graphic illustration of the frightening complexity of the whole problem of foreign economic control. I hoped that Herb Gray could get his paper completed soon so that we could try, at least, to remove ourselves from the predicament of having to make far-reaching decisions on an ad hoc basis.

Wednesday, March 10, was not a particularly complicated day in terms of major issues. At the usual morning meeting of the Transportation Council, we discussed at considerable length the problems involved in operating ferry services between mainland Canada and Prince Edward Island, and the island of Newfoundland. I learned to my surprise that although the CNR had been responsible for operating the ferries to Newfoundland since Confederation, as well as coastal boat services, there had never been a formal contract with the federal government, which, of course, was paying for the very substantial deficits these services incurred. As a result, there was enormous confusion over who could make major decisions. I gave most emphatic instructions that this ridiculous situation be ended, and that clear lines of responsibility be established. I could see now why there has been such a long-standing controversy over ferry services; in effect, no one had ever had the ultimate legal responsibility.

I spent over an hour of the morning with Warren Reynolds of the Warren Reynolds advertising firm in Toronto. Warren was an old friend, and I made arrangements for him to visit Joey Smallwood with a view to handling the advertising and promotion during Newfoundland's upcoming provincial election. Warren wanted some background information from me as to the best approach to take with Joey, and I filled him in as best I could. We also spent considerable time discussing his views on what the likely consumer response would be during the current year. Many of our hopes for a resurgence in the economy in 1971 were based on assumptions with regard to consumer spending. It was clear that savings had now reached an unusually high level, and this was a circumstance that usually set off a wave of consumer buying, especially if confidence in the economy was improving. Warren tended to confirm the views of economists that there would be an upsurge in spending during the current year. He indicated there had been an increase in advertising expenditure, and this usually reflected a belief that the public was in the mood to buy.

At lunch hour, I attended an interesting presentation arranged by Memorial University of Newfoundland. Under the direction of Don Snowden, the Extension Department at the university had taken videotape equipment to Labrador and had taped interviews with residents in order to get their views on their needs in the field of communications. The objective of the luncheon was to show Eric Kierans and me the taped interviews and to get our response to the various requests made by coastal residents. I taped my answers immediately following the showing, and these were to be taken back to the coast and shown to the people concerned. It was an exercise in what Snowden called circular communication, and I could see that it was an idea that had a good deal of promise. I was also impressed by the nature of the demands of the people on the coast. These were not outrageous by any means; mainly, they reflected a lack of proper liaison between officials in Ottawa and elsewhere who made the decisions and those who ended up being affected by their actions. It was another graphic example of the failure of our system to find a means through which effective communication could be established, and such failure could probably be held accountable for much of the unrest and dissatisfaction so evident among those whom we tried to serve.

During the day, Jack Pickersgill told me that Guy Roberge would be available to become vice-chairman of the Canadian Transport Commission. An old hand around the Ottawa scene, Roberge had held a number of positions. In recent years, he had worked for the Quebec government as head of their special office in London. Now, apparently, Guy wished to return to Canada, and Jack suggested to me that he would be a good replacement for Taschereau who was leaving his post to join Canadian National Railways.

This exchange provided another classic example of the way Pickersgill operated; superficially, he observed all niceties of consulting with the minister on such matters and of refraining from doing anything himself to recruit appointees, as this was a cabinet responsibility. Nevertheless, because he had been around so long, Jack understood the system thoroughly. Already, before he spoke to me, he had determined from Roberge that he was ready to come, and he had spoken to Gordon Robertson, the Clerk of the Privy Council, to alert him of the possibility of such an appointment. To keep the intrigue from getting out of hand, I consulted with the Prime Minister in the House of Commons during the afternoon question period, asking him if he thought that Roberge would be a good appointment. He agreed, and the two of us held a small conference with Jean Marchand, the outcome of which was a decision that I should make formal representations to Roberge to see if he would be available.

I record this incident simply to show how such appointments could be engineered in Ottawa and to point out how difficult it had become to recruit good people for many of the top jobs. This I expected to continue as long as the public continued to object to the payment of executive level salaries to those who agreed to enter any area of the public service.

As the time neared for the Victoria conference on the constitution, all ministers were aware that it would be in some respects a do-or-die session. Yet from a cabinet point of view, there was no great degree of involvement or excitement as Trudeau prepared to leave for the coast. There were a few issues which assumed more than normal importance, and of these, the key one had to do with Quebec's position on various aspects of social services. The Prime Minister had sent John Munro to Quebec on a number of occasions to try and determine just what Quebec was looking for in terms of concessions on various welfare programs. The general consensus brought back by Munro, and confirmed by Jean Marchand and top officials, was that it might be possible to get a deal on the patriation of the constitution if the federal government was prepared to make concessions on key issues in the social welfare field such as family allowances. The basic question for the federal government was whether to give up the right to distribute family allowances to all children in Canada. This was rejected out of hand, but a compromise emerged involving, among other things, an agreement that Quebec or any other province could, within certain limitations, indicate to the federal government how monies earmarked for family allowances in a province were to be distributed. In other words, the federal government would set down certain sums which would be available to each province. Within this framework, the federal government would be guided to a degree by how the provincial government felt the money should be distributed, for example, among different age groups. There would be a national minimum below which no province could go in its payments to individual children, but there would be a certain amount of flexibility.

Another possibility advanced at the conference was the prospect that, under the Canada Assistance Plan, changes could be made which would enable Quebec or any other province to use the Canada Assistance Plan as a base for the establishment of a form of guaranteed income. However, any province wishing to follow this route would have to dip deeply into its own coffers.

Both measures were discussed in cabinet, first in the presence of the Prime Minister and, on other occasions, in committee meetings where he was not present. I think it is fair to say that there was no great enthusiasm on the part of ministers for the creation of federal social service programs which would result in wide discrepancies in payments to citizens in different parts of Canada. Here, once again, emerged that unspoken feeling that we were taking special actions in order to accommodate Quebec since, from all accounts, no other provinces were seeking similar concessions. Yet there was a real desire on the part of all of us to assist the Prime Minister in carrying out the Victoria conference successfully, and to have as one of our accomplishments the patriation of the constitution prior to the next federal election. So it was that, after prolonged and intricate discussions at the federal level, as well as exploratory talks with representatives of the province of Quebec, it was concluded that if we could get Quebec to agree to a formula on the constitution, the Prime Minister would be prepared to offer concessions in exchange. Others of us insisted that there be a quid pro quo of Quebec agreement, and that any variations agreed on with regard to social welfare programs would be offered to all provinces, whether or not they were interested in them. This was the situation as the Victoria conference opened, and much of what happened from that point on is now history. Quebec politicians, and particularly Bourassa, vacillated considerably during the discussions; unable to make up their minds, they finally asked for two weeks for further consultations at the provincial level. Ultimately, when the period was up, they announced that they could not accept the formula as proposed in Victoria and agreed to by all other nine provinces and the federal government.

In the interim between the conference itself and the end of the two-week period, there was a great deal of exchange between Ottawa and Quebec, and many cabinet meetings aimed at devising some method through which Bourassa could not only save face, but agree to the constitutional proposals as well. Personally, I had no hope whatsoever that he would be cooperative or that he would be able to sell any compromise to his colleagues in the Quebec government.

At that time, there appeared to be general agreement that Bourassa's government was exceedingly weak, and that Bourassa himself was incapable of making up his mind or of carrying through with the commitments he personally made to the federal government. Jean Marchand in particular was consistent in denouncing Bourassa as a weak character. This worried many of us, as it appeared that Marchand, who was assuming a most important role at the provincial level, and who was clearly a liaison between the federal government and Quebec, might soon find himself in the impossible position of having to represent two fundamentally opposite points of view.

When the Victoria conference ended, Trudeau reported to cabinet briefly on what had transpired, but as was customary on such occasions, did not engage in a lengthy post-mortem. Nor did he give us any personal assessment of the key issues. Indeed, he tended to brush the whole thing aside, saying, in effect: you heard what went on; there is really not much more that I can report.

Trudeau did virtually the same thing with his trip to the Soviet Union and his earlier discussions with Commonwealth leaders it Singapore. He was not disposed to brief his colleagues in detail, rehash what had been done, or even explain some of his statements while abroad on official business. In this regard, a most difficult moment occurred as a result of his Moscow announcement that he was preparing to sign an accord with the Soviet government. On the morning following the appearance of this item in the news, there was a cabinet meeting presided over by Mitchell Sharp. Some of us queried how the Prime Minister could make such an announcement when, as far as we were aware, no such decision had been made in cabinet, and there had been virtually no discussion of such an accord or policy. Mitchell Sharp was obviously embarrassed by these questions and said that the whole business had come up at the last moment. Most of us had the impression that even Mitchell himself had not had a great deal of prior notice. Don Macdonald, especially upset by this particular turn of events, indicated that he felt that the Prime Minister should not have signed the accord in

Moscow without consulting his colleagues since this marked a significant change in policy. He said that it might be a change for the better, but that, nonetheless, we could not judge this because the matter had not been thrashed out at the cabinet level. He went so far as to ask that the minutes record his displeasure with the way the Prime Minister had handled the matter, a move of the kind that is rare in cabinet.

When Trudeau returned, he made some off-handed reference to this aspect of his Russian trip, but he did not go into detail. I had no doubt that he and Macdonald discussed the matter privately and probably with some acrimony. In late June, when I asked Macdonald how he was making out with the Prime Minister, he replied that their relationship at the moment was distinctly cool.

This coolness, incidentally, was not due entirely, or even largely, to the Russian incident; it sprang more from Don's frustration over his inability to get detailed cabinet consideration of his white paper on defence. On two or three occasions during the spring, this item was on the agenda of cabinet and cabinet committee meetings, but on each occasion, for some reason or other the Prime Minister was not prepared to deal with it. Either there was another matter of greater urgency or, perhaps, there was something about the paper itself he did not particularly like. In any event, on one occasion when Don Macdonald showed up in cabinet prepared to discuss the matter only to find that it had been postponed again, he left the room, and it was quite clear that quite a huff had developed between him and Trudeau.

The real highlight of the spring was, of course, the bringing down of Ben Benson's budget which incorporated the final decisions regarding tax reform. The actual presentation was scheduled for Friday evening, June 18, after the banks and markets had closed. There was an enormous amount of expectancy evident in and around the Commons and, certainly, the speech itself lived up to its advance billing. Ben was not the world's greatest orator and was simply not capable of injecting a large amount of drama into his speeches. In this case, however, the document made up for any deficiencies in the reader. Even those of us who had worked on tax reform for the best part of two years and who could claim authorship of particular reforms or changes, did not comprehend the magnitude of the package we had been putting together or the general appeal it would have. The opposition parties were genuinely shaken by the decisions announced by Benson. Apart from the occasional catcall, they listened in silence through what turned out to be a nearly four hour address by the Finance Minister. Our own troops, the Liberal backbenchers, were positively ecstatic as they heard the various announcements, proving with what amazing speed the mood of the government's supporters can change when they get even a hint that things are going their way. Time after time, they cheered the

Benson proposals and directed caustic remarks in the direction of the opposition which, of course, had been forecasting a much more gloomy document than the one presented.

All in all, it was a night of triumph for Benson. I doubted that he would ever experience anything like it again during his political career; nor did he expect to. He received nothing but congratulations afterwards in his office where the usual party was held, and on the following day at a special caucus of Liberal supporters, we were treated to the unusual spectacle of a Minister of Finance entering a room to a standing ovation from the backbenchers.

Ironically, less than a week before, there had been bad blood in caucus, so much of it that you could practically cut the atmosphere with a knife, and much of it was directed toward Ben Benson. Such is the lot of the Minister of Finance, and Ben was entitled to revel in the brief respite that the occasion offered him.

Looking back on the exercise of tax reform, I doubt very much that it should have been undertaken in the first place. Granted, the initial decision was that of the Diefenbaker government. However, having received the report, we were perhaps making a mistake in deciding to put together a total package and presenting it in one legislative lump. In retrospect, I think that we would have been better off had we proceeded over a period of time to introduce measures piecemeal. Yet the exercise was by no means a failure. I believe that its main usefulness, apart from the changes to the tax system, was that it made it possible to advance proposals and trust that they were merely for consideration and that the government was prepared to change them in light of public opinion. In terms of real value, I would say that the tax reform exercise did more to advance the cause of participatory democracy than all of the other projects that we had undertaken during the previous three years of our administration.

Following the introduction of the budget accompanying the tax reform proposals, there ensued the usual budget debate. However, this did not generate very much heat; nor was there a great deal of negative media and press reaction.

It was now mid-June, and everyone was looking forward to the closing of the House at the end of the month and a break from parliamentary activities, even though ministers would work even harder during the month of July. There were one or two last minute developments. John Munro finally managed to get clearance to announce a ban on cigarette advertising, but not until I had won my point that the ban should not be confined to broadcast media only, but should extend to all forms of advertising. While John accepted this view with some reluctance, it was the one that carried the judgement of the cabinet members, most of whom would have probably been happy if

John had shelved the matter, falling back on the valid explanation of a crowded calendar. In any event, he managed to get the bill in for first reading.

In the dying days of the House, John Munro also announced changes in the family allowance plan. Although this required approval of an additional allocation of one hundred and fifty million dollars more than what was foreseen in the White Paper on Social Security, the additional funds would allow for a more palatable package where the cut-off point for family allowances would not be as low an income level as previously. I continued to be concerned over the growing tendency of so much of social legislation to zero in on what might be called the middle classes—that is, the middle-income earners who had both limited cash and considerable obligations in terms of mortgages, education, and other family responsibilities. Through one piece of legislation or another, they were being clipped for an extra few dollars here and there so that we could give more to those on the lower end of the income scale. And while I have never been opposed to helping the poor, I felt in this instance that we must soon move to assess the total impact of all our programs on the middle class. They were, after all, the majority of the population, and if we were to be perfectly selfish in our motives, some of them were consistent supporters of the Liberal Party.

During the spring I had an exceedingly busy time in the ministry. While no purpose would be served in attempting to record the day-to-day developments in the Ministry of Transport, there are two achievements—if I may call them that—which gave me considerable satisfaction at the time. I was able to convince my colleagues to undertake experiments involving short-takeoff aircraft, and while I could see numerous pitfalls ahead for this project, I was convinced that it had merit, and I was glad to be able to secure the necessary funds for it. As well, I finally managed to make some kind of breakthrough in terms of a new harbours policy for Canada. Again, while I was sure there would be trouble ahead in trying to make this policy work, I at least had it past the hurdle of cabinet approval and in a position where it was largely up to me whether or not it worked.

It was with considerable relief that I and, I suspect, all of my colleagues saw the House of Commons rise for the summer at the end of June. It had been a rough session, the worst in many respects that we had had; so many issues seemed to break more or less simultaneously for the cabinet, and for each of us as ministers. These collectively made up what could properly be described as "the winter of our discontent." I hoped that we had, indeed, passed through the worst of it and could now start to get ourselves in shape for the next election.

Eleven

I resumed my writing on September 11, 1971. During the period since mid-March, it had not been possible for me to record my recollections on a regular basis. The period in question was without a doubt the most hectic and, in many respects, the most difficult one the government had experienced. Personally, I found it to be a very trying phase of my political career, and one which I was sure I would look back on without any degree of enthusiasm or joy.

From notes and from memory, I attempted to record what had been the undoubted highlights of the four or five months since my last writing. The overriding impression I retain from the period is one of considerable uncertainty and a great deal of frustration within government because the economy did not respond in the way that some of our advisors, and at least some ministers, thought it would.

What was probably the low point for the administration came during the early spring from mid-March until June. It was then that unemployment figures reached their highest point, fuelling the opposition's efforts to discredit us. I must say that I felt that the Tories were scoring points on the issue of unemployment, and were looking good for the first time since the election. I do not think that Stanfield could take much credit for the situation; in fact, his own handling of the issue in the House of Commons and on various public platforms had been something less than brilliant. But we had laid a ready-made issue in his lap, and the Party would have to have been even more incompetent than it was if it didn't make some progress as a result.

I had been interested in observing the performance of John Lundrigan during this period. Assigned to the job of unemployment critic by Stanfield some months ago, he had, in terms of the narrow interpretation of the role of opposition spokesman, done extremely well in needling the government and in getting the Prime Minister's goat. The result, of course, had been a sizeable amount of publicity against the government in the news media. Lundrigan was by far the best known and most active of the Newfoundland Tories during this period, and this raised questions in my mind as to how the hierarchy of the Newfoundland Tories would develop should its fortunes improve.

The difficulties we encountered as a result of economic issues had produced an interesting phenomenon as far as the media were concerned. I had been fascinated by the near unanimity of the press gallery writers, columnists and editorialists. The situation continued to confirm my growing conviction that there is a kind of "group think" that takes place within the press gallery, that the newsmen and editors do not really understand most of the complicated issues, and that they tend to draw on each other for support for what they write. There appears to be a certain amount of protection in numbers and in unanimity. Thus, we found that on almost every major issue, there was very little of the old-fashioned taking of sides that used to make newspaper reading such an interesting experience. Now, if it was established that there was an economic crisis and that the government was responsible, virtually every newspaper and radio and television commentator tended to take the same line.

There was throughout the spring no special meeting at which the economic situation and the employment figures were discussed. Instead, these matters ran like a thread through practically everything else that was done, and we were all kept hanging on, waiting for the doldrum months of winter and spring to pass, and for the inevitable upturn, at least in public mood, to take place. This did not happen as rapidly as anticipated. In fact, as the spring wore on, there was one month when the figures released by Statistics Canada were actually worse than the previous month, and this naturally caused great consternation. I felt that the Prime Minister adopted the proper course under the circumstances when he refused to be stampeded into any precipitate action or crash program. Such action would not have had significant impact, but might have actually been harmful to the government's position and image; it would have suggested both a reaction to the opposition, and a loss of control over the situation. From April on, I kept repeating at every opportunity that the big chance we had to change the public's impression of us regarding the economy and unemployment occurred when Ben Benson finally brought in his tax reform package and related budget. I was also determined to the best of my ability to prevent the House of Commons from sitting during the long summer months in order to deal with the tax measures. Early in the spring, I wrote a letter to the Prime Minister expressing my view, and urging that he support my position calling for a summer recess after the budget was introduced. Subsequently, he told me that he agreed with my position, but that he did not wish to raise the question of timing in cabinet while preparation of the tax reform speech and the companion legislation was still under way. He said that if officials received even a hint that the pressure of a June deadline was off, then we would never get the work completed. I agreed with him, but we had a private understanding that, at the appropriate time, the question of our subsequent strategy would be brought forth and the idea of a summer recess would be fully supported by him.

Throughout this period, we were also getting the customary reports from officials regarding the likely performance of the economy in the months and years ahead. I have recorded on previous occasions my lack of satisfaction with these sessions. It is not that the officials were incompetent or even that they were inclined to put the best face on the general outlook. It was simply that they were still far too conventional in their approaches and techniques, and that they had not recognized sufficiently the new forces at work in the world which made many of the old forecasting techniques ineffective. Be that as it may, the general forecasts we had been shown in recent months tended to predict a strengthening of the economy and a general decline in levels of unemployment. Of course, this would not be a dramatic decline, and it would mean that during the coming winter, we would have just as many unemployed as the year before. Any reduction of the percentage unemployed would be offset by a larger work force. The question that remained unresolved was whether or not the government could accept a level of unemployment of about six percent, or whether, before winter, we would be prepared to examine new and perhaps even drastic measures that might cut the figure significantly.

There was no doubt that the economic issue—or to be more precise, the unemployment issue—had become the overriding concern of most ministers, who saw it as the basis on which we would be judged by the public regardless of anything else we might do. It was ironic that so much of the Trudeau image had been tarnished by what was one of the oldest political issues used by opposition parties to score on the government. On the non-economic side, ours had been a most innovative and liberal government, and we had a good record to our credit with more to come. Yet so much of this was lost and forgotten as day after day the media and the politicians kept harping on the jobless figures. My own view was that we could live even with the high levels of unemployment except for the fact that the Prime Minister, with his usual candour and with what I still feel was an abnormal degree of political naïveté, had not assumed responsibility for the unemployment situation. Some of his utterances of the last year or so had given the opposition the opportunity to damn us as the conscious creators of unemployment because of our fixation with inflation.

This, of course, was a gross misinterpretation of Trudeau's and the government's attitude, and it may very well have been that the Prime Minister's frankness in this matter improved his credibility on other questions of substance when he commented on these publicly. But as things stood at the moment, it was very easy for the opposition to point to the jobless figures and then tie these to Trudeau's on-the-record comment that he would tolerate unemployment at six percent in order to lick inflation. No doubt future students of political history will examine this period and this issue with fascination.

It was interesting to observe the reactions of my cabinet colleagues toward everything that happened during those months. I haven't the slightest doubt that most of them felt, as I have said above, that much of our difficulty at that time was due both to Trudeau's ineptness in making public comments and to his fixation with the issue of inflation. In ranging across the ministers, I cannot think of many who were intellectually on the side of Trudeau in this overall exercise, or who did not feel that he had committed a gaffe in some of his public comments. The exceptions might be Ben Benson, Bud Drury and, to some extent, myself. But Trudeau's domination of the cabinet was all but complete, and there was no minister that I can think of who would have been prepared to come out at a cabinet meeting and say that it was Trudeau himself who got us into so much of our trouble.

There were occasions when, although no comment was made publicly, I could sense that the Prime Minister was sensitive to the possibility of such a charge. He often commented somewhat ruefully on the lack of wisdom involved in public utterances, but in a more serious vein, he sometimes asked rhetorically what else we could have done over the previous two years if we had not chosen the strong anti-inflation route. He and I had exchanged words on this question on two or three occasions. For example, when discussing the posture we were to adopt in the new budget, I made some references to this being a good time to introduce new policies. His retort was that he could not conceive of very much in the way of new policies that we could bring forward and that, in fact, we would simply reaffirm that we had been right all along, and that we had no choice but to move against inflation as we did. I argued that it was pointless for us to try and defend the past, and that what I had in mind was that the budget could be presented and delivered in such a way that it would give the government a new look. It could indicate that we were willing to pursue more expansionist policies, and that we had a sympathetic concern for the unemployed and a determination to do everything possible to alleviate their problems.

Arising out of this and similar discussions came what was for me the most fruitful and beneficial part of the whole dialogue—a growing awareness that, realistically, we had to find new, or at least additional, ways of determining the economic health of the country. Raw statistics on unemployment were no longer very meaningful since so many types of people could register as unemployed and since unemployment itself did not necessarily mean poverty, given the range of social welfare measures in place. By the same token, there were people who were actually working who were in more difficult straits than those who showed up on the unemployment rolls. I and several other ministers had been quite surprised by the unsophisticated ways in which we continued to measure unemployment, and by the lack of statistical information we had with which to assess the health of the economy. This would have to be corrected as quickly as possible because, with the new unemployment insurance measures passed during the year and the improvement of other social welfare schemes, it would be possible in future to have large numbers of people on the unemployment rolls in the traditional sense and yet not have widespread deprivation. It might even be possible at the same time to have a healthy and highly productive economy.

There were some silly anomalies in the statistics we were using; however, it was impossible to expose them publicly because we would simply be accused of trying to doctor the books. Nevertheless, the Committee on Priorities and Planning directed Otto Lang's Department of Manpower and Immigration to start preparing new data that would give us a more realistic profile of the unemployed. We had also asked Finance to try and devise new yardsticks through which we could better measure the general relationship between unemployment and productivity.

Once again, I must reiterate my objections to what I can only describe as the conventionality of many top level officials. Throughout all our troubles with the unemployment issue, they did not appear to be the least disposed to pursue the kind of routes I have outlined. They were content to keep on doing things the routine way no matter how many distortions new developments brought to the final results.

Apart from a period during the Easter holidays when my wife and I made a fascinating and thoroughly enjoyable visit to Israel, my main preoccupation during the spring, outside of departmental responsibilities, was with the final stages of tax reform. It is pointless to attempt to record here all of the individual subjects discussed at a whole series of meetings of the Committee on Tax Reform. It is sufficient to say that, in the majority of cases, I was able to have my own views prevail when the proposals of the committee differed from what I felt ought to be done. I must say that this success was due at least in good measure to the fact that Ben Benson himself was convinced that many of the more dramatic aspects of his white paper could not be implemented at that time, and that he would not get either parliamentary or public acceptance of the package without substantial revision of some of its basic schemes. In any event, over a period stretching from early winter until May, the committee met regularly and we were able to take the sharp edges off most of the controversial issues such as capital gains and credit arrangements. Perhaps the most significant decision of the committee was to have the federal government withdraw entirely from the estate and gift tax fields. This, I was sure, would be very popular, not perhaps with large numbers of people, but with most of the opinion makers. It was, I think, one of the things which helped us to sell the package eventually.

Once the final version of the tax reform paper was put together and polished, there arose the necessity of deciding on a parliamentary timetable. In the Committee on Priorities and Planning, there was a good deal of argument, with Ben Benson feeling at first that we should abandon at summer recess and press on with the budgetary measures until completion. Eventually, however, he came around to what was a more widely held committee view and one which I supported—that we should have the House rise for the months of July and August and come back immediately following Labour Day to begin the debate on tax reform. I think that everyone was pleased that this was the ultimate decision, and it later went through cabinet with very few objections. Caucus, too, welcomed the plan when Ben advanced it to them.

At this particular point in time, the caucus was in a most difficult mood. The unemployment figures and resultant criticism were making them anxious, and there was a general feeling that we were, in some way or other, out of touch with the public. Some of the more vocal members were flatly forecasting that we would be defeated in the next election. There were one or two caucus meetings in particular where the mood was very nasty, and where veterans like Paul Martin said that they could not recall a similar situation during all their days in Parliament. It was during this time that the first open criticisms of Trudeau were voiced in Parliament; unfortunately, this was done while the Prime Minister was in Russia. Perhaps it was his absence that made some members bold enough to speak out against some of Trudeau's statements and actions. In any event, it was not a good period, and about all that experienced members could say was that it was inevitable during the life of any Parliament that there be a down time for the government and the caucus, and this was undoubtedly it. Also, it was far better to have such a low point in the third year of the administration rather than in an election year.

During the winter and spring, the mood of caucus was also soured by the government's failure to act on the question of pay raises for members of Parliament. This was a very problematic issue, but one with overtones of comedy. In many respects, it revealed how bad most of us in politics can be when it comes to assessing likely public reaction.

The pay issue had been around for a number of years, and immediately after the Trudeau government was elected, demands for an increase started all over again. The first year or two, when it might have been easier to make a decision, saw us in the midst of the anti-inflation fight and the government judged, quite rightly in my view, that it could not ask for restraints from the public and then turn around and grant itself a significant pay raise. Then there was the problem that the NDP became holier-than-thou over this kind of issue, even though they wanted the money as much as anyone else. One could never be sure when putting a proposal forward whether the NDP would denounce it or not. In any event, after fudging the question for a couple of years while the discontent of the caucus grew, and while we waited for the Beaupré Commission's report on the question, we finally realized that we had to make a decision one way or the other.

There is no point in recording all of the controversies that arose. There were divisions in cabinet. British Columbia members were largely opposed to an increase at this time, whereas Quebec members were unanimous in wanting to put it through. Between these two extremes, there were perhaps a dozen variations of opinion. A key figure in getting the matter resolved was Harold Stafford, our member for Elgin, Ontario, and chairman of the Ontario caucus. He not only lobbied our own members but was active with the opposition, and finally, when we learned that there would be no strong criticism from the Tories, cabinet decided in principle to go ahead. Having done so, however, there was the question of what kind of increase to introduce, and Allan MacEachen had the thankless task of trying to produce a formula that would meet with everyone's approval.

Perhaps the most troublesome matter of principle centred around whether or not members of Parliament should be accountable for their expenses. The Beaupré Commission had recommended that members should be paid certain expenses for living and travel in their constituencies, but that vouchers or receipts for such expenditures should be submitted before payment was made. A number of ministers expressed strong objections to this technique. They questioned who was going to pass judgement on whether or not a member's expenses were legitimate. Should it be the Speaker of the House or a committee established by the Speaker? Or would it be left to some civil servant to tell a member whether or not a particular claim would be allowed. I personally could see some logic in this argument, but I was not overwhelmingly in support of it. I objected to the voucher system for a more practical reason. I said that I was quite sure that it would only be a matter of time before some member would try to cheat on his expense account, and once this happened, it would become a cause célèbre throughout the country, and we would all be tarred with the same brush. Also, I saw the inevitability of a member of Parliament demanding that the expense accounts of all MPs be made public. This would result in unfair comparisons, and MPs would be put in the position of having to explain either why they had spent a great deal of money or, conversely, why they had not done enough travelling in their constituencies to have accumulated sizeable expenses. Because of this, I agreed with those who favoured a fixed amount for expenditures without a direct accounting procedure. I do not have an accurate account of how many hours cabinet and cabinet committees spent on this issue, but I do know that on many occasions, I found myself frustrated and even a little amazed. Here we were—the twenty or so men charged with running the country—consuming hour after hour of valuable time debating a relatively minor question while vital issues remained unresolved.

From the outset, Trudeau was very anxious to do something for members of Parliament. He believed that unless pay was increased, we would lose a number of good members in the next election because they simply would not run again. Also, we would find it increasingly difficult to get new, competent candidates to run if we did not make the job sufficiently attractive. The upshot of the whole tortuous, protracted and sometimes silly exercise was that, in the end, all of the complicated formulae were tossed out, and we decided on a straightforward increase both in basic pay and allowances.

It was interesting to observe Trudeau's final reaction to all of this. I have noted time and time again that, where an important issue was concerned, he would allow an interminable amount of time for debate, far more, I think, than was necessary. During the period of debate, he made few personal interventions and usually refrained from expressing a definite point of view which would require dissenting colleagues to cross swords with him. Finally, however, as in the case of the pay increases, Trudeau would often act impetuously and, at a given point would say, in effect, what the hell, let's do it in such and such a way. Generally, before he reached this point, he would have noted from the discussion that there appeared to be a significant majority in favour of the point of view eventually adopted. Even now, I am far from certain whether this constituted a well-planned technique whereby, having reached certain conclusions privately, he seized the appropriate moment to solidify them into a cabinet decision, or whether he simply got fed up with the discussion and decided that the moment had come to end it.

Reaction to the announcement of the pay increases was predictable. The NDP expressed their opposition as did some of our own members, one or two Conservatives, and, in a rather brazen fashion, the Creditists. However, I had no doubt that they were all taking the increases and were darn glad to get them. There was not as much public outcry as some had expected. Harking back to my earlier observation about the failure of many politicians to forecast accurately, a number of British Columbia members who had predicted problems if they took the raise later confessed privately that their noble stand did them no good whatsoever, and they regretted their commitment to hand the money over to charity or return it to the government.

Another interesting observation on this whole exercise is that, prior to the decision, many people said that the reason caucus was proving difficult and critical of the government was that members resented our failure to give them a raise. Yet the pay raise decision was well known prior to the rough caucus meetings where the government was raked over the coals unmercifully because of its economic policies. The lesson is presumably this: when things are bad at home, and the MP is getting pressure from constituents, nothing the government does for him is likely to reduce his concern for his own skin; he will proceed to roast the government, at least in caucus, whether or not he gets a raise, additional office space, or whatever.

While the dominant issue of the economy and unemployment was building to a climax, and while we were putting finishing touches on the tax reform policies and legislation, Trudeau was in the Soviet Union. There was more than the normal amount of reporting of this visit because a very large press corps travelled with the Trudeaus. Yet it did not appear that the visit aroused any great amount of interest on the part of the Canadian public. If the public was interested, it was more concerned with what Margaret Trudeau was doing than with her husband's diplomatic exploits. Nevertheless, it can be said in retrospect that the trip was very successful.

While the trip was under way, Paul Hellyer took his inevitable last step out of the Liberal Party. He announced in the House of Commons that he wanted to be identified as an independent Liberal, and during the days that followed, he launched a strange new movement called Action Canada. The cabinet was at least mildly concerned over the first rumours of what Hellyer intended to do. There was no panic or feeling that we should devise a strategy of our own against Action Canada, but before the details were known, there was an understandable degree of concern that a significant number of influential people might join Paul in denouncing the party and in criticizing the government. For these reasons, the reports of Paul's first press conference to launch Action Canada were awaited with something more than the normal curiosity. Once the conference was held and turned out to be a failure, there was considerable incredulity among cabinet ministers that Hellyer would go to such extremes and create such expectations for so little ultimate result. The Hellyer movement was especially intriguing because it apparently had the support of some who were known to have a long association with the moral rearmament movement. This tended to reaffirm in my mind the view that I had held for some time: that, despite all of the public protestations he made regarding his reasons for leaving cabinet and subsequently the Liberal Party, Hellyer's basic reason was a conviction that the Prime Minister and a number of those around him were dangerously left wing, if not outright communists.

Some of Paul's statements following his resignation recalled for me an encounter I had with him during the cabinet debate on the question of Canada's role in NATO. Paul and I had met in the hall outside the cabinet room following one of the special meetings held on the subject. I confessed to being a bit perplexed and uncertain about what ought to be done in the circumstances. Paul immediately suggested that he and I should waste no time in having a private meeting because, he said, there were things going on which were quite alarming. He was quite enigmatic and made no specific accusations and identified no individuals, but he felt that there were sinister leftist elements at work within government and, particularly, in the Prime Minister's Office. If my assessment is correct, this probably explains to some extent why supporters of moral rearmament were among those backing Hellyer's new cause. In any event, it appeared to be pretty much of a fizzle; from all accounts, Paul had been drawing sparse crowds at his public meetings, and there had been a number of key people, such as Reid Scott of Toronto, who had left his party already.

At a cabinet committee meeting subsequent to the Hellyer resignation, Jim Davey of the Prime Minister's Office expressed the view that we should not underestimate Hellyer, and that, in fact, he might very well have identified one of the problems of our time and could conceivably become the catalyst for many dissatisfied and disaffected people. This may have been true, but I had definite doubts that Paul Hellyer was the man to polarize this undoubtedly widespread attitude. He was sincere in his beliefs, but devoid of a sense of humour. There was a coldness and aloofness about him that, in my opinion, made him very doubtful leadership material for a protest movement, let alone a type of missionary undertaking that would lead Canadians into a promised land.

Potentially more troublesome for the government in many ways was the late April resignation of Eric Kierans. I had had mixed feelings about Eric ever since we both joined the cabinet at the same time. He was my seatmate in cabinet, and I think it is fair to say that we developed quite an affection for each other over the nearly three years that we sat together. Kierans' resignation did not surprise me at all; what was ironic was that a year or so before, during the crisis surrounding the Lapalme drivers in Montreal, I received a frantic phone call one morning from Kierans' special assistant, Richard Quinn. Quinn told me that Eric had decided to resign, and he asked me if I would get in touch with him and try to talk him out of it since, Quinn maintained, I was one of the few people to whom he might listen. At that point, Eric's reputation as a minister was at a low ebb. He was being roundly condemned for his handling of the Post Office situation, and both Mackasey and Marchand were very much opposed to his actions, particularly in the province of Quebec. As a result of the Quinn phone call, I did contact Eric and initially got a commitment from him that he would at least consider my advice. During the same morning, there was a meeting of the Committee on Priorities and Planning chaired by the Prime Minister. Late in the meeting, Trudeau, who had left for a time, returned and asked, "Well, which one of the ministers do you think has resigned?" I, being aware of the background, immediately replied, "Kierans."

There was, I think, a feeling of genuine regret amongst the ministers present that Eric was pulling out, and Bud Drury and myself got the Prime Minister's blessing to attempt to talk him into changing his mind. We contacted him at home by telephone, and Bud and I each spoke to him through a loudspeaker phone arrangement in Bud's office. Eric was obviously agitated and said repeatedly, "I appreciate what you fellows are trying to do, but I wish you'd leave me alone." Nevertheless, I think that our conversations with Eric had a beneficial effect, and later that afternoon Eric met with the Prime Minister and decided to withdraw his resignation. It was probably Trudeau himself who really clinched matters, but he might not have been able to do so if Bud and I had not softened Eric up first. In any event, had he gone at the time, he would have been classed as a failure, and I have sometimes thought that it was quite a twist to see columnists and others referring to Eric Kierans as one of the most capable of the Trudeau ministers.

I suppose the writing was really on the wall for Kierans during the cabinet shuffle of the fall of 1970, when Trudeau split Kierans' department and took responsibility for the Post Office away from him. No matter how many explanations were given for the reasons for this change, it had to be a blow to Eric Kierans, and I would be willing to bet that he made up his mind then that he would get out when the proper moment presented itself. I believe that there were two major developments that contributed to his decision. First, there were the revisions to the tax reform white paper which, in his view, were too lenient to the resource industries, and particularly to mining, oil and gas. Then there was the Home Oil deal which, although it didn't go through, revealed that the government would have been prepared to take the kind of action recommended by Joe Greene and buy the company to keep it

Canadian. Kierans felt that from a business standpoint, the government was really getting the worst of that proposition. But the matter of principle to which he objected was that the offer made by the government to Brown, the principal shareholder, would not be available to all other shareholders. This, he felt, was morally improper even if it was legally acceptable. As it turned out, we did not have to move in the Home Oil case but I am sure that discussions surrounding the issue soured Eric still further.

Despite all of this, what is most surprising is that Eric, though a member of most of the cabinet committees dealing with economic matters, was not particularly active in any deliberations and did not in his cabinet interventions express with vehemence the views that he subsequently uttered about how the government was deciding economic policy. I myself must have been present on a hundred or more occasions when Eric and the rest of us engaged in discussions with key officials such as Simon Reisman, Bob Bryce and others. I do not recall any serious disagreement between Kierans and these officials who, I presume, were the ones he subsequently referred to as being too long in their jobs, too unimaginative and, for all practical purposes, unfit for the important positions which they held. The point I am making is that I believe Eric had plenty of opportunity to challenge the proposals put forward by the officials and others, but that with one or two exceptions, notably the Home Oil case and some aspects of tax reform, he was not one of the more active members of either the Economic Policy Committee or the Government Operations Committee. I can only assume, therefore, that in the last year or so, he had already made up his mind as to what he wanted to do. Having concluded, as he later told a newsman, that he was going to get out, he had lost much of his drive and interest. This, I suppose, is consistent with his history. He had never remained very long in any one spot, and whenever he had, he had tended to rock the boat to a great extent. In fact, in the case of his years in the Quebec government, there were many who held him primarily responsible for the defeat of Premier Jean Lesage.

Eric Kierans was one of the most interesting people that I met during my years in politics, a likeable man with an undoubtedly brilliant mind. However, apart from his lack of staying power, there was also his temperament, which tended on many occasions to prompt him to a dramatic course of action without thinking through all the consequences. I have said repeatedly to various people and in various forums, when talking about my own approach to politics, that a successful and effective public man must not only be able to act; he must have a highly developed ability to anticipate reaction. This I would class as Eric Kierans biggest failing. When a course of action commended itself to him with glaring and irresistible logic, he felt compelled to pursue it to the end, regardless of what difficulties were created in the process. In other words, he did not see politics as the art of the possible, but as a series of dramatic moves which must be taken, although the end result might be the fall of the party from power and the prevention of its being able to carry out its objectives.

As a side note to the Kierans story, I recall that in the summer of 1970, the Prime Minister called me to a private luncheon at his home to discuss a possible shift in the composition of cabinet. We agreed that Don Macdonald had served his time admirably as President of the Privy Council and as House Leader, and that it was time for him to get another portfolio as Trudeau had promised him. As with most cabinet shifts, taking one man out of a particular spot in the line-up usually sets in motion a whole series of changes, and the exercise becomes increasingly complex. On this occasion, Trudeau asked me who should succeed Macdonald as House Leader. I had heard already that there were those who felt that I would be suitable for the job, but having been in Transport for only a year, I had no wish to change. Furthermore, although I got by reasonably well in Parliament, I was a long way from being a House of Commons man in the traditional sense. Therefore, I quickly took advantage of the Prime Minister's offer to choose a portfolio of my own liking by saying that I wanted to stay where I was. I then recommended Allan MacEachen for House Leader and told the Prime Minister that I would help him in every way I could to get Allan to accept. We then moved to the question of who would be moved into the Manpower portfolio and what other changes might be possible.

The Prime Minister felt that it might be wise to move John Munro from Health and Welfare; this was, in fact, his first choice for Don Macdonald's new portfolio. He told me, too, of Léo Cadieux's interest in the job of Ambassador to France, and we discussed briefly the possible retirement of such cabinet members as George McIlraith and Arthur Laing. But the interesting part of the discussion as it relates to Eric Kierans is that, although we agreed that Eric could not remain as postmaster general, given the problems that had developed during his tenure, we could not, for the life of us, see another portfolio which Eric could hold down without causing even greater potential difficulty.

Twelve

I began to write again on December 11, 1971, following a period of almost six months during which, for a variety of reasons, I had not been able to record my impressions of events in and around government and Parliament. What I have included here, therefore, is not meant to be a complete and detailed record, but a general recollection of a most remarkable period in the life of the Trudeau government.

Immediately following the adjournment of the House at the end of June, most ministers and their wives, including Pierre and Margaret Trudeau, flew to Victoria for the July 1 ceremonies connected with British Columbia's Centennial. It was not an especially memorable occasion; the various events were dull and unimaginative and lacked the life and sparkle of the celebrations held a year earlier in Manitoba.

During the visit, I had to meet with a number of protest groups and spend a day in Tom Good's riding. Although apparently I give the impression of being "hail fellow, well met," I do not really enjoy back-slapping, handshaking sessions. And as for the protest groups, I had, as time went on, less and less faith in this particular form of "participatory democracy." In any event, it was not a very happy beginning for the summer.

The following day, however, was the beginning of three or four of the happiest days of the year for me. Barbara, Allan Baker and I flew to Calgary where we were joined by Al and Marg Waters. After I had opened a nearby airport, we flew north to Yellowknife and then, having transferred to a DC3, to Great Bear Lake for the night. The hope had been for a few hours of fishing, but although the two Allans went out under the midnight sun to try their luck, they got nothing and my decision not to join them was vindicated. On the following morning, we travelled on to Inuvik where we picked up Pat Pierce of the CRTC and flew on to Tuktoyaktuk, the small Inuit village on the shores of the Arctic Ocean. Allan had been persuaded by Dick Roaumer, who was travelling with us, to provide the community with a radio station, and we all participated in the official opening. It was funny, yet regrettable in some ways, that after I had declared the station officially open, the first record played was an American country and western tune. And although the old patriarchs of the village, marvellous looking men of great character, brought their native drums to the assembly hall, and the local priest urged the young people to dance to the native music, none did so. We were told that hardly any of them knew or were interested in native culture. They preferred the music and dancing of the rest of North America. I could not help but feel that most efforts at retaining their culture and way of life were doomed to failure. Modern influences had become pervasive across most of the Arctic that I had seen, and the native people were really a most tragic group—caught between the old and the new, and not really capable at this stage of grasping either.

The highlight of the trip was a voyage from Tuktoyaktuk, which everyone calls "Tuk," back to Inuvik along the Mackenzie River by tug and barge. The cruise took about two nights and a day but, of course, it was daylight all the time in July. The river and the surrounding scenery were magnificent, and I remember hoping that the time would come when more Canadians would see the wonders of this magnificent part of the country.

For Barbara and I, however, the trip would be marred by sadness. While on the tug, we learned that Jack Beck of Swift Current had died. We had known it was coming, of course, but it was still hard to imagine a world in which Jack Beck no longer existed. Some time, perhaps, I will write more of this remarkable Newfoundlander, my first cousin and official agent during the 1938 election. We got back to Swift Current for the funeral, a naturally depressing affair. I was proud to deliver the eulogy. Perhaps it was Jack's death and the subsequent events that put me in a mood that I found myself unable to shake in the months that followed.

My mood of depression, sometimes deep but usually superficial because of my naturally optimistic makeup, was not helped in July as we resumed an intensive series of cabinet meetings, planning for the fall and winter. The euphoria that followed the introduction of Ben Benson's tax bill evaporated rapidly. The Prime Minister, though correct enough in conducting the meetings, showed a certain remoteness. He displayed little capacity for warmth, or for providing the word of encouragement or little joke that can ease the burden of a dull, serious meeting.

Much of the talk early in the month was of the constitutional conference of late June in Victoria. There was a general feeling of depression over Bourassa's rejection, but even more, I think, over the widespread approval in Quebec of the province's actions. Trudeau was frankly puzzled by Bourassa. Basically, he told me, he thought that Bourassa was a weak man who feared his cabinet, especially Claude Castonguay who had great ambitions both for himself and for the welfare programs he wanted to run more and more internally within the province of Quebec. And yet, Trudeau told me, he was sometimes of the view that Bourassa was a shrewd bargainer whom we were grossly underestimating.

The key issue which preoccupied cabinet during most of July was what to do about the offer made to Quebec at Victoria regarding the province sharing in the responsibility for family allowances. I say "offered Quebec," but in truth, if we were to do this for Quebec, we would have to make the same offer to all the provinces, and leave it up to them whether or not they should accept.

The basic proposition was that the federal government would establish certain minimum sums, based on population, to be spent on family allowances in each province, and set a per child minimum allowance below which no province could go. If Quebec wished to augment the program or change the amounts for different age groups, it would be free to do so. The cheques, including any additional amount contributed by Quebec or any other province, would continue to be sent out by Ottawa with some appropriate reference to provincial participation and contribution.

One result of this whole debate was that John Munro managed to get the basic allocation for family allowances, already augmented in his white paper, increased by another one hundred and fifty million dollars. It was a neat ploy; once the general proposition became known, there was no way we could withdraw the money even if Quebec did not come through on its side of the bargain.

The bargain was initially, of course, that Bourassa would agree to the patriation formula for the constitution. Now, however, we were in the position where the offer on family allowances was out in the open, yet we had no commitment from Bourassa. Indeed, what we had received was, for all practical purposes, a rejection.

The Prime Minister was clearly both disappointed and angry at this turn of events. Yet the Quebec ministers, headed by Jean Marchand, were strong in advocating that the family allowance deal proceed anyway. Consequently, what was at first a bargaining position involving give and take on both sides became a matter of Quebec taking while still uncommitted to give on the constitutional issue.

I voiced strong exception to this approach. I had never liked the idea of the bargain in the first place, feeling that a federal measure designed to give all Canadian children equal treatment could and probably would become distorted in people's minds. They would not understand the subtleties of the situation, and mothers in Newfoundland, for example, would wonder why children in Quebec were getting more. Or an even more likely alternative would be that the poor provinces would be forced to follow Quebec's example. Then we would be back, if only indirectly, to the federal dictation of provincial spending priorities, something which we had previously said was undesirable and should be discouraged.

Nevertheless, before and during the Victoria conference, when the negotiations with Quebec were going on, I was prepared to accept the compromise if it meant getting the constitutional matter settled. Now in July, Victoria was over, Quebec had said no, and we were still talking about the family allowance proposal.

At a cabinet meeting in late November, I talked frankly when the subject arose about the need for the government and the party to reassess its attitude toward the provinces, especially Quebec. I told the Prime Minister that, after extensive travels around the country and based on other evidence, I felt that there was still considerable goodwill toward Quebec among English-speaking Canadians. But there was a growing feeling also that we appeared to be bending over backwards to accommodate Quebec, and Bourassa was showing no disposition to return the favour. I said that this position was becoming increasingly difficult for ministers from the rest of Canada to defend. At some point, we would have to start hitting back, just as we would have to do if the government of Quebec was not Liberal. Trudeau did not disagree, but held to the faint hope that Bourassa might yet come around on the constitution. He said that Bourassa had told him he had a group of ministers working on a possible solution who would advise Trudeau shortly on the results.

Jean Marchand, however, had no hope that Bourassa could persuade his cabinet to change its views. Nevertheless, Marchand saw no alternative to federal acceptance of Quebec's proposals in the welfare field. On the contrary, even without the constitutional and other divisive issues, it was plain that he regarded the Quebec proposals not only as acceptable, but desirable. He saw them as an example of the kind of flexibility that must become commonplace if we were to defuse the power of the separatists.

I had often found Jean as hard to read as Trudeau. Obviously, he was a Quebecer first and a gut politician to boot. His main objective, perhaps the only one in which he believed strongly, was to do everything in his power for Quebec while in office. I, of course, felt the same way about Newfoundland, but I think that I had much more of a feel for the country as a whole than did Jean or any other Quebec minister. As for Trudeau, I simply did not know. Obviously, he had a great preoccupation with Quebec. This was only natural. But I felt that he did see the bigger picture, even to the point of being global in his thinking rather than nationalistic. But as the Scottish saying asserts, "Still the blood is strong." And I am sure that it was difficult, if not impossible, for the Prime Minister to seriously oppose Marchand and Pelletier. And these two, the first passionately, the second in a more detached way, were preoccupied with the separatist problem. I, for one, found it impossible to measure the correctness of this.

Shortly before Christmas, 1971, we were scheduled to meet in the Priorities and Planning Committee to lay the groundwork for the next election and for our position in the period that would follow. There was no doubt that the two overriding issues, in the minds of English-speaking ministers at least, were the economy and the reputation of the party as it related to Quebec. All of us, but particularly John Turner, were concerned about the effect of bilingualism on the public service. We were concerned that we would lose one of our traditional political bases in the Ottawa region as a result of the issue. Would the Quebec ministers agree to a softer line and, if so, was it already too late? This issue was bound to surface in cabinet with more frankness than in the past; it already had in caucus.

I must now revert to the events of July. Apart from the post-mortem on the Victoria conference, the dominant subject for discussion again and again was the economy. There had been a general upsurge in the country following the June budget, but it dissipated quickly as the unemployment figures remained stubbornly high. There were also the first reports of bad handling of the Opportunities for Youth Program with, inevitably, the major mistakes initially getting far more publicity than the overall success of the program.

There was great tension in cabinet and in cabinet committees over Bryce Mackasey's new labour bill and Ron Basford's Competition Act. I saw from the beginning that these would agitate the business community even more than tax reform. A few of us, including Bud Drury, Mitchell Sharp and, lately, Don Macdonald, were concerned about the combined effect of these measures on the business community and on the middle class in general. John Turner had been consistent in voicing his fears about the cumulative effect many of our measures would have on the broadly based middle class.

It was difficult, however, to argue with Mackasey. He became indignant when his judgement was questioned and was not above the odd bit of personal abuse. With many ministers either not understanding his proposals or unwilling to engage in debate with him, there inevitably came a time when I was no longer able—or perhaps willing is a better word—to carry the battle alone. Consequently, when the relatively small vocal opposition evaporated, bills like Mackasey's usually went through with members who had doubts consoling themselves that changes were bound to be made once public opposition emerged.

That is how it was with the competition policy bill. Basford worked very hard on it, and it must have come to committee a dozen times. My complaint, joined by those of other ministers, was that this enormous and important matter had been written largely by people who did not know how the business community operated, and how unreasonably concerned they could be about government actions, and, above all, who were unaware that a great deal of business growth was really discretionary and could be put off indefinitely if the climate was wrong and the business mood one of uncertainty and indecision.

None of this made much of an impression except that, finally, Basford agreed that his bill would get first reading only, and he would make it plain that he was prepared to make changes. In effect, he was using the legislative route to introduce what amounted to a white paper. I felt that even this would cause another furore and further undermine the confidence of business in government. But Basford, like Mackasey, could be very determined, and there usually came a time when all opposition melted away. After all, when a man is chosen to run a department, his views have to take on a certain priority even with the Prime Minister. In this case, I doubt that the Prime Minister fully understood the implications of the two measures; if he had, he might have sent them back for further study. In any event, they were introduced and the rest is history. There can be no doubt that, despite the disclaimers and assurances that changes would be made, these bills combined with high unemployment and the uncertainty over tax measures resulted, over the summer and fall of 1971, in a depressed and depressing period for the government and a resultant rise in the fortunes of Stanfield and the Conservative Party.

As July moved toward its close, the pace of cabinet activity quickened even more. Committees and full cabinet were meeting every day and night, with every minister bringing forward something to be dealt with before the August holiday. This produced the usual performance from the Department of Finance. Throughout all of the early Trudeau administration, but particularly since Simon Reisman became deputy minister, there had been a reluctance by the department, endorsed by Ben Benson, to reveal all of the facts. I had consistently objected to this. Each year, I had predicted accurately that the limits on spending and the general budgetary position outlined by Finance at mid-year would not stand up. I had said, and had been proven right, that petty expenditures we quarrelled about in July would be dwarfed by October when someone pushed the panic button on unemployment. It might have been said that the approach then in use was prudent money management, the only way to keep a reasonable curb on the spending ambitions of various departments. But the result was a charade in which, periodically, keen ministers had to go through a selection process to determine what projects would proceed based on imaginary limits of what funds were or could be made available.

It was in this situation that, at the end of July, a group of exhausted ministers working until two in the morning divided up the supposedly available funds. Fortunately, I was able to get my way on an amount of about sixty million dollars for roads in the Atlantic provinces. Without this allocation, the roads in my own constituency would have remained uncompleted, and my chances for re-election would have been virtually nil. But such is the process of determining government spending, and though I was told that it was now infinitely more sophisticated and forward-looking than in the past, it was far from perfect.

During the last days of July, we also examined and approved Don Macdonald's white paper on defence policy. I had come to admire Don, both personally and as an administrator. In this instance, he had done his homework well and there was little serious opposition in cabinet. One incident, however, serves to reveal a peculiarity of the Prime Minister.

Macdonald wanted a minor revision of a few million dollars in his budget. Most of us saw this as routine; with such a large budget and with the inevitable short-falls in certain types of expenditures, the odds were that by the end of the year, Defence would not have spent all of its allocation. Yet Trudeau made a big issue out of the fact that this represented a departure from the earlier decision to freeze defence spending at 1968 levels for a period of three years. Mitchell Sharp, Ben Benson, myself and others argued that the proposed procedure was insignificant. Trudeau, however, took a great deal of persuasion before he agreed, and then only after words were added to the paper that cosmetically covered the situation. I did not really know what to read into this incident, except that it reinforced my general impression that once Trudeau had made up his mind, or had joined cabinet in making a decision, he was inordinately reluctant to change. He might take a long time to reach a conclusion and to explore all shades of opinion, but having moved—as with the War Measures Act—he was tenacious even to the point of unreasonable stubbornness.

The hectic series of July meetings finally ended, and there remains only for me to recount a personal conversation between the Prime Minister and myself. He called me into his office where he indicated that he was interviewing all ministers regarding their future plans. It was a strange encounter—more formal than any other I had had with him. He had a loose-leaf notebook in front of him, presumably with a page for each minister. After the usual pleasantries including references to his pending visit to Newfoundland, he asked me if I intended to run again, adding that he presumed that I would. I replied that at the moment that was my intention, but it would only be once more and then, win or lose, I would quit. He appeared surprised and asked if I were not going to offer myself for the leadership. I answered no, that I was fifty years old—at which he commented, "almost as old as I am"—and that I had no intention of hanging around after fifty-five at the latest.

He then asked me if I had any preference with regard to another portfolio. Again, I appeared to surprise him by answering that I was perfectly happy in Transport. He responded that there were likely to be major changes after the election, and asked what I did have in mind if there were? I answered that I had not seriously thought about it, but perhaps I would be interested in Treasury Board. During all this time, he made notes like an interviewer filling out a questionnaire.

But now he said that my comments made it difficult to discuss the other subject he had in mind—an immediate change for me to Finance with Ben Benson taking my place in Transport. This did not come as a complete surprise, as Ben had put the same proposition to me earlier.

My answer was that I would, of course, do as he asked. But I went on to say that I thought until tax reform was completely through the House, a change would be ill-timed. I pointed out that although I had been on the tax committee, I did not know the details of the legislation intimately. He reminded me that I would have a month to bone up before the bill was introduced. He told me that he favoured me for Finance because he thought that I could sell our policies better to the public and that I could control officials. He expressed mild disappointment with Ben's performance in this regard.

I repeated that I thought the timing was wrong, but that the matter was in his hands. I also expressed doubts that Benson should go to Transport, since Ben had already told me that he was interested in taking over the presidency of the CNR. If that were to happen, it would look bad politically if he moved from Transport to the head of a corporation for which Transport had responsibility. I cited the Jack Pickersgill case as an example. But I had another reason for my hesitation—my doubts that Ben would be as tough in Transport as the job demanded.

Trudeau did not discuss in detail Ben's possible move to the CNR, but said that he saw the wisdom of my observations. He then dropped the matter, except for the final comment that perhaps Jean-Luc Pepin might be suitable for Finance at some point.

Next, he asked me my views on the CDC and the job of president, telling me that he was considering two candidates—Jack Austin, the

Deputy Minister of Energy, Mines and Resources, and Marshall Crowe, the Deputy Secretary of the Cabinet. I expressed a preference for Crowe on the grounds that he had been privy to all the discussions concerning the composition of the corporation and the government's objectives for it. I believed that he could be relied on not merely to carry out government policy, but to understand the underlying motivations for it. Subsequently, of course, Crowe received the appointment, but I had no way of knowing the effect, if any, of my advice.

After a few more pleasantries, the interview ended with my assurance to the Prime Minister that as long as I was in politics, I would do whatever he wanted, at whatever time he wanted. He expressed his appreciation, commenting that Finance was something of a graveyard for the politically ambitious, at which point I again reassured him that for me it was one more time around, and then I would quit.

Thirteen

As the end of July approached, we took off for what all of us hoped would be a month of comparative rest. I returned to Newfoundland to prepare for the Prime Minister's visit the following week. I suspect that the last thing on any of our minds at that moment was that within two weeks, President Richard Nixon would disrupt our vacation plans—and a lot of other things as well.

Except for a weekend in Swift Current, my return to Newfoundland did not provide much real rest; Trudeau was to start his tour of Newfoundland on the Tuesday following my return. Earlier, my own staff had had their share of frustrations trying to work out the Prime Minister's schedule with those in his office who attended to such matters. Finally, however, there was agreement that the Trudeaus would circumnavigate the island of Newfoundland by Coast Guard ship. I won my point that my riding should get special attention since it was the only one which had voted Liberal. I had some problems with Joe Smallwood who, as usual, wanted to cram too much into the schedule; in the final analysis, I chose to ignore his plans and to do things my own way.

In retrospect, both myself and the Prime Minister's staff were overly ambitious and too optimistic about the Newfoundland weather, and, indeed, it was the weather which turned out to be our nemesis in the long run. This situation was complicated by the fact that the Prime Minister went to St. Pierre first. The plan was to fly him to the Burin Peninsula from St. Pierre after lunch. I should have known that there would be fog; there almost always is. As it turned out, the Prime Minister's party had to come all the way to Fortune by Coast Guard. This put everything about three hours behind schedule and made it necessary to omit half the itinerary. Still, in Fortune and Grand Bank—the places we did visit—the greeting was tremendous.

It was quite an amusing affair, and one which revealed a side of Trudeau which was both endearing and baffling. Most of the Newfoundland welcomers, especially the mayors and other officials, were decked out in their Sunday best. When the ship finally berthed in Fortune, Trudeau was waiting for me at the gang plank. It is not difficult to imagine my reaction when I beheld him in a pair of faded jeans and a French-style striped sailor's sweater, a scarf knotted around his neck. The people of Fortune, especially the mayor, councillors and clergy, did not know what to make of him. Usually, distinguished visitors arrived in great solemnity and splendour with accompanying uniformed aides and other attendants. But here was the whole bunch, newsmen included, looking for all the world exactly what they were: a bunch of tourists returning from St. Pierre, some of them showing the wear and tear of a wild night on the famous islands.

The Prime Minister's first words to me were about Margaret. She would not make a public appearance, he told me, but would like to take the helicopter with my wife directly to our home in Swift Current where the Trudeaus were to spend the night. I knew that the people would be disappointed, but argument was useless. So the Prime Minister and I went ashore and received an unbelievably warm welcome from a large crowd assembled on the school grounds. The disappointment that Margaret was not present was obvious. We had a repeat of the same scene at nearby Grand Bank. Then, after taking close to half an hour to get through the friendly crowd to the other helicopter, we took off with a security man for Swift Current.

I had been in a state of concealed agitation for the previous hour. I could see the fog rolling in and was worried that if we delayed much longer, we would not make it to Swift Current where Margaret had already arrived. But thanks to our pilot and a slight bending of Transport regulations, we finally made it. We had to cancel two other stops on the peninsula, much to the disappointment of the residents and with the risk of political backlash.

When we arrived at Swift Current, the young people we had assembled to meet the Prime Minister rushed to the helicopter. Margaret hurried forward as well, looking not unlike the rest of the young people around her. She greeted her husband with obvious relief and, subsequently, my wife told me that as soon as they had arrived in Swift Current, Margaret, showing great agitation that some newsmen and photographers were present, went into the guest house we had prepared for her and Trudeau and remained there alone for more than two hours until her husband arrived. The affection the Trudeaus had for each other was obvious. Invariably, they walked arm in arm or hand in hand, almost oblivious to everyone around them.

We spent half an hour touring the grounds, but Trudeau rejected the idea of any time to himself, and he and Margaret immediately became involved with the young people. There were fifty or sixty of them, and the fresh lobster meal was a perfect icebreaker. The discussion that followed was brisk and satisfying. I confess to some personal satisfaction that my own children participated fully and knowledgeably and that there were few present who were even slightly in awe of the Prime Minister, even though there was no lack of respect. For the first time since I had known her, Margaret took a full part in the discussion, sometimes, as in the discussion on drug policy, disagreeing with her husband.

Trudeau was extremely gracious and interested in what was being said, and he performed his usual role of asking pointed questions and then listening intently to the responses. I took on something of the role of moderator and tried to avoid having only a few young people monopolize the conversation. The talk went on for about three hours, after which the Trudeaus spent a few minutes at our house before retiring to the guest house for the night.

A humorous side note to the event came to light subsequently. Barbara had made special preparations in one of the guest house rooms—new bedding, electric blankets, a special supply of towels and other amenities. After the Trudeaus had left, she discovered that they had not used that room at all, but the adjacent one. Later, I asked Margaret why, and the answer was simple and mildly embarrassing. They had not been able to open the window in the room we had prepared for them, so they moved to one where the window would open. This just goes to show how difficult it is indeed to think of everything.

On the following morning, the schedule called for a helicopter trip to St. John's for the annual regatta. The first word we got was that the regatta had been cancelled due to bad weather, and although the weather was good in Swift Current, the helicopter pilots figured we could not get through to the city. There was nothing to do but to go by car, as Joe Smallwood had laid on a luncheon with "the heads of church and state."

It was obvious that the Trudeaus were in no rush to leave. Swift Current was close to being its most attractive, and we spent a long time over breakfast with the table drawn close to the big picture window which gave a superb view of the mountains and the river. I had never seen Trudeau more relaxed, and both he and Margaret ate heartily.

Finally, there was nothing to do but leave. The Trudeaus took the back seat, and I rode up front with the security man who acted as driver. There was the usual collection of accompanying cars front and back.

Since there had been a real argument in cabinet about the merits of paving roads in Newfoundland a few days before, I confess that I was pleased that the first twenty miles of our journey were over the roughest dirt roads imaginable. Two cars in the cavalcade were knocked out of the procession, and there were jokes to the effect that I had arranged matters that way on purpose. I had not, but I voiced no objections either.

At the point where we turned onto the paved Trans Canada Highway, an interesting incident occurred. We stopped momentarily to regroup our shattered caravan, and the Prime Minister spied a group of hitchhikers on the side of the road, complete with knapsacks, bedrolls and three or four young children. With genuine interest, he beckoned them over to chat. It turned out that they were two American couples, well-spoken and tidy, who said that they had fallen in love with Newfoundland and were out to see as much of it as possible. They told Trudeau that Newfoundlanders were the friendliest people they had ever met and said that, despite their large group and the amount of gear they were carrying, they were having no trouble hitching rides. It was not hard to imagine the Trudeaus doing the same thing, as they had in the past, and I detected a note of nostalgia in the Prime Minister's comments to the travellers. He referred to the incident in several of his short speeches during the tour.

With some interventions from Margaret, Trudeau and I talked constantly on the trip to St. John's. He was interested in my account of the Newfoundland Confederation struggle. We discussed religion, particularly the differences between his background of classical training by the Jesuits and my Presbyterian roots, which were tempered by constant youthful exposure to Irish Catholics and the more earthy and superstitious approach of the Irish Christian Brothers. It was a memorable conversation, with Trudeau throwing in casually, without any attempt to impress, quotes from various scholars and writers, some extremely obscure. On arrival in St. John's, we went straight to the Arts and Culture Centre where Joe's luncheon was being held. Earlier, while I was still in Ottawa, Joe had told me over the phone that the lunch would be his only public contact with the Prime Minister during the visit. I did not know if he had heard that this was my wish and, less directly expressed, that of the Prime Minister. But Smallwood stuck to his word. I had three reasons for wanting minimal provincial involvement during the visit. There was a provincial election coming up, and I did not want the Prime Minister's tour interpreted as an effort to boost Joe's fortunes. Also, the Prime Minister himself wanted a low-key visit. And finally, I feared that Joe's involvement would necessitate a hectic schedule with long speeches and all the other trappings that Trudeau so disliked.

When we arrived at the Centre, there was a substantial crowd waiting, and Joe himself was at the door. There were also a few demonstrators supporting the striking fish plant workers of Burgeo. Among them was Richard Cashin, a former member of Parliament and now president of the striking union. Smallwood asked Trudeau if he would say a few words to the protestors, and when he readily agreed, Joe called Cashin forward. Richard was mildly embarrassed by this encounter with the Prime Minister and his former House colleagues, but he stated the union case well, and the meeting between the four of us amidst the crowd was amiable and friendly.

The luncheon was supposed to be an entirely "stag" affair, so Margaret remained in the car while all of this was going on. She looked genuinely frightened as the crowd surged around the car, evidence once again of her fear of crowds and her discomfiture in the back-slapping, hand-grabbing world of politics. Finally, her car was driven off and she had a quick, private tour of St. John's before going to the Coast Guard ship to await her husband's return.

The luncheon was unlike anything else ever held in Newfoundland. In the first place, Trudeau retained his casual attire: open-neck sports shirt, slacks and sneakers. The rest of the guests, cabinet ministers and the heads of all the religious denominations were as formal as could be. I had managed to strike the happy medium: sports coat and slacks, but with shirt and tie. A few sherries while waiting had made Smallwood more ebullient than ever. He was especially anxious to please the clergy and, above all, the spokesman for the Pentecostal Assemblies. Ever since 1968, he had had the conviction that it was the Pentecostals' fear of Trudeau that had cost us at least four federal seats. There is some truth in this, but it is only part of the story. On this occasion, however, Smallwood was determined that Trudeau should make the best possible impression on the clergy in general. As is often the case, he tended to overdo his efforts.

It was a hot, humid day, so Joe suggested that everyone emulate the Prime Minister and get down to his shirt sleeves. At this suggestion, the clergy, especially the Roman Catholic Archbishop and the Anglican Bishop, looked acutely embarrassed, and few of those present took Joe's advice.

On top of all this, Joe had invited to the luncheon, amidst all the dignitaries, a St. John's taxi driver. During his speech, the premier admitted that he had done so because the taxi driver was a long-time Tory who controlled many votes and who was now switching to the Liberals. The original plan had been for the taxi man to drive the Prime Minister to the regatta. Since this plan had failed, the luncheon was the next best way for him to meet Trudeau. Also, despite the fact that the luncheon was supposed to be male only, Joe invited two women to attend—his sister, who was visiting from the mainland, and the wife of

Andy Crosbie, the local businessman who subsequently became Joe's campaign manager.

It was, in all respects, a mixed bag. Trudeau handled himself well, impressing the Roman Catholic Archbishop next to him with a short speech ideal for the occasion, emphasizing the distinctiveness of Newfoundland and the friendly character of all the people he had met.

After the luncheon and innumerable farewells and special introductions, we went directly to the ship. This was the major error of the tour. No one, including my own staff, had thought of an alternative plan in the event that the regatta was cancelled. Consequently, with the exception of those who came to the Arts and Culture Centre, few in St. John's saw the Prime Minister. In retrospect, the least we should have done was to have moored the ship in a prominent place where we could have arranged a small ceremony instead of on the almost inaccessible south side of the harbour. As it was, we whisked through St. John's to the ship, and that was that. There was considerable local resentment, something which the political opposition was not averse to using to their advantage.

I left the Prime Minister at the ship and returned to Swift Current for the night while the ship travelled north to St. Anthony. I joined him there the next day by helicopter. The scene was a repeat of Fortune and Grand Bank, and the mayor of St. Anthony made the best speech of the trip, saying that this was the first prime minister to visit St. Anthony, and that this made the people feel closer to Canada and more Canadian than ever before.

At St. Anthony, Margaret, for the first time, was actively involved in the ceremonies and in the memorable visit to L'Anse aux Meadows, the site of early Norse settlement in North America. It was memorable not only for historical reasons; the weather was miserable with flying conditions well below acceptable limits. At St. Anthony, Ed Roberts, the Minister of Health and provincial member for the area, told the Prime Minister that it would be possible to get through by helicopter to L'Anse aux Meadows, but that the weather was "dicey" and he did not know if the security men would permit it. Trudeau retorted somewhat testily that he himself made these kinds of decisions, and he wanted to go.

The two helicopters took off in the fog and literally followed the road at a height of only a few feet. Both got there safely, and in the biting wind and fog, the Trudeaus toured the entire site which, I confess, I did not find very impressive. Then it was through the fog again to St. Anthony for the usual speeches, and then back aboard the ship. I flew with most of the newsmen to Corner Brook and entertained them while we awaited the Prime Minister's arrival on the following day.

The ship arrived at mid-morning, and the Corner Brook reception was quite remarkable. First, I went aboard ship and persuaded Margaret to join us. Then a motorcade travelled through the town to the park, where an incredible throng of people were waiting to hear the standard speeches. Trudeau's speech referred to the gentleness of Newfoundlanders and the fact that they did not push and shove, but offered their hands almost diffidently. Ironically, moments later, the Corner Brook crowd gave the lie to his words. They pushed and shoved and were particularly insensitive to Margaret. After a few moments, Trudeau asked the RCMP to get her out of the crush. I helped, and we moved to a relatively open area near the swimming pool. But the crowd soon caught up with us, and it took quite an effort to get Margaret back to the parked open car where she remained until her husband returned. She was visibly shaken and embarrassed as the crowds gaped at her and pressed in to shake her hand and touch her.

Finally, the event ended and we headed back to the helicopters. After take-off, on our way to Port aux Basques, the helicopter with the Trudeaus and myself aboard landed on a beautiful and secluded headland so that we could have a light lunch. The location was near Robinson's and, inevitably, a few residents drove out to see what was going on. Here, the visitors were most gentle and courteous and were reluctant to come forward even when I invited them to do so. It was a delightful and happy occasion. Again, when Margaret got too far away from her husband, she would stop until he caught up and there was the usual hand holding as they viewed one of the most beautiful scenes in Newfoundland—the coast at the edge of the Codroy Valley and the imposing outcrop of Cape Anguille.

Following this pleasant interlude, it was on to Port aux Basques where my special assistant, Eric Facey, had done the best organizational job of the entire trip. A large crowd had gathered at the landing site. Again, Margaret agreed to accompany us to the ceremonies in the stadium, but the instant she left the helicopter for her car, she was literally besieged and someone walked heavily on her foot; once inside the car again, she was understandably reluctant to get out. Both inside and outside the stadium, the crowd of several thousand was well-controlled. Trudeau and I shook hands all the way to the platform, and when Trudeau saw that there was a little girl present with flowers for Margaret, he made sure that his wife was rounded up after the speeches so that the girl could make her presentation. Then came our usual plunge into the crowd until, finally, we were back in the helicopter and on our way to the last stop, Stephenville.

This portion of the flight I remember fondly; the pilots flew low over the sea and close to the steep cliffs, offering us a truly spectacular view. At Stephenville, there were a few protestors objecting to reports that we had plans to downgrade, or perhaps even close, the airport. I assured them that they were false. They gave no trouble and the general mood was friendly.

A delightful incident occurred during this particular stop. Some of the French-speaking families in Newfoundland live on the west coast, and they greeted the Prime Minister with "O Canada" in English and French. They also gave him—of all things—an antique spittoon! He conversed with them in French, but there were no formal speeches at Stephenville. After the handshakes, and after it had again been necessary to escort Margaret back to the helicopter by car to avoid the press of the crowds, the Trudeaus left to meet the Coast Guard ship with an en route stop on board the icebreaker, the *St. Laurent*.

I said good-bye to the Trudeaus at the helicopter, and after meeting briefly with the protestors, I had the Department of Transport DC3 take me back to St. John's. It was now the afternoon of Friday, August 6, and I thought at the time that the rest of the month would be virtually free for me and my family. Little did I know that this was not to be.

Was the Trudeau visit worthwhile? I am sure that it was although, as subsequent events showed, it did nothing for the fortunes of the provincial Liberals. And it was too far away to influence the next federal election outcome. But it did bring Newfoundlanders in many areas closer to Canada, and it enabled the Prime Minister to see some of Newfoundland's needs and issues and problems firsthand. For me, it made talking to him about these issues less difficult than it had been in the past. And as for Trudeau, despite some of the rough spots of the trip, I am sure he took away not only a new awareness, but also a greater affection for the tenth province.

Index